RUNNING AND ME

RUNNING

AND ME
THEN AND NOW

MARY BUTTON

For permission requests, please address
Iconic Press
PO Box 292055
Los Angeles, CA 90029-2055

Published 2019 by Iconic Press
Printed in the United States of America
21 20 19   1 2 3 4

ISBN 978-1-7323265-0-7
Library of Congress Control Number:
2018961962

This book is dedicated to the two "Geralds" in my life. My father, Jerry Button, showed me the way and was my guiding light during my younger years. My husband, Gerry Hans, has been with me every step of the way during my running career, and in the aftermath as I wrote this book.

TABLE OF CONTENTS

INTRODUCTION

I WROTE THIS book to let other runners know an insider's perspective of long distance running, since I lived the runner's life from many different angles.

In the chapters of this book I will share first-hand experiences of my life as a competitive runner. This book is a memoir combined with a recent history of long distance running.

I was drawn to the sport as a high school freshman in 1972, the year of "Title IX," when I ran with our school's male cross country team in southern New Jersey. (A female cross country team did not exist until after I graduated high school.)

In 1986, my husband and I moved to Los Angeles where I joined a local grass roots running club and became part of the running community of long-distance running. I discovered we runners have a special bond and are able to strike up instant dialog regardless of our religious or political views. Whatever our differences may be, our love of running brings us together and breaks down formidable barriers.

I am fortunate. I led a full, productive, successful, and enjoyable running life. I became an elite marathon runner, an active member of a grass-roots running club, and the co-owner and founder of RaceReady, a successful running apparel manufacturer. I traveled to dozens of cities far and wide for business and pleasure. I met many of the heroes of our sport, as well as thousands of average runners over the course of my 20 years as a runner and business owner. I witnessed the sport grow and evolve.

I no longer run due to knee problems. I miss running, but I am appreciative of the friends and running partners I have met over the last two decades. I cherish the memories and the laughter we shared. Years ago, I referred to them as my "running buddies." Then it became obvious these people were much more than that. They were in fact my real, true friends.

It's been an incredible journey.

CHAPTER ONE

"Got You Last"

OUR FAVORITE GAME during childhood was called "Got You Last." It wasn't complicated, just your basic game of tag with a different name. We played it quite often that summer of 1972, the year of the Alice Cooper hit song, "School's Out." We ran around our yard, the soft grass between our toes, and belted out the lyrics:

School's out for summer
School's out forever
No more pencils
No more books
No more teacher's dirty looks
Out for summer
Out till fall
We might not go back at all

I often started our game by running after my older brother Paul. Then it became his turn to chase after either me or one of my younger sisters, Eileen or Anne. Any one of the four of us closely-knit siblings could and would randomly start the "Got You Last" game. We played it often. It didn't require any equipment and not much planning – except for making quick getaways.

We grew up in the small town of Merchantville, New Jersey. Everyone knew everyone else on the block. There were no neighborhood scrooges. Doors were not locked at night. We felt secure. Paul was 14 years old that summer. I was close behind and would turn 13 in September. Eileen was 11, and "baby" Anne was 7.

My mom is full-blooded Italian; my dad is a mix of English and Irish. Paul and Eileen looked Italian. They were both dark-haired, with olive skin. Anne and I were blonde, and proud of it. I taught Anne the chant, "Blondes are best, from east to west. Brunettes are beast, from west to east." I can't remember their comeback, but Paul and Eileen most assuredly had one. Paul was a bit pudgy back then, like he could stand to play a little more "Got You Last." He was not one to turn down seconds on Mom's pasta.

It sucked to be Paul back then because we would always gang up on him. My sisters and I would stretch the rules of the game and turn the "tag" into a mean shove when we were pissed off at Paul, but he couldn't do the same back. One of my parents' firm rules was that Paul was never allowed to hit one of the girls under any circumstances, even when we sisters mercilessly shoved and punched him.

Good call, Dad! Despite Paul's pasta poundage, he was strong, and could very easily have knocked us out. Today Paul is 6 feet 5 inches tall and an expert kayaker. He also cycles, skis, and hikes.

Another favorite game was kickball, which we played in our side yard. It was your typical pick-up game. This was before the era of "play dates." We were ruthless and unaccountable to authorities. We kicked, fought, and screamed without supervision. It was great.

The only time my dad intervened was in defense of the poor 100-year-old azalea bush that we skidded into time and time again. "Use something else for first base," my dad screamed at us from the kitchen window. But we couldn't.

The way our yard was laid out, that beautiful azalea with its brilliant bright red blossoms was destined to be first base. There was no escaping the azalea. It was the only way to set up the perfect home run. Home plate was next to our house. You stepped up and, if you gave the ball a good swift kick, it flew into the yard of the old lady next door, and you scored.

Mom and Dad didn't go out very much back then. But when they did, we would break the household rules. After we heated up frozen Swanson's TV Dinners (the best part was the little dessert square of apple pie in the top center of the foiled "dinner"), we inevitably played a few rounds of "Got You Last" indoors, which was strictly forbidden.

Our house was more than 100 years old, and it had two separate staircases which connected the first and second floors (a regular staircase and a hidden back staircase that led up from the kitchen). It was a perfect set-up for our game. We could run up one staircase and down the other, similar to running circles around a track, though it was a vertical track in our case.

One hot and humid August evening, we played a game of indoor "Got You Last" that I'll always remember. I tagged Paul and then ran up the front staircase, did a skid along the second floor hallway carpet, and then ran down the back staircase. I fell down hard and landed on my right knee as I tried to make the sharp turn to exit the kitchen. I got up and carried on with the game, but I was a bit wobbly. I slowed down my pace because my knee stung.

I didn't think much of it at the time because minor injuries were common. But weeks went by, and summer turned to fall. The pain in my knee got worse. It began to make a quite audible clicking noise. It clicked whenever I flexed the knee, such as when I walked up stairs. My parents noticed.

"Mary's knee doesn't sound good," my mom worried.

"I think you should take her to the doctor," my dad suggested.

I hate needles, especially long fat ones like the doctor used to inject blue dye into my knee so he could diagnose the problem. I was lying on a cold metal table that September afternoon at the clinic in Philadelphia's Thomas Jefferson Hospital. The walls were a bleak grey color. It was a windowless room with no artwork, no perky plants or sweet-smelling flowers, or anything else to disguise how clinical and sterile the room was.

"Don't worry, the shot will only take a few minutes," the doctor explained. "The dye will naturally remove itself and disappear within the next day or two." The two-minute shot seemed to take hours. I grasped the metal rails on the side of the bed and tried to stay calm, but I was scared. It hurt.

A week later, I returned to Thomas Jefferson for the results and learned what the nasty blue dye injection had revealed.

"You have chondromalacia patella."

This sounded scary to me. "I have chondro – what?"

These were big words for a 13-year-old to comprehend. I learned that chondromalacia patella is the softening and break-down of the tissue (cartilage) that lines the underside of the kneecap (patella).

"So now what do I do?" I asked.

He addressed my mother, "My advice is we remove the en-tire piece of the cartilage, via surgery. It is the best option for your daughter. The cartilage will not repair itself on its own. You should probably schedule the operation soon, before it can get any worse."

My parents were sticklers about any of us kids missing school. While most of my friends could skip out of class to see the dentist, the Button kids always visited the dentist after the last school bell rang at 3:00 p.m.

Back in 1972, knee surgery like mine required a week's stay in the hospital. Naturally, my parents scheduled the surgery during our Christmas vacation so I wouldn't have to miss even a single minute of a day of school.

School let out for the holidays on Friday, December 15. My classmates were excited about the upcoming vacation weeks, but I was dreading it. That evening, I checked into Thomas Jefferson Hospital. I knew what Santa would be dragging down the chimney that year for me on Christmas Eve: a brand new pair of crutches. I was forewarned by the doctor that these crutches would become my closest friend for the next few months.

Surgery was scheduled for Saturday. In the morning, the anesthesiologist visited me shortly after I was wheeled into the operating room. There I was once again, lying upon a familiar cold metal table. This time, a mask was rubber-banded around my head and the anesthesiologist told me to relax and take deep breaths. "You will wake up and the surgery will be over. You won't even know it happened."

———

"Where am I?" I was awake, but fuzzy. I then remembered. "I am in Thomas Jefferson Hospital, and I just had my knee fixed."

I glanced at my right forearm. It was heavily taped with a bunch of tubes and needles. *(I later learned this was an IV hookup.)* Near my bed was a tall pole with plastic bags of fluid attached to the top. I noticed that the tubes in my arm were attached to this apparatus. It made no sense to me.

I thought that the hospital must have made a huge mistake. I concluded that they switched me with another patient by accident. I was to have had surgery on my right knee, not my right arm! My knee was heavily bandaged, but it did not have tubes and needles attached to it.

I panicked, and I yanked the needles from my arm. Suddenly, I became the center of attention. The medical staff on the floor was instantly by my side.

"I can't believe she took out her IV…"

"What is she thinking?"

"Whose patient is this?"

All nurses have dealt at some point with PITA (Pain-In-The-Ass) patients like me. It goes with the job. I still maintain my childhood innocence today. We weren't allowed to watch much TV, just the occasional sitcom when homework was done. We were allowed an hour tops of TV time. It was *Bewitched*, *That Girl*, *Mary Tyler Moore*, *I Dream of Jeannie* …not *E.R.* Naïve as it may seem, I had no idea what an IV was or what purpose it served.

A few hours later, I was wheeled out of the recovery unit and back to my hospital room where I stayed for another six long days and even longer nights. Many friends came to visit. They pulled up chairs to play games of gin rummy. Mom came every day. She read to me until I dozed off, which didn't take too much time. I was under heavy pain medication, which made me dopey and drowsy. My dad would come in the evenings after work. His office was in Philadelphia, only a few miles from the hospital.

Every day, a nurse got me out of bed to practice walking. I was informed that I had to master the walk across the room to the bathroom (using my crutches) before they would dismiss me from the hospital and let me return home. The first day, it was agony to simply stand and put weight on the leg. But the next morning, I was able to walk a few steps.

My favorite part of the day was when the nurse handed me a menu checklist. I felt almost like I was in a restaurant. I could choose whether I wanted chicken or beef, potatoes or rice, ice cream or fruit. I penciled a checkmark in the appropriate box and then my meal was "made to order." I got to personally select my meal, which made me feel privileged. It tasted like crap, and it was crap!

I dreaded night time. I've always been a light sleeper. I heard when the nurse stations switched shifts at midnight. I was awake when, every three or four hours, the nurses walked by each of the half-dozen beds in this children's ward to record the patient's blood pressure, heart rate, pulse, and God knows what other vital signs.

I missed home. I didn't want to be here at Thomas Jefferson Hospital in Philadelphia. I desperately desired to be like my friends: playing with new Christmas toys, sledding, having snowball fights. I missed my siblings more than I ever thought possible. Each day in the hospital dragged on longer than the previous one.

Finally, a week after the knife, I *was* home and sleeping in my familiar bed in the first room at the top of the stairs. My crutches leaned against the wall. In the morning, I took hold of them and hobbled around the room. I couldn't manage the stairs for several days, but either Anne or Eileen came to my room at mealtime to keep me company. We set up card tables and ate. Afterwards, we played card games for hours. It took a week, but finally I was strong enough to walk up and down the stairs. Slowly but surely, I made progress. The doctor was satisfied that my recovery and recuperation were going well and according to the predicted timeline.

Two months post-surgery, I attended swim practice with my doctor's approval. He thought swimming was an ideal, non-weightbearing exercise. Eileen, Anne, and I swam year-round. Our summer club, Woodbine Swim Club, was one of the top in the South Jersey Tri-County area. Swim team practice was held at Woodbine twice a day, Monday through Friday. Swim meets were every Saturday morning. During the school year, we swam three times a week at an indoor club, the Wahoos. Most weekends, we traveled to cities throughout the state for swim meets.

I was thrilled to resume swim practice, though my knee swelled up severely after the workout. I felt like a victim of elephantiasis, the condition in which a part of the body (my knee) swells to massive proportions.

Follow-up doctor visits became less frequent. By early summer of 1973, the doctor "signed off" and deemed my surgery a success. The doctor's parting words of advice to my mom were, "Mary can be active and play like any normal kid. Swimming is great for her. In the future, she will probably want to avoid sports such as basketball and running, where there is too much pressure and pounding on the knee."

CHAPTER TWO

Title IX

THE LOUD DING of the school bell startled me and got my attention. This was my usual cue to get up from behind the desk of my seventh period biology class and walk down the hall to eighth and final period, history. History was taught by tall, thin, bespectacled Ms. Pamela Reddy. With her demeanor and activism, she could have passed as the famous songstress Ms. Helen Reddy. I could just as easily hear our Ms. Reddy belt out those lyrics:

"I am woman, hear me roar, in numbers too big to ignore."

But I didn't go to history class because it was Friday. Instead, I walked downstairs to the gym. The entire student body of Camden Catholic High School (CCHS) was headed in the same direction. Like a stampede. It was time to worship and pay homage to the football gods.

These were our heroes!

It was fall of 1973 and I was a freshman in a class of 225 at CCHS, a high school in Cherry Hill, New Jersey. Our school boasted a total of 900 students. Every Friday before a Saturday home game, all eighth period classes were canceled. Instead, we held a roaring pep rally in the gymnasium.

The gym wasn't even big enough to seat us all. We squeezed in knee-to-knee, shoulder-to-shoulder, and still extra folding chairs had to be brought in to accommodate everyone.

The band marched in playing our school's theme song, "When the Saints Go Marching In." They were followed immediately by the cute cheerleaders who wore their short skirts in the colors of the Fighting Irish. They raised their green and white pom poms in the air and led us in the chant, "Let's go, Fighting Irish. Let's go. Let's go. LET'S GO!"

The applause became deafening as in walked our boys who were dressed in full uniform (shoulder pads, helmets and all).

"Two bits, four bits, six bits a dollar. All for the Irish, stand up and holler!"

The bleachers rumbled as everyone stood up to cheer and stomp their feet. The idea was to make as much noise as possible. The band played and we screamed and yelled for the next 40 minutes. Finally, our boys exited to the locker room. Somehow, they squeezed their big heads through the doorway.

We didn't *have to* go to the game the next day. It was not as if they took attendance. In fact, I never went, but I heard about football first thing Monday morning in homeroom. The intercom buzzed on. "The Fighting Irish fought hard and played well. They lost by a slim margin, 24 to 14. We'll get them next time!"

I was a swimmer. I swam AAU (Amateur Athletic Union) since our school lacked a pool and a swim team. Meets were scheduled throughout the Tri-County South Jersey area on Saturdays. So I had a good excuse for missing the stupid football games.

I had a crush on my swim coach Steve, as did most of the girls on our team. He was twenty-three years old and a former competitive swimmer whose stroke had been the butterfly. He had a well-defined chest and broad shoulders. Our indoor pool was in a small enclosed room, which was hot and stuffy and reeked of chlorine. I don't know how Steve could bear it as he stood poolside with his stop-watch in hand for 90 minutes. But *WE* got to view his gorgeous bare upper body when we finished each lap. He was in graduate school and no longer trained, but he found time to coach us through vigorous 1 ½ -hour practices on Monday, Wednesday, and Thursday evenings. Steve was smart, funny and good-looking with his bleached-out light blond hair and sparkling blue eyes. He put his heart and soul into coaching our team, the Jersey Wahoos.

One Saturday afternoon in late September, Steve had a pow wow with us after the meet. The topic was "cross-training." (It wasn't the catch-phrase it later became.) He implored us, "You'll become stronger swimmers if you spice it up and take up another sport. You do have plenty of options. Try out for basketball, or perhaps soccer. Or just jog around the block a few times every evening. You girls are really fortunate and should take advantage of Title IX."

Title IX? I was vaguely familiar with the term. I remembered that Ms. Reddy talked about it one non-Friday afternoon in history class. She had explained, "It's the law President Nixon signed last year in June of 1972. It makes it illegal for schools to discriminate against girls in education and sports. Girls are entitled to the same funding and opportunities as boys."

On Monday afternoon, I got up my courage to approach Mr. Cormier, the coach of the boy's cross country team. Unlike football, his team got no respect. Runners weren't considered cool, and not once were they given a pep rally. They were the misfits, just a few dozen lanky boys who ran on the hills and trails after school. Mr. Cormier, a math teacher, had been at CCHS forever. He was probably in his sixties; a serious, no-nonsense type of guy who never cracked a smile.

I finally got his attention. "Umm, Mr. Cormier, I want to join the cross country team. Umm, I think I can because of Title IX. And... and...I really have to run so I can become a better swimmer."

He stared me in the eye but didn't say anything for several seconds. Maybe he was hard of hearing? Finally, he said, "Don't expect any special favors. Practice begins at 3:00 p.m., and that does not mean 3:01 or 3:02. You show up on-time, or you don't show up at all."

On Tuesday afternoon, I sat on the locker room bench and laced up my running shoes. Another girl, Megan, whom I barely knew, walked in. She was also a freshman, very petite and skinny with short, curly, light brown hair. Her legs were half the length of mine. "My older brother Michael is on the team. Yesterday at practice, Mr. Cormier told the team a girl would be joining them. Michael knows I love to run, so he asked Mr. Cormier to let me join too."

We exited our crappy locker room with the scummy floors, dented lockers, and three or four barely-working showers. Megan confided, "My brother says the boy's locker room is so much better, nothing like this."

Camden Catholic is a single two-story building. The school sits on a well-manicured large grassy lawn. A narrow dirt foot path, which is about ¾ of a mile around, circles the campus. This is where practice was held. Our typical workout was three or four laps around the loop. Toward the south end of the footpath looms the football field. As I ran by, I overheard a guy in their huddle say "Check *HER* out," which was followed by catcalls, laughter, and whistles. I ignored them.

Early October was our first meet, a "home" meet. The three-mile course was a combination of grass and trail on familiar terrain. My main concern was to dodge the half-hidden gopher holes. In one half-mile stretch, they seemed to be everywhere, and I came close to twisting an ankle. I heard both cheers and jeers as I kicked up my heels on the dusty trail and headed toward the finish line. Thirty spectators, mostly parents and friends of the runners, crowded the side lines. I heard someone's mom say, "I didn't know they allowed girls to run."

I came in 22nd out of 27, ahead of a handful of the boys. Some of the boys made a big deal out of it. Before practice the next day, Megan filled me in. "My brother told me that several guys in the locker room bullied those boys who finished behind you and wouldn't shut up. They said, 'I can't *BELIEVE* you let a girl beat you.'"

The next week was an "away" meet at a school half an hour away. I had never run the course at this location. We gathered in a big circle on a dirt field adjacent to the start line. The official stood in the middle holding a stick. He bent down and drew out a map on the ground as he described the course to us. "It's pretty simple. Turn left here, ¼ mile later make another left, then make a right after ½ mile, and you will be in the woods. Got it? Two lefts, one right, and then the woods. Just keep your eyes peeled for the bright pink flags in the trees on your right which will mark each and every turn for the next two miles. The final ¼ mile is a clear straight shot to the finish. Any questions?"

"Nope," we chimed.

"OK, we start in 60 seconds."

Ten minutes later, I was alone in the woods, not a soul nor a pink flag in sight. A minute ago, three boys were within sight. Where did they go? "OK. Don't panic. Keep running. Someone will come from behind any second." My self-talk didn't do much good. I was alone in a fragrant pine forest. I heard the rustling of leaves and my hopes surged, but it was only a couple of squirrels playing amongst the pine cones. Five minutes later, I turned around and tried to retrace my footsteps.

Finally, up ahead I spotted a bright pink flag on a tree branch on my left. It was *SO* obvious. "Shit. How could I have missed that? I'm such an idiot." I finished that race dead last, thirty minutes behind the next-to-last runner. The boys never let me hear the end of it the rest of the season. Cross country ended a month later.

I swam that winter, but it didn't seem as fun as it once was. I missed running. Doing lap after lap, while I stared at the bottom of the pool, bored me. I hated the nasty smell of the chlorine and the sting in my eyes when my goggles leaked, which they often did. The car ride home late at night after practice was pretty miserable too. Maybe the moms in our car pool were going through hot flashes because they *always* cranked up the air conditioner. I sat in the back seat, my wet hair dripped down my back, and I shivered. Dads never did the car pool; it was always the moms.

———

My senior year, spring of 1977, Camden Catholic *finally* had its very own girls' track team! I had run cross country with the boys the past four years, but never ran track with them. Two dozen girls signed up, including my sister Eileen who was two grades behind me in school.

Some archaic rules were on the books back then. Most ludicrous and frustrating was the two-mile limit. That was the maximum total distance a girl could run in any single track meet, period. I heard rumors, "If girls exercise too much, there may be serious negative effects to their reproductive organs. It may affect their hormones."

Did they think our uteruses would fall out or we might grow a mustache? And how about the fact that the cross country distance I raced for four years was *three miles*? Now I was limited to *two?* This whole thing reeked.

Most meets *didn't even offer* the two-mile option. The longest race often was the one-miler. But on the rare occasion when the two-miler was scheduled, that was the race I wanted to run (although it meant I couldn't run the half-mile an hour later, nor could I be part of the mile relay, since I was forbidden to run another step).

Our coach, Mr. Coleman, was fresh out of college. He taught history, and nearly all the girls at CCHS prayed to have him as their teacher because he was so handsome. He sported a year-round tan, pearly white teeth, and a winning smile which showed off his cute dimples. The reason many joined track was *because* Tom Coleman was the coach. Good-looking he certainly was; a brilliant coach he definitely was not.

Pennsauken High, our main rival team, hosted our first meet of the season. We arrived at their campus, jogged a lap on the 400-meter track, and stretched in our designated corner of the grassy infield. Mr. Coleman read our team lineup, and told us who was in what events. I sat quietly. I leaned forward in a horizontal position, touched the top of my shoes, and held that stretch. My gaze was on the ground when I heard Mr. Coleman announce that I was entered in the two-miler. I thought, "Good, I get to run my event."

Then I heard my sister's voice. I stopped my stretch and looked up at Mr. Coleman and my sister Eileen who had interrupted him mid-speech.

"Mr. Coleman, doesn't it make more sense to scratch Mary from the two-miler if we want to win? Come on, think about it! Take her out of it, and put her in the mile, the 800-meter, the 400-meter and the mile relay. That way she can run four times, not just once." This meant more opportunities to score points for our team.

Both teams could enter up to three runners for each event, for a total of six runners on the track. Each event from the 100-yard dash to the two-miler was scored exactly the same: five points for first place, three for second, and one for third. Coach Coleman reworked the roster to maximize the number of races of our fastest runners.

I silently fumed. Once again, I couldn't run my best event, and I was furious at the unfairness of it all. I knew that I was capable of running nearly every event on the damn schedule. I ran four events instead of one that afternoon and helped lead our team to victory over Pennsauken. Yet, I felt I had been gypped.

One afternoon in May, track practice was delayed thirty minutes because of after-school parent-teacher conferences. In our dilapidated girls' locker room, we changed into our shorts and tried to figure out how to kill time before practice. Eileen, always hungry and nicknamed String-beanie Eileen-ie suggested, "Why don't we go to McDonald's?"

Mickie D's was only two blocks away. Ten of us were onboard with the idea. We stuffed a few dollar bills into our socks, laced up our shoes, and jogged over to McDonald's. We scarfed down our Big Macs (Two-All-Beef-Patties-Special-Sauce-Lettuce-Cheese-Pickles-Onions-On-A-Sesame-Seed-Bun), faster than you would think possible, then we jogged back toward school. We began track intervals ten minutes later. Midway through, I barfed up this pinkish-colored Special Sauce. Never again did I eat a Big Mac!

———

Not once did I make the Honor Society at Camden Catholic High, even with report cards of mostly A's sprinkled with a few B's. Honor Society was a desired title to include on one's college application. The Honor Society didn't do anything; it was simply recognition, voted upon by a select group of teachers. Their committee reviewed a student's grades, extra-curricular activities, and everything else deemed "honorable."

I should have been a shoo-in. I participated in cross country, track, and orchestra. I played clarinet and was first chair my junior and senior year. I might even have been first chair my freshmen year. The woodwind instructor confided in me back then, "You play as well as Kathy

Rourke (a senior). But we can't have a first chair freshman. It is simply not done."

I spoke my mind and argued with teachers, which were points against my being inducted into the Honor Society. My freshman algebra teacher, Mr. Phipps, was a chain smoker. He was nearly bald, had a pasty complexion, and wrinkly skin. He looked near retirement age. A cigarette constantly dangled from his mouth as he wrote algebraic formulas on the black board. One morning, I coughed and raised my hand to speak. "Please can you put out your cigarette? The smoke is bothering me. Can't you wait until you get to the teachers' lounge?"

I never entered the teachers' lounge because it was, after all, a teachers' lounge, not a students' lounge. Yet as I walked by its open door, this tiny dank room reeked of smoke. It was such a cloud of smoke that I could barely make out which teachers were inside. I nearly gagged each time the lounge door swung open to admit or belch out a teacher.

I touched a nerve with Mr. Phipps that morning. His face turned from pasty white to beet red within five seconds, and he shouted, "This is *MY* class. I set the rules. If you don't like it, GET OUT."

I obeyed him. I exited the classroom and walked down to the principal's office where I told the principal my story. From then on, Mr. Phipps never lit up in algebra class. However, Mr. Phipps was on the committee which had the final say in the selection of the Honor Society. I am sure he cast a "no" every year when my name came up for consideration.

Decades later, I am glad I wasn't part of the bogus so-called Honor Society.

But I remain grateful for Title IX.

It opened doors for me.

CHAPTER THREE

College to the Canyon

I ENTERED SHIPPENSBURG University of Pennsylvania in the fall of 1977. The school accepted me, despite the fact I did not list Camden Catholic Honor Society on my college application.

Shippensburg (the Ship) is located in the tranquil and scenic Cumberland Valley, about an hour drive west of Harrisburg. Many of the old homes and barns in this pastoral farmland date back to the previous century. I fell in love with this small, quaint college town. The Main Street of Shippensburg boasted two or three restaurants, a grocery store, a handful of churches, and even more bars. I had followed my brother Paul's advice, *"Pick a college town where the bar/church ratio is equal or greater than 1 to 1."*

Beyond a doubt, the best part of the Ship was Natalie. I met her within a few weeks of my freshmen year. She lived across the hall from me in Kiefer Dorm, an all-female dormitory. (Only one of the seven dorms on campus was co-ed in 1977.) Natalie and I became roommates spring semester and have remained close friends ever since.

Natalie's major was social welfare while mine was accounting. We were opposites in many ways but got along perfectly. Natalie put down her books and picked up needlepoint or another handicraft for a break from studies. I changed into my t-shirt and shorts and pedaled my 10-speed bike on the hilly roads of the Cumberland Valley, or I ran a few miles when I needed a breather.

My longest run at college happened by accident in the fall of sophomore year. My intent was to do the roughly three-mile scenic loop, which I had discovered the previous week on my bike. I left our dorm room at 4:30 p.m. for my run. "Natalie, I'll be back in an hour or so."

I ran along and approached the end of the three-mile loop. I was within a half mile of campus when a ferocious dog took me by surprise. He leaped out from a barnyard and had an angry bark as he approached me. It terrified me, and I froze. I feared the beast was about to sink his fangs into my foot or lower leg. There was no way I was going to step another foot in his direction. I turned around and retraced my steps. I thus wound up with an unexpected six mile run.

Cell phones didn't exist in 1977, so I couldn't call Nat and explain my delay. She was visibly worried when I arrived back at the dorm 45 minutes later than expected. "Where were you?" she asked. I explained and then quickly showered so we could make it to the dining hall for dinner before it shut its doors at 7:00 p.m.

I tossed in my bed that night and couldn't sleep. Thoughts were spinning in my mind. *"Wow. I can't believe I ran six miles!"*

————

I graduated magna cum laude from Shippensburg in May of 1981 with a degree in business administration and a major in accounting, but I was not eager to enter the corporate world. I couldn't picture myself sitting at a desk crunching numbers all day. I knew this is what I had studied and prepared to do, but I didn't want to do it quite yet.

The economy in 1981 was fairly stable. As a magna cum laude graduate, I think it probable I could have found a good entry-level accounting position with a decent salary, but my heart wasn't in it. I put my accounting career on hold. Instead, I sent applications to several National Parks, and hoped to land a "fun" job for the summer. In those pre-Internet days, it took hours to research the parks, get the contact info, and mail typewritten letters and forms. I craved an adventure and hoped a National Park far away from Merchantville, New Jersey, would come through with a job offer.

Early May 1981, I glanced at the postmark stamped "AZ" before I ripped open the envelope. The enclosed letter offered me a job as "KU" on the South Rim of the Grand Canyon! KU is the abbreviation for Kitchen Utility. I read the job description and learned the translation of Kitchen Utility is Dish Washer. I was a bit hesitant to spend the summer washing dishes but the location of the Grand Canyon was irresistible.

My parents weren't thrilled, but they were supportive. My dad advised, "It's OK to take a break and do what you want for the summer. You deserve a vacation. Your career can wait a few months."

Two weeks later, I flew from Philadelphia to Phoenix. I spent a sleepless night at the Phoenix airport and then boarded a tiny aircraft for the hour flight of 230 miles to Tusayan, the tiny village ten miles outside the entrance gate to Grand Canyon.

My career as KU lasted only a week before I was promoted to work the line of the employee cafeteria. I dished out servings of fried chicken or baked fish, mashed potatoes, green beans, and applesauce to fellow Canyon workers, mostly college kids like me who were happy to be Canyon bums for the summer. That job lasted three weeks before I moved up again and became a waitress in the Bright Angel, the family restaurant.

The salary wasn't much, but (all modesty aside) I was a great waitress and made a killing in tips. I worked the night shift, 2:00 p.m. to 10:00 p.m., which was ideal. It allowed ample time to hike in the mornings and early afternoons before I clocked in to work. I almost always hiked and camped on my rare days off.

I met people from all over the world, both on the trails and at work. I gave special attention to my customers who hobbled into the restaurant with red dirt stained upon their face, arms, and legs. We were kindred spirits and shared our love for the Canyon. I greeted them, "How was your hike today?" They be-

COLLEGE TO THE CANYON

came animated as they described their recent time on the trail. I didn't have too much time to jabber on the job, so I saved it for after 10:00 p.m. when I got off work and met up in the Bright Angel Bar next door.

Musicians from Phoenix, often folk singers with their acoustic guitars, held gigs there most nights. Nothing's better after an eight-hour waitress shift than to unwind, drink a beer, listen to talented musicians, and talk trails. I did this night after night. I often returned to my dorm room after midnight for some shut-eye and then awoke in the morning for a pre-work hike. I burned the candle at both ends.

My most memorable tip was the two dollars I received one evening from a young hiker about my age who was fresh off the trail. The bills were enclosed in a folded napkin upon which he had posed a multiple-choice question.

After you get off work, will you:
A) Have a Beer with me
B) Smoke a Joint with me
C) Both A & B
D) None of the above.
I chose "A."

———

My "summer" in the Grand Canyon began in May of 1981 and didn't end until January 1983, an unforgettable glorious "summer." Early in October of 1981, I rode the bus to Flagstaff, a town 80 miles south of the Canyon with the mission to buy a bicycle. I had cash, tip money pocketed over several months. A friend had clued me in that I could purchase a 10-speed bike for not much money in Flag. I found my bike for less than $200, which proved to be a worthy investment. I often pedaled along the rim of the Canyon, except in the winter when the roads became sheets of ice.

One spring evening in 1982, we organized a full-moon hike. Three of my friends and I brought our sneakers and shorts into work and stored them in the employee lockers. We clocked out at 10:15 p.m. and stripped from our waitress uniforms and into our hiking gear. We hiked the four-and-a half-miles down to Indian Gardens, along the Bright Angel Trail by moonlight. No flashlights were necessary. We made it back to the rim, slept a few hours, then went to work as usual.

I didn't run one step during my 18-month tenure in the Canyon. Yet, I was constantly on the go, working, hiking, and cycling. Best of all was in July of 1982 when I was lucky enough to have four days off in a row. This was the one and only time that ever happened, and I milked it for all it was worth.

I planned a solo four-day, three-night excursion to the North Rim and back. Day one, I hiked roughly eight miles down to the floor of the Canyon via the South Kaibab Trail. I entered the employee bunkhouse, a log cabin called Phantom Ranch, where I guzzled down glass after glass of lemonade, which was "all-you-can drink" and free to employees. I was offered a bed in the bunkhouse, but declined and slept 200 yards away outdoors, under the stars, beside Bright Angel

Creek. The second day was a strenuous 14-mile ascent to the North Rim, where the temperature plummeted when I arrived after sunset. Now I understood why the North Rim was shut down half of the year because of frigid temperatures. A fellow hiker lent me a blanket for the night since all I had packed for bedding was the sheet from my dorm room. Still, I shivered on my "bed," a cheap inflatable mattress. Day three, I descended back to the bottom of Canyon. I was hot and sweaty when I arrived, and refilled my water bottle multiple times with the lemonade. Day four, I climbed out of the canyon at the South Rim with a wide grin on my face. I was filthy but thrilled to have completed this 40-plus mile Rim-to-Rim-to-Rim hike.

I was a no-frills hiker. I didn't wear hiking boots or own a camera. I carried only what I could stuff into my daypack. My heaviest equipment was my 32-ounce water bottle. I packed minimal food since I had connections with the employees at Phantom Ranch and ate with them. The sheet I stripped from my dorm bed served as my sleeping bag. I wore a tank-suit style bathing suit, a pair of shorts, and sneakers. I pulled my long hair back in a ponytail. I didn't even own sunglasses. I cringe now to think I seldom even applied sunscreen.

I never regretted my time in the Canyon. The Grand Canyon was GRAND!

CHAPTER FOUR

"We Love L.A.!"

B Y JANUARY 1983, it was time for me to move on. My college degree did *not* increase in value while I waited tables at the Grand Canyon. It was difficult for me to break away because of the deep connection I felt with the Canyon. I prized my carefree lifestyle and my spectacular "backyard." I never tired of the scenery. Most of my cohorts in the Bright Angel were roughly my age, but some were older, in their forties and fifties. They appeared content with their long careers in the food and beverage industry. I admired them, though I knew I owed it to myself (and my parents) to give the accounting profession a try.

I became nervous. Where would I go? How would I explain myself in interviews and justify the 20 months as a Canyon bum?

I dialed my brother Paul, who lived in the town of Lakewood, a suburb just west of Denver. He worked as a mechanical engineer for the National Park Service in their Denver regional office. He too had been an avid hiker post-college. Whereas I waited tables at the Canyon, Paul worked in housekeeping at a lodge in Yellowstone National Park. Like me, he had put his career on hold. Unlike me, he left the National Park after one summer to begin his professional career.

"There's great hiking in the Rocky Mountains, Sib! You would love it here!" (Our nickname for each other is Sib, short for sibling. We began to call each other "Sib" when we were teens, and have yet to stop.)

"I am in the mountains nearly every weekend. Often, I hike both Saturday *and* Sunday. Even in the winter, I trudge the trails in snowshoes. Downtown Denver is booming. There must be a need for accountants in all those high-rises."

Sib and I shared a few more conversations over the next weeks. He convinced me I should give Denver a shot. Our plan was to find a suitable two-bedroom apartment in the downtown area, which teemed with young professionals in their twenties and thirties.

In February, I gave my two-week notice to the manager at the Bright Angel. I placed an ad in the local fish wrap, the *Pinion Press*, to sell my 10-speed bicycle. It was the most expensive possession I owned. I received my asking price of $150.

I had lived in a small apartment at the Canyon for the past year with my roommate Michelle. It was cheaply furnished, but it did include a well-stocked kitchen, a bed with bedding, a living room sofa and chair. I had very little personal stuff to pack up; only a handful of books, a few trinkets and knick-knacks, my clothing, and shoes. It all fit in a four-by-four-foot box, which I shipped home to Merchantville, New Jersey. My plan was to fly home for a brief visit with friends and family before I headed west to Denver.

I said my Canyon goodbyes. Teary-eyed, I hugged my friends. I knew we would probably never see each other again. (The Internet didn't exist and there was no social media. Even cell phones were a thing of the future.)

I spent a week in Merchantville and reconnected with high school friends I hadn't seen in years. Ninety percent of my high school graduating class still lived within a ten mile radius of Camden Catholic. I was the oddball when I headed west after college. My friends were quizzical why I wanted to return to the West *again* in less than a week to find a job. "What's wrong with Philadelphia?" they inquired. I tried to explain. "Nothing is wrong with Philadelphia. I just want to live near the mountains."

Paul and I revised our game plan and agreed we better wait to find our two-bedroom apartment until after I found a job. I had saved $10,000 from my stint at the Canyon, but I didn't want to blow the money on rent while I had no source of steady income. I decided to live with my grandfather, P.L., in Sterling while I conducted my job search. It seemed a prudent plan since I had no idea how long it would take me to find a suitable job.

Late February, I flew from Philadelphia to Denver. P.L. picked me up at the airport and drove me back to his home in Sterling. Sterling is in the northeastern part of Colorado, 110 miles from Denver. Sterling harbored roughly 11,000 residents - triple the size of Merchantville in the 1970s and 1980s – yet it still held small town appeal.

Merchantville was quite urban, surrounded by other towns and boroughs. When you stepped outside the city limits of Sterling, you were in the boonies, with nothing but wide-open space and farmland for miles and miles. You could drive for thirty minutes on the two-lane highway before a car approached from the opposite direction.

When I was a kid, my favorite time of year was the two weeks in August when we visited our grandparents, P.L. and Nell, in Sterling. My grandfather's given name was Percy Leroy, a name he despised. As a young adult, he adopted the moniker P.L. Nearly everyone called him P.L., except his wife Nell. My grandmother Nell chose to call him Red for the thick reddish-color hair he sported in his youth. She continued to call him Red long after his hair had turned to gray. When I knew him, he had just two tiny thin patches of white hair on either side of his crown. He was her Red until she died in April of 1980. They had been married for nearly 54 years.

If I were asked, "What is the most loving marriage you ever knew?" I would answer in a flash, "My grandmother and grandfather, Nell and P.L." They adored each other; it was obvious when you saw them together.

My grandmother and I shared a special bond. She was my favorite person in the entire world. Perhaps because I was so close to her, I didn't know P.L. very well as a kid. My focus had always been on my beloved grandmother. Now as a young adult ready to embark on my professional career, this was to change.

P.L. was in his early eighties in 1983, still as sharp and stubborn as ever. He chauffeured me to all my interviews in Denver. He insisted I sit in the passenger seat and relax on the two-hour drive. I used the time to psych myself for the pending interview. When we arrived in Denver, P.L. would find a shaded place to park the car, and there he sat and waited for me. He spread the *Wall Street Journal* or the *Denver Post* across his lap and read for the hour or so I was away on my interview. He never objected or complained.

We made trips to Denver twice a week that spring. By May, I had become discouraged; the repeated rejections took their toll on my self-esteem. P.L. offered his moral support and encouragement. He was witty and had a dry sense of humor.

We were on the return drive to Sterling one day after an interview I had with Colorado National Bank. P.L. asked, "How did it go? Did they ask you any tough questions today?"

"They caught me by surprise when they asked me to describe my weaknesses. I struggled to think fast and come up with a good answer. I responded to the man, 'I tend to be an overachiever and take on too many responsibilities.' I think that was an OK answer, since I turned a so-called weakness into a positive."

My grandfather frowned, clearly displeased. "I think it was a silly, inappropriate question for them to have asked. The next time some wiseguy asks you that, tell them your weakness is strawberry shortcake!"

In June, I scheduled an interview with L.C. Fulenwider, a prestigious real estate firm. They were pioneers in the field and had been in business since 1904. I met with Phil, their company controller, who was looking to hire an entry-level accountant. Phil was roughly ten years older than I, in his mid-thirties. He was tall and slender, and looked Italian with his dark hair and olive skin tone. Phil was clean-shaven and wore an expensive suit and tie. He appeared solemn and serious when we shook hands.

The interview went well from the get-go. His face lit up and I noticed a sparkle in his eyes when I discussed my time in the Grand Canyon. "I wish I had done something like that after college. You showed real guts and determination. It took self-confidence to go to the Canyon and stay for a lengthy time with no guarantee of a career job in the future."

Phil offered me the position and asked me to begin work in two weeks. P.L. was ecstatic. He knew of Fulenwider and their stellar reputation as a classy, reputable real estate firm. *He had done HIS job when he helped me secure MY job.*

I coordinated with Paul who located an ideal downtown apartment for us within ten days. I was excited to move to Denver, though sad to leave P.L. Our time in Sterling had been precious. I would miss him as well as his homemade strawberry shortcake. Truth be told, it was my weakness. P.L. passed away one year later in July.

———

Sib and I lived in the area known as Capitol Hill. Our apartment was located on the fourth floor at 999 Ogden Street, a building named the "Ogden Nines." The address was within two miles of the Colorado State Capitol Building and City Hall. It took me 30 minutes to walk from the Ogden Nines to the Fulenwider offices on bustling 17th Street.

Beautiful Washington Park is a mere two miles south of the Ogden Nines, and the park became my refuge. It is sizable, covering 165 acres. A three-mile paved road circles the perimeter and is a popular circuit for walkers, joggers, and cyclists. Volleyball nets were set up on the interior grassy lawns of the park. Dozens of volleyball games were played nearly every evening after work.

Sib and I often bicycled to Wash Park in the early evening. At 6' 5" height, Paul was a natural at volleyball. He joined a league with games or practice four times per week. Although I am tall (5 '10"), I lack hand/eye coordination and did not take to volleyball. I was content to pedal the circuit while Sib spiked the ball.

When Friday evening rolled around, we retrieved our guide books and selected one of the dozens of glorious hike options to do the next day. Saturday morning, we arose before daybreak and drove a mile to Denny's for a breakfast of poached eggs and toast. Then, we headed to the mountains. Our early start ensured we were off the 13,000-foot peak prior to the typical dangerous afternoon thunderstorms. The Saturday hikes became the highlight of my week.

––––––

Sunday, April 28, 1985, I awoke early, picked up the newspaper and sat outside on our balcony to read. By 10:00 a.m., the sun was intense, with not a glimpse of a cloud in the bright blue skies. I felt antsy, so I got on my bike and pedaled over to Washington Park to ride the perimeter circuit three or four times. Midway through my second loop, the chain slipped and disengaged from the gears. Ugh! I didn't wear bike gloves back then, and (like most recreational cyclists in the 1980s) I didn't even own a helmet. I carried no tools, not even a rag for this type of minor emergency.

I stopped, got off my bike, and walked over to the grassy interior lawn. I really did not want to do this - fix the chain and get my hands all greasy. I glanced to my right, and noticed a handsome guy with dark hair and blue eyes, perhaps in his late twenties. He looked athletic; I noticed the well-defined muscles in his calves. He sat relaxed, his bicycle by his side. I approached him, and cradled my "broken" bike under my right arm. I asked him if he could help me. This is how I met Gerry.

He quickly fixed my bike, getting the chain on its proper sprocket. "Thanks!"

"Sure. No problem. Why don't we ride a loop together? Might as well test it to make sure the gears work properly and the chain doesn't slip again."

"Sounds good to me," I replied.

We rode two or three loops and talked the entire time. Toward the end of our ride, I thanked him again for his help. We exchanged phone numbers, and said goodbye.

Two days later, Tuesday afternoon, April 30th, I answered the phone in my office cubicle.

"Hello, this is Gerry, the guy from the Park on Sunday. We should get together again. Do you happen to like Vietnamese food? I know of a great little place that serves fabulous Vietnamese. Are you free this Thursday evening?"

"Sure. I love Vietnamese. Thursday will be fine. I look forward to it."

I walked home from work that evening in a jubilant mood. I greeted Sib when I opened the apartment door, "Have you ever eaten Vietnamese food? What does it taste like?" Paul was as clueless as I was. We figured it must be similar to Chinese food. Back then, it wasn't possible to do a Google search or ask Siri.

Gerry lived in a small brick house on Dahlia Street, less than five miles from the Ogden Nines. He arrived in his red Subaru at 7:00 p.m., Thursday evening. Off we went to the Vietnamese restaurant located on South Federal Boulevard.

We entered the tiny restaurant and noticed half a dozen tables, a few booths, and a tiny kitchen in the back. Our waiter suggested several of their specialties. We feasted on spicy ginger chicken breasts, marinated pork, and sautéed veggies, with heaping bowls of rice to soak up the sauces. Truly delicious!

We were stuffed when we walked out the door two hours later. But we were gluttons and drove over to Lickety Split, (Denver's notorious ice cream shop) for a nightcap of double-decker cones. We ended the evening at El Chapultepec, a smoky, dark, and dank bar famous for their nightly live jazz music. Musicians take the stage and perform until last call at 2:00 a.m. We stayed until midnight. By then, the smoke had gotten to us. We left with blood-shot eyes, not from liquor but from the cigarettes.

The next day, Friday, the Fed Ex delivery guy arrived at our office as usual at 3:00 p.m. He dropped off a handful of urgent envelopes to my boss. Then, he walked over to my cubicle and placed a gorgeous bouquet of a dozen peach-colored roses on the corner of my desk. I opened the enclosed note card and read, *"I hope we spend much time together this summer....Gerry."*

I called home to Merchantville that weekend, as I did every few weeks to catch up with mom and dad. Mom answered the phone. I gushed, "You'll never believe this! I met a nice man in the Park last weekend on my bike ride. He asked me out to dinner Thursday evening and we had a fabulous time. He sent me a dozen roses the next day!" I went on and on about Gerry.

My mother and I share an uncanny "sixth sense." I later learned that, after we ended our conversation, she leaned toward my father and predicted, "Gerry Hans is the man Mary is going to marry. I just know it."

Gerry and I saw each other often that spring and summer. Neither of us had any interest to date anyone else. We shared many similar interests in addition to bicycling, ice cream, and jazz music. Everything seemed better with him by my side. On Friday afternoons, we headed to the mountains for weekend camping and hiking trips. Or we stayed local to bicycle. We went out to dinners and parties with friends, or we simply snuggled up on the couch at his house and listened to the stereo. By the fall, I rarely lived at the Ogden Nines with Sib. Instead, I spent most of my time on Dahlia Street with Gerry.

———

My sister Eileen married in late December of 1985. Gerry flew back east with Paul, Anne, and me for the holidays. We celebrated Christmas with my parents in Merchantville. Paul and Anne had gotten to know Gerry over the past several months, and they liked him. (Anne was a student at the University of Colorado in Boulder, a 45-minute drive from Denver.) Mom, Dad, and Eileen now finally got to meet Gerry and they also gave him their thumbs-up vote.

I showed Gerry my childhood haunts: the swim club, Camden Catholic High School, the Community Center, historic Centre Street in Merchantville. We also did the typical tourist routine and explored Philadelphia. We visited Independence Hall to see and touch the historic Liberty Bell.

In early 1986, Gerry began to mull over a career change. Gerry had graduated with a biology degree from the University of Illinois. He moved to Grand Junction, Colorado and worked in medical sales for six years. By the time I met him, he had already switched careers and had entered the corporate world of finance. Now, he considered switching firms and taking a job with a company in Los Angeles. In February, he flew to Los Angeles for two interviews. He was offered a position in March. The company wanted him to relocate to Los Angeles and begin work in June.

I was apprehensive. I had heard Los Angeles described as nasty, smoggy, overcrowded, and having horrendous traffic. I wasn't sure I wanted to live there. Yet, Gerry and I were in love and our priority was to be together. I couldn't fathom a long-distance relationship with Gerry in Los Angeles and me in Denver.

We became engaged and set our wedding date for May 24. Neither of us desired a fancy ceremony. We preferred a simple celebration in the tranquil setting of Gerry's back yard. It would be just the two of us, the required witnesses, and the justice of the peace.

We flew to St. Louis the first weekend in April. It was my turn to meet Gerry's family. His parents lived in the southern Illinois town of Edwardsville, 25 miles from St. Louis, Missouri. Edwardsville, incorporated in 1818, is the third-oldest city in the state and is the county seat of Madison County.

Gerry grew up on a 140-acre farm on the outskirts of town. He was the third of eight children, sandwiched between the only two girls in the family (his older sister Ginny and his younger sister Jane). Cattle, sheep, chickens, ducks, and geese could all be found on their land. Yet, the main focus was the crops: wheat, corn, soybeans, and alfalfa. The farm was a success, but his family gave it up and moved into town when Gerry was in junior high in the 1960s.

He has great stories about the mischief he got into on the farm. He and his older brother were playing Boy Scouts one afternoon. They accidentally set a huge haystack ablaze and nearly started the granary on fire.

I liked Gerry's family from the get-go. Most of his siblings lived within a few hours of Edwardsville and I was able to meet all but one brother that weekend. It was a challenge to remember the names of the siblings and spouses, not to mention a dozen nieces and nephews! I have grown very fond of the Hans family over the years, especially Gerry's mother Ann, who reminds me of my beloved grandmother Nell.

Although it wasn't our original intention, both sets of parents were in attendance when we exchanged our vows on May 24th. When they learned of the date, they invited themselves. "We'll be there!" they promised. It all worked out for the best. Paul, Eileen, and Anne also joined us on our special day. Gerry and I stood in the shade under his large maple tree on a bright sunny afternoon and pledge our "I Dos" at the end of the twenty-minute ceremony. In the evening, our party of nine celebrated with dinner at The Normandy, a gourmet French restaurant located on historic Colfax Boulevard in Denver.

Gerry and I headed to Vancouver and Vancouver Island for our honeymoon. Gerry handled the travel plans and reservations. He booked us into a bed and breakfast in Vancouver for three nights in the home of a sweet elderly retired German couple. They served us hearty breakfasts each morning: pancakes, eggs, bacon, pastries, and juices. We explored the quaint, clean downtown area and also the exhibits at the World Fair, held in Vancouver that summer.

Next, we sailed to Vancouver Island for four nights. We rented a private house located on a secluded beach. It was peaceful and quiet with no TV, no radio, no stereo, (and of course, no iPhones and no Internet). One day, we chartered a boat and guide for a deep sea fishing excursion. Gerry landed two good-sized salmon, roughly ten pounds each. We arranged to have the salmon smoked on the island and shipped to Denver.

We threw a going-away party for ourselves a week after we returned to Denver. The invitations were inscribed, "We Love L.A., or At Least We Will Try!" Nearly a hundred friends attended. The party started in the early afternoon and carried on to past midnight. The smoked salmon was a huge hit.

The next two weeks were a whirlwind as we packed up everything for the move to Los Angeles. I felt excited, yet nervous. Gerry and I made a pact, "We'll give it five years. If one (or both) of us doesn't love Los Angeles by then, we will return to Denver."

CHAPTER FIVE

The "Los Feliz Flyers"

"California Here We Come!"

Not just a song lyric, but my reality! By the end of June 1986, we were settled into our temporary digs, a furnished apartment in Marina del Rey, a coastal town just south of popular Venice Beach. I remained guardedly optimistic that I would adjust to the Californian lifestyle.

Gerry's company covered the expenses of our move. They even footed the bill for our first two months' rent at the Oakwood Apartments (temporary corporate housing). Amenities at the Oakwood included an outside pool, spa and barbecue area, laundry facilities, and a fitness-exercise gym room.

We were given a $40-per-day allocation for food, an extravagant amount in 1986. The time at Marina del Rey, living at the beach for a few months, felt like an extension of our honeymoon.

Within a few days, I soon realized the oven didn't work. I followed a simple recipe and placed a small chicken along with a handful of red potatoes seasoned with rosemary in the 375-degree oven for an hour. When we sat down to eat, the chicken was pretty much raw and the potatoes still hard as rocks. It took another hour before we could sink our teeth into our dinner.

So, we took advantage of the $40 perk and dined out often. I discovered sushi. The very idea of eating cold cooked rice with raw fish was unheard of in Merchantville, the Canyon, and in Denver. Kifune, a Japanese restaurant located a block away from the Oakwood, employed a master chef whose sushi and sashimi creations were delicious and works of art. We became regulars there.

Our Marina del Rey neighborhood offered every ethnic cuisine imaginable. My favorites were the dozens of mom and pop Thai restaurants within a few-mile radius. We tried nearly all of them. Most were tiny places with limited seating of perhaps a dozen tables. They offered extensive menus with a fine selection of authentic spicy Thai cuisine.

I wasn't in any particular hurry to find a job and took advantage of living two blocks from the beach. I would walk from our apartment and five minutes later dip my toes into the ocean surf. I strolled the boardwalk, rife with joggers and runners, for hours. I hadn't run much since my college days at Shippensburg, and suddenly I missed the sport.

One morning, I laced up my sneakers and ran a mile on the boardwalk. A few days later, I ran again, only a little further.

Within a week, I built up my mileage to three or four miles every other day and felt exhilarated and energized. The running also calmed my mind and helped me relax. I never tired of the sounds of the surf or the sights of the waves as they crashed ashore.

I awakened with Gerry when the alarm rang at 3:45 a.m. He was out the door by 4:30 a.m. since he needed to be downtown at work by 5:00 a.m. I waited until sunrise before I left for my morning jog.

After a month of being unemployed, guilt weighed upon me. I also felt isolated and lonely. It was a challenge to make friends in the Oakwoods. I had acquaintances, other young adults I chatted with poolside in the afternoons. But the very premise of the Oakwoods - *temporary corporate housing* - is not conducive to lasting friendships. Most residents lived there for mere weeks. Rarely did a tenant stay for longer than a month. We were the exception.

"I need to get a job," I told Gerry one evening in early August. "I don't want to wait another month until we leave the marina." I am happiest when I am busy and productive. I registered with Accountemps, the world's first and largest specialized temporary agency for accounting, finance, and bookkeeping professionals. Accountemps assignments could be as short as a one-day stint or as long as a three-month commitment.

My first job was at a small electronics company in Beverly Hills. It was boring, tedious work, but at least I brought home a paycheck and brushed up on my accounting skills. And I got to interact with other professionals. I kept the job for about a month, until we left Marina del Rey in September and moved inland.

———

Gerry had worked with his friend Geoff in the early 1980s in south Denver. Geoff attended our "We Love L.A. or At Least We'll Try" farewell party in Colorado. He gave us the contact information for his older sister Diane, a pediatrician who lived in the Hollywood Hills. Diane had planned a six-month sabbatical in Australia from October 1986 until March 1987. She had the jitters about leaving her house unattended and unoccupied for half a year and hoped to find a house sitter while she was away.

The timing was ideal for us. We met Diane one sunny September afternoon at her home on North Knoll Drive. The address was a mile from the Hollywood Reservoir and close to the Burbank studios and Griffith Park. The tree-lined streets in her neighborhood were narrow with many a blind curve and no sidewalks. The houses were Spanish-American architecture with white-washed walls and terracotta patios. Well-manicured lawns landscaped with native plants caught the eye. Vibrant pink and red bougainvillea vines draped over the driveways. Quiet and serene, it was quite the contrast from the noisy hustle-bustle of Marina de Rey.

We were thrilled to live in Diane's hillside home, a gorgeous moderate-sized two-bedroom house built in the 1960s with a newly-renovated modern kitchen. It gave us an additional six months' time to explore and decide, "Where in the massive metropolis of Los Angeles do we want to make our home?" (Our furniture and fixtures from Denver remained safe and secure in a storage unit in downtown Los Angeles.) We found we preferred to live in the hills instead of by the beach. We hiked the trails in nearby Griffith Park for hours and ran loops on the three-and-a-half-mile paved road which circled the Hollywood Reservoir.

In February, a realtor showed us a two-bedroom house less than five miles from Diane's. "This place definitely needs some work," Gerry and I agreed, after we toured this 1957 house. It was the original kitchen with yellow Formica countertops, a black-and-white checkered linoleum floor, and scant cabinet space. Wood floors throughout the remainder of the house were stained a deep almost-black brown. Hideous ugly shutters covered all the windows. Closed, they blocked every ounce of natural sunlight. The entire interior needed a fresh coat of paint.

But the location was perfect. You could scramble up the hillside from the back yard and be in the Park. We made an offer and closed the deal in March of 1987. This is the place I have called "home" ever since. I love it here.

———

Things looked rosier for me career-wise. My temporary Accountemps position with Marvin Davis Companies turned into a permanent job. Oil magnate billionaire Marvin Davis, a Denver transplant like me, lived in Beverly Hills. His corporate offices were just west of there, in Century City. They occupied the 28th and 29th floors of a high-rise building on Avenue of the Stars.

It was a pretentious but appropriate street name. Marvin Davis's offices were "Star" quality, posh and swanky. I never saw a more glamorous office suite. Lobby floors were marble, hand-picked slabs imported from Italy. Decorative furnishings included ancient Chinese vases worth thousands of dollars. My spacious private office on the 29th floor featured a plush cream-colored carpet and large picture windows. I sat in a high-backed, black leather swivel chair behind a massive walnut desk.

The executive offices on the 28th floor were even more extravagant. Mr. Davis's office suite included his private bathroom. Rumor was it featured a gold-plated commode.

A strict dress code was enforced at Marvin Davis Companies. Women were required to wear dresses, or blouses and skirts, and pantyhose. Bare legs were verboten, as were trousers. We did not partake in a "casual dress" Friday, common at the various companies where my professional friends worked.

My claim to fame during my Marvin Davis tenure took me by surprise when I shared the elevator ride to the high floors of our building with President Ronald Reagan. President Reagan was retired from his second term in office. He established his post-presidential office suite on the 34th floor of our building.

It was an early Friday morning in May of 1989. I showed my ID to the security guard (standard protocol), and approached the elevator lobby. I pushed the "25–35" floors button. I glanced to my right and recognized the President who stood nearby with two official looking men. His reported height was six foot one inch when he took office in 1980. I stand at five foot ten inches, perhaps six foot with my dress heels. Yet, I towered over President Reagan. Maybe he had shrunk over the years from the pressures of being our Commander in Chief?

The elevator doors opened within seconds. I was bashful and murmured, "Please Mr. President, go ahead, I'll wait for the next elevator." He looked me in the eye and replied, "No, no, no. We both have to get to work. Please step in." So, I rode up to the 29th floor with President Reagan and his two security guards.

Marvin Davis was enormous, six feet four inches and 300-plus pounds. He had a huge appetite and the resources to satisfy it. Davis thought delis in Los Angeles were subpar to those in New York. Once, he called his wife Barbara before he stepped aboard his private jet to return home from New York. "I'm bringing home $1,000 of pastrami sandwiches from the Carnegie." He tired of schlepping deli food from New York and opened his own restaurant in Beverly Hills. Davis hired famed designer Pat Kuleto and gave him a budget of $4 million to "build me the best deli in the world." The west coast version of the Carnegie Deli opened August 9, 1989. The *Los Angeles Times* described it as "the most hyped deli opening in history."

I was one of Davis's five staff accountants who reported to the controller Grace. At first, I enjoyed the work. I learned the oil business and then helped manage the books of the Carnegie Deli. I was intrigued with the food and beverage industry and harbored hopes of my own restaurant or other small business someday.

By September, I was no longer happy with my job. I had given up three Saturdays straight and had put in 15-16 hours per week of unpaid overtime; but even that wasn't enough. Grace often showed up at 7:00 a.m. and worked until midnight. She expected similar dedication from her staff, which was ridiculous. Marvin Davis, with a net worth of $1.7 billion, was among the wealthy in Los Angeles. Why didn't he hire more staff?

Grace was an attractive, single Italian woman ten years older than I. She was stylish, with impeccable taste in clothes. Her dark black hair was perfectly coifed, her lipstick always fresh. One Tuesday morning, she called the five of us into her office. She was furious as she screamed at us for leaving "early" at 6:00 p.m. the previous evening. I stared at her as it dawned on me she was dressed in the same expensive Ann Taylor suit she had worn on Monday. "I worked on the Deli books until 4:00 a.m. I might have been able to go home and get some sleep if some of you had a stronger work ethic." I was stunned that she had spent the whole night at the office.

I resigned the following month.

I became an independent contractor and started my own consulting business, Button Accounting Services. Davis Companies didn't miss me. When I left, they continued to thrive. Marvin Davis prospered and died at the age of 79 in September 2004. He left his descendants a fortune of $5.8 billion.

———

In 1986 when I lived in Denver, my sister Anne and I entered a local 5K charity race in Boulder to raise funds for breast cancer. It was the first race I had entered since my high school days at Camden Catholic. We registered in the special category, "Sisters Division." The race allowed such divisions as mother/daughter, father/daughter, roommates, aunt/niece, brother/sister, brothers, and sisters. Anne and I both ran the 5K in less than 20 minutes and we won the "sisters" division. I had fond memories of that race and decided to find a 5K to run in Southern California. A blurb in the *Los Angeles Times* caught my eye.

The fourth annual Star Festival 5-K run and fun walk will be held Sunday, July 17, 1988 at Pacific Square, 1630 W. Redondo Beach Blvd., Gardena. The 5-K will start at 8 a.m. Entry fee is $12 with t-shirt or $7 for the run only. There will be an extra $3 charge for registrations received after July 1.

Late June, I mailed in my race registration. Gerry drove me to the race, a half-hour drive. We arrived before 7:00 a.m., more than an hour prior to the start. It was chaotic and crowded. I became nervous as I milled around, talked with fellow runners, and stretched my legs. I couldn't believe the number of people. There were easily a couple thousand runners - roughly 75 percent men, 25 percent women.

I later learned the Gardena Star Festival was one of the more prestigious certified 5K races in the nation. The race drew an elite field of the top runners in the world; it was quite possible a world-record 5K would be run. Prize money was doled out to the top ten finishers, male and female.

Thousands of spectators lined the race course. Gerry squeezed in with others on the sidewalk about a block away from the finish line. He saw the top finishers and also caught a glimpse of me when I rounded the final corner for the home stretch.

I finished 11th woman, just shy of the prize purse. I was elated that I finished the race in 18 minutes 55 seconds. (I had achieved my goal: a sub-twenty-minute 5K, like Anne and I ran in Boulder a few years earlier.)

That day marked a turning point in my running career. My time placed me fifth in my age-group division (25 to 29-year-old females). Top six age-group finishers were awarded a commemorative beer mug engraved with the race date and the Gardena 5K logo. I cherish this mug.

Local running clubs congregated after the race. They stood under canopy pop-up tents in their team jerseys. I overheard much laughter and talking; I envied their obvious camaraderie.

We drove back home shortly after noon. A world record had not been set, but Gerry reported it had been a neck-to-neck sprint to the finish. Then he remarked, "You didn't appear as exhausted as most of the other runners as they finished. You barely broke a sweat. It looked like you could have kept on running. Maybe you should consider the 10K."

I took his advice. A month later, August 21, I ran my first 10K race, the Tom Proctor 5K/10K in West Hollywood. Once again, Gerry chauffeured me to the race and cheered me on.

Tom Proctor didn't draw the crowds of the Gardena 5K. Fewer than 500 of us were registered. I spotted a shaded place to stretch, beneath the branches of a sycamore tree where other runners were gathered on this scorching morning.

"What race are you doing?" I asked the tall lanky guy who stood next to me as he bent down to touch his toes. "I'm doing the 5K. No way would I do a 10K in this heat. How about you?"

"I'm doing the 10K – my first one."

"Good luck. Make sure you drink water at both aid stations. It's going to be a hot one!"

The majority ran the 5K that day. Their course was one loop, and the 10K runners ran this same loop twice. Our race bibs did not differentiate between the 5K and 10K runners. Often, when a race featured two distance options, bibs were unique colors. The 5K bib might be yellow and the 10K bib blue. Runners knew their competition. It also helped race officials steer the runners in the correct direction.

As I completed the first loop, most runners ahead of me veered off to the right to the finish line. A handful of runners continued on their second loop. It was only guys as far ahead as I could see.

Maybe I was the first woman? The thought crossed my

mind. I had set a goal to run the 10K under 40 minutes. When I caught a glance at the large electronic time clock to the right, the illuminated letters blinked 19:06. I was on pace for a sub-forty. I could even slow down a bit the second lap and still achieve my goal.

Many runners despise races with repetitive loops because it can be boring to do the same circuit twice. But it is conducive to running an evenly-paced race since there are no surprises on the course. The second half is the same as the first. Elite runners may run a "negative split," which is when you run the second half of the race *faster* than the first half. Challenging, difficult to do! Statistics back up the wisdom of the negative split. Competitive long-distance runners learn to master it. Often, the marathoner who goes home with the gold medal ran a negative split race.

The sun beat down on me as I approached the finish line at Tom Proctor and I caught a glimpse of the time clock.....38:35, 38:36, 38:37, 38:38... I stepped over the line...<u>38:39</u>!

I finished first female and came pretty damn close to a negative split, with a 19:06 first half and a 19:33 second half.

I was ecstatic as I approached the awards stage 30 minutes later. The race honored the top three finishers in both the 5K and 10K, male and female. The emcee handed me my trophy as well as a complimentary entry into next year's Los Angeles Marathon, scheduled the first Sunday in March 1989.

The Los Angeles Marathon? Why give the winner of a 10K race an entry to a marathon? A marathon is more than *four times* the distance. Surely most 10K runners don't run marathons. I tucked the free entry into a desk drawer when I got home that afternoon.

Tuesday after work, I went to the Bally's gym as usual. I saw my friend Joe, a runner roughly my age. He spoke with a thick New York accent, and had arrived in Los Angeles five years ago straight from the Bronx. He knew I had registered for the Tom Proctor race.

"How did it go? Did you actually do it? It was a sizzler Sunday. I don't blame you if you decided to bail."

"Actually, the heat didn't bother me. I ran a 38:39 and finished first female."

"Congratulations, but that is so unfair. I've raced more than a dozen 10Ks the past five years. I got serious about it a year ago and upped my mileage from 30 to 40 miles per week with the hope to break 40 minutes in a 10K. And you go out and run a 38-minute 10K the first time? Take advantage of your gift, this talent. Work hard and you could be a world class runner."

I took Joe's advice to heart. I bought a journal to keep track of my mileage. The first week, I scribbled down 15. The next week, I upped it to 18. Then, it was 20...25...30.

I opened my desk drawer once in a while to verify that the Los Angeles Marathon entry was still there. The notion of a marathon wasn't quite as ridiculous as I first thought.

In October, Gerry and I both entered the "Run for the Homeless," a 10K in Griffith Park.

The proceeds benefitted Chrysalis, a nonprofit Skid Row

organization which helps those down on their luck find jobs and turn their lives around. Crowds turned out despite overcast skies and occasional drizzle. The field included several dozen former drug addicts and former alcoholics.

The course was hilly, unlike the pancake-flat streets of my first 10K on the streets of West Hollywood. The roads in Griffith Park are rolling, with a few steep inclines. I ran 39:54, more than a minute slower than my first 10K. At least, I squeaked in under 40 minutes and I was the first female to finish.

Gerry and I mingled with fellow runners as we awaited the awards ceremony. We were drawn toward a group of three guys and one gal who wore red shorts and matching singlets. The words "Los Feliz Flyers" were embellished on the front of their jerseys. I was curious about their club. The woman, Eva, looked to be Gerry's age. She was Hispanic and very attractive with her shoulder-length thick dark hair and the strong lean body of an athlete. She beamed a bright smile as she enthusiastically told us about the Flyers.

Los Feliz Boulevard is a beautiful tree-lined street, three-miles long, near the southern border of Griffith Park. The Los Feliz Flyers, aka "Flyers," was a grass-roots running club with two dozen members. The club was founded in 1986 by four friends who trained together for the Los Angeles Marathon. They were coached by Gary, a native of Torrance, CA and a former competitive high school track star. The Flyers raced frequently in Southern California. Any given weekend, a handful of them entered a 5K or 10K. Their favorite venue was Griffith

Park, their local training ground.

Eva suggested I join them Tuesday evening. At 6:00 p.m., the group gathered at The Sport Shoe, the running store located a half mile away from the Park. They stretched and chit-chatted there for a few minutes before they ran into the park. "We run to 'The Tree' and back," explained Eva. "It's about five-and-a-half miles." The park has thousands of trees; the Flyers "tree" was a massive oak. The rule was: you touched the tree, and then you turned around and ran back to the store.

The Sport Shoe was "rustic." The building dated back to the 1950s. The owners didn't seem to care about the upkeep and appearance. Paint peeled from the walls. The wooden floor was uneven; half of the floor boards were rotting. The store was divided into two rooms. The display room in the front was marginally nicer than the inventory room in the back where boxes of shoes were stacked haphazardly from floor to ceiling. The back room stank of Steve's body odor.

Steve was the store manager. A decade ago, he was one of San Diego's top distance runners. He had switched from being a competitive runner to a heavy beer drinker. He boasted of his six-pack-a-day habit. His unkempt appearance fit in with the store. Steve stood six feet tall and weighed more than 250 pounds. He was unshaven and seldom bathed. Rumor had it that he slept among the towers of shoes, which explains why the air in that room was infused with his rank body odor.

With three or four of the guys, I ran to the Tree that Tuesday at a steady seven-minute-per-mile pace. Gerry joined me the next week. Each Tuesday evening, at least ten Flyers met to run to the Tree.

I considered Los Angeles a not-so-friendly place until I met the Flyers. My co-workers lived miles away and we didn't socialize. Most of our neighbors were elderly and didn't go out much. I ran and hiked by myself. I had a fair number of acquaintances, but very few friends. Gerry and I became active with the Flyers for the next fifteen years which provided us with a fun and busy social calendar. The timing was right for I was just about to give up on Los Angeles. The running club changed my life.

We met to see a movie, go out to dinner, attend a concert, or explore the latest exhibit at the art museum. Best of all were the glorious summer Saturdays at the beach. We ran seven miles, ate breakfast at a local café, and then played volleyball for hours. We took dips in the ocean to cool off between games.

"Los Feliz Flyers Running and Adventure Club" was our appropriate and official name. In June 1989, a mere nine months after I first met Eva, we joined the Flyers on their Rosarito Beach adventure. Rosarito Beach is a coastal town on the Baja peninsula of Mexico, a three-hour drive south of Los Angeles.

Thirty Flyers shared this memorable weekend together. We ran the race – a 5K, 10K or 10-miler – Saturday morning. We lazed about on the sandy beach in the afternoon. Saturday evening, we celebrated with a delicious dinner of fresh lobster. Later, we danced the night away at Calafia, an outdoor nightclub perched high on the beach above the surf of the Pacific. It required a climb of a hundred uneven wobbly stone steps to reach the dance floor. There's no way a club with this dangerous footing would be legal in Los Angeles. The experience was surreal – the music, the scenery, and the surf.

I first met my dear friend Chuck on a Tuesday when he showed up at The Sport Shoe after Gerry and I had been with the Flyers for about a year.

"Where are you from?" I asked this new person. He was stocky, several inches shorter than I. He looked to be ten years my senior and seemed shy.

"Denver," he answered.

"Wow, what a coincidence! That's where I'm from. How long have you been here?"

"Two weeks, and I hate Los Angeles. I'm ready to move back."

"Give it some time. I couldn't stand Los Angeles either at first."

Chuck and I have been friends ever since our initial conversation.

Ours was a tightly-knit running club. What began as a group of four friends in the mid-1980s, expanded to a membership of nearly forty by the early 1990s. Yet, we remained very much loosely organized. The club grew, mostly because of our coach Gary who was the most charismatic person I ever knew.

On a sunny Sunday morning in April 1991, seven of us tackled the hilly six-mile trail run starting from our backyard. Afterwards, we sat in our patio drinking Gatorade and eating my homemade banana bread. We got into a philosophical discussion about the future of the Los Feliz Flyers. We agreed we lived in a society which was becoming more and more litigious (especially here in Los Angeles, a city where neighbor sued neighbor).

Of course, Chuck would never sue me. Even if he stumbled over a rock in my backyard, tripped and broke his back, he would not file suit. Nor would I ever sue him. But our club was expanding. Every Tuesday, more runners showed up to run to the Tree. We didn't know these newbies very well. Just suppose one of them tripped and suffered an injury. Could they sue our club? Could they even sue us personally? These were serious questions.

We had researched membership in the Road Runners Club of America (RRCA). The RRCA, formed in 1958, is the oldest and largest organization in the United States dedicated to distance running. Over 1,000 running clubs, (representing nearly 200,000 runners) are members of the RRCA, the official governing body of our sport. A key perk is the liability coverage RRCA provides at a bargain-basement price.

We took a vote and it was unanimous. The seven of us decided the Flyers should join RRCA. The next week, we filled out the paperwork and mailed in the $300 annual membership. It was well worth the peace of mind. The Flyers were now insured; we had no more worries of lawsuits.

However, our club was no longer free. In late 1991, after

the Flyers joined RRCA, we charged $35 annual dues. Most of this money went to the RRCA. We also paid a fee to Caltech (California Institute of Technology) of Pasadena to reserve their track for three hours each Wednesday evening for our speed work intervals. We registered as a non-profit corporation. The spirit of the Flyers remained the same as before we became organized, and Coach Gary never accepted a dime.

Running boomed in the 1990s. Clubs sprouted up throughout the country. Most were highly official, with Boards of Directors, lengthy by-laws, and written policies. Sadly, many grass-roots clubs gradually disappeared, replaced by corporate-like machines.

Marathons surged in popularity. Small towns and big cities alike began to host races. In the 1980s, only serious high-mileage runners attempted a marathon. By the mid-1990s, it seemed nearly every long-distance runner harbored the goal to experience the 26.2 mile event. Running clubs formed with the sole mission to train their members to safely finish a marathon. These new-age clubs signed up runners several months in advance of the marathon date.

The L.A. Leggers Running Club was founded by Bob Scott in 1989. His goal was to offer the Leggers an eight-month training program to complete the March 1990 Los Angeles Marathon. Membership was free. To the best of Scott's knowledge, such a program had never before been offered. At 8:30 a.m., March 4, 1990, 249 Leggers were among the 18,000 gathered on Figueroa Street in downtown Los Angeles for the start of the marathon. One Legger was forced to drop out at mile 15 because of an injury. By late afternoon, 248 Leggers finished the race. Tears streamed down the faces of some as they approached the finish. Scott was ecstatic; his program had proved to be an undeniable success.

Casual runners and walkers have joined the ranks of marathoners. It is no longer verboten to walk during the marathon. Old-timers never walked in the race except as a last resort when they had "hit the wall." "Hit the Wall" is runner slang for when the body becomes depleted of oxygen. It usually happens after mile 20 when it is impossible to put one foot in front of the other. When you hit the wall, it is time for the "marathon shuffle;" you stagger, walk, stumble, or crawl your way to the finish.

In 1980, there were roughly 143,000 marathon finishers in the United States. A decade later in 1990, that number had jumped to 224,000. By the year 2000, the number reached 353,000. The statistics for 2010 is 507,000 finishers. The numbers continue to skyrocket.

CHAPTER SIX

My First Marathon

I LOOKED FORWARD to Tuesdays and our run to the Tree. Our club attracted runners of all abilities, from the faster six-minute-a-mile pace runners to those who plugged along at a sixteen-minute walk/jog. We adhered to our strict Flyer policy: *no one runs alone, ever.* Safety was top priority; to run alone to the Tree at night was forbidden.

We returned to the Sport Shoe after the run. Steve greeted us with his dumb-blonde jokes. (I tried not to take offense.) Then, he handed us plastic cups of Gatorade from the huge vat container. Hydrated, we walked into Giamela's, the mom-and-pop pizza joint next door, and ordered several pizzas. I consumed mega-calories to support my 40-to-50-mile per week running habit.

One evening mid-October 1988, I sat next to John at Giamela's. John was 30 years old, six-foot tall, Irish, fair-skinned and freckled, with the sinewy runner's build. I glanced at him as he spoke while the parmesan pizza cheese oozed down his chin.

"Why don't you ever attend the Wednesday night track workout at Caltech? It will make you a faster runner." He grabbed his napkin to catch the dribbles of cheese.

"I have no interest in track. I haven't set foot upon a track since my high school days at Camden Catholic back in 1977. It doesn't sound like much fun to me. I am not a sprinter and don't have the 'fast-twitch' muscles."

"Mary, all elite middle-distance and long-distance runners do track workouts. Believe me, if you 'do track,' your 5K and 10K times will improve. Trust me."

The next Wednesday, I showed up at Caltech. When I arrived, fifteen other Flyers were well into their two-mile jog warm-up, eight laps upon the spongy rubberized (a gentler surface than asphalt) track.

Then the workout began. We ran 800 yards (two laps) at a quick, uncomfortable pace. The goal was to reach oxygen debt at the end of the interval. I heard Coach Gary shout out times as he read from his watch, "2:55, 2:56." I gasped for air as I finished under three minutes. I bent forward, hugged my knees, and caught my breath. Coach Gary yelled, "OK, Everyone. Good Job. Take a recovery lap." I jogged the one lap, 400 yards. "See if you can do the rest of the intervals in less than three minutes."

I came close. I heard Gary call out "3:05" as I finished my sixth and final 800-yard interval. I left the track weak and worn out. Thirty minutes later, Gerry and I were seated at a Thai restaurant, which was located within a mile of Caltech. I devoured my Pad Thai when it was placed in front of me.

Long Beach Half Marathon was on the upcoming local-race calendar. Six Flyers had already registered, including my friend John. We talked at Giamela's Tuesday evening in early November, and he encouraged me.

"You should do it, Mary. You look strong. We can run it together." The longest I had ever run was ten miles. I remained skeptical, but I registered for the race.

I called my friend Shari and asked her to join me at Palermo's for dinner Saturday night before the race. Palermo's, a neighborhood Italian restaurant was known for its generous portions of pasta, reasonable prices, and friendly service. Maitre d' Tony greeted us with a smile when we walked in and an animated, "Hey, how you doin' tonight?"

There was a wait, so he made his standard offer, "Have a seat in the lobby and enjoy complimentary glasses of vino until your table is ready." I passed on free wine this pre-race evening. Shari and I feasted on salad, homemade lasagna, and a basket of buttery, garlic bread. I was stuffed when we exited and feared the heavy meal might keep me up all night.

I tossed and turned, but managed a few hours of sleep. I got behind the wheel of my Honda Civic at 6:00 a.m. for the 40 minute drive to Long Beach. I allowed enough time to find a place to park and find John in the crowd of 3,000 runners before the 8:00 a.m. race start.

We found each other and staged ourselves a few rows behind the elite fast runners at the front of the pack. John thought we were where we should be, with the seven-minute-per-mile runners. Our goal was to finish under 90 minutes, a 6:52 pace for the 13.1 race.

At target pace the first six miles, we ran side by side with identical strides. I did most of the talking. John listened, chimed in an occasional word or two. As we neared the half-way mark, he huffed, "Go ahead. I need to slow it down a bit for the next mile. I'll catch up with you later."

"Are you sure?"

"Yes! Go on."

I missed John the second half of the race. I was nervous without him beside me. I hoped he would rejoin me, but it didn't happen. My official time for my inaugural half marathon was 1:26:45, a 6:37 pace, placing me sixth female overall, third in my 25-29 year-old age division.

Exhausted, yet thrilled and proud to have run Long Beach Half Marathon, I smiled as I drove back home. The marathon distance still seemed daunting, but not impossible. I opened the desk drawer that evening. My free Los Angeles Marathon entry was still there.

——

Hooked, I entered races twice a month. In the late 1980s, you could run a race in Los Angeles every weekend, and it didn't cost much. I paid $20 or $25 tops for a 10K race.

We spent Thanksgiving weekend 1988 with Gerry's family in Southern Illinois. We stayed with his parents in Edwardsville. The Great River Road Run, a 10-miler, is held Saturday morning in nearby Alton, Illinois, a 30-minute drive from Edwardsville. The race and I share the same birth year - 1959. Gerry's uncle, Mike Brazier, ran the inaugural race in 1959 when he was a senior in high school and has run every year since.

Mike is a legend in the running community of Alton. I met him Saturday morning when we arrived at 9:30 a.m. a half hour before the 10:00 a.m. start. Southern Illinois is chilly late November. Temperatures hovered in the low 30s, and I shivered along with Mike and several hundred runners as we jogged in place to keep warm pre-race. I seldom ran in tights back home, but I gladly wore them this morning.

The pancake-flat course was a simple out-and-back. We ran five miles along the River Road which parallels the banks of the Mississippi River; circled the orange cone at the turnaround, then ran back to the start/finish line. I raced with a time of 1:04:39, a 6:28-minute-per-mile pace, second female to finish. My weekly Caltech track practices had paid off.

Historic downtown Hotel Stratford hosted the post-race celebration. Uncle Mike and I chatted and got to know each other over a couple of bottles of Coors and bowls of the Stratford's famous homemade chili in the downstairs bar.

A few years later, the post-race party moved upstairs to a much larger room to accommodate the growing number of participants. Registration had skyrocketed to more than a thousand. Coors remained a sponsor, but sadly it was no longer chili and beer post-race. Instead, jelly donuts and coffee filled the bill.

November 28, 2009, marked the 50th annual Great River Road Run. The race director made a big deal about Uncle Mike before the start of the race. Mike stepped up to the mike to thunderous applause from the crowd of runners and spectators. "I won the first race in 1959. There aren't too many races that have lasted so many decades, but I love that this race has. I'm excited to be here." He was 68 years young.

The starting gun fired. Mike wore race bib #1, his honorary race number which he has worn the past 10 years. He finished faster than his goal time of two and a half hours, with two seconds to spare. "I was happy to do a 15-minute pace. I did a combination of a jog and walk, but I jogged the entire final mile!"

———

John and I met on a morning in early February 1989, and he introduced me to a new running trail near the Rose Bowl in Pasadena. We ran fifteen miles on the dirt path just north of the Bowl on cross country-type terrain, plenty of rocky uphill and downhill. My feet became soaked as we crossed the streams, which meant blisters afterward. But it was well worth it!

I recorded the run in my journal, "Fun! Longest I have ever run; a wonderful morning." Days later, sick with the flu and a fever of 101, I wrote in the diary, "No running. I am tired and miserable. I can't get enough sleep." I didn't run a step the next ten days.

Later in the month, I joined the Flyers for another 15-miler. This time we were in Palm Springs, the desert town two hours east of Los Angeles where older people retire. Parents of our friend/coach Gary owned a vacation home here. Gary invited a dozen of us for the weekend. "Bring your sleeping bags. There is plenty of carpeted floor space to unroll them and sleep."

Saturday morning, we got up at 6:00 a.m. to run while it was "cool." Eighty degrees in the morning is preferable to the 100-degree temps in the afternoon. We ran at a brisk pace, and strangely no one broke out in a sweat. *We were sweating*, but since it quickly evaporated due to the dryness, we didn't notice. We drank gallons of water when we returned.

This was my first trip to Palm Springs, a posh, well-planned, gated community. A manicured golf course sat within 200 yards of Gary's back door. The golf course meandered behind all the mansions on this three-mile circular street. Swimming pools were on every block. We dipped into at least five of them. At sunset, we whipped up a batch of frothy margaritas and fired up the backyard barbecue grill for a delicious Mexican-themed meal of carne asada tacos, chips and guacamole, rice, and beans.

Back in Los Angeles, I awoke early Tuesday morning and felt feverish. I stumbled out of bed to the medicine cabinet, found the thermometer and took my temperature. It read 102 degrees. Damn. For the second time, a 15-miler had kicked my butt.

I "called in sick" to Marvin Davis Companies, which was

a first, though I had been with them for over a year. I spent the day in bed and tried to read and rest. With no appetite, I forced myself to eat bowls of chicken noodle soup and saltines.

Thursday, I was back in my office on Avenue of the Stars. I was my healthy self within a few weeks, able to run. I felt strong enough to go to Caltech for the Wednesday evening track workout, though I didn't push myself. I ran the intervals at a slower pace than usual. Gary jogged next to me as we did our four laps, one-mile easy cooldown. We talked about the upcoming Los Angeles Marathon.

"Eight Flyers are running 'Los Angeles' this year. Maybe you should register. You have the free entry you won last August."

"Gary, the furthest I have ever run is 15 miles. I did it twice and got sick a few days later, both times."

"Just a coincidence. You probably caught the flu and would have gotten sick anyway."

"I doubt it. I never get sick."

"Well, think about it. I really believe you can do it. You'll get swept up in all the hoopla and excitement of the marathon. Worst case scenario, you drop out of the race."

I left work Friday, March 3rd, and drove to the Hilton Hotel near LAX airport. Los Angeles Marathon registration and the expo were in two adjoining banquet rooms of the hotel. The rooms were jammed with thousands of runners who came to pick up their race packets, t-shirts, and goody bags. I found the line for late registration and turned in my free entry, filled out the application, and signed the liability waiver. It was official. I had entered the race.

I left the expo with knots in my stomach over what I had just done. I called Gary when I arrived home. "Mary, I'm so glad you registered! And, just so you know, no Flyer has ever entered and then dropped out of the marathon. All Flyers have finished."

"Thanks for the pressure, Gary. Not your message of two days ago."

Sunday morning, March 5, I rubbed shoulders in the crowd of nearly 19,000 runners on Figueroa Street, near the start line of the Los Angeles Marathon. The Los Angeles Times reported, *"The temperature at the start was 63 degrees, not bad, but not likely to hold. It did not hold and it was tough going for the 18,861 entrants. A fine sunny day burst out, sending temperatures up to the mid-70s, about 20 degrees above a marathoner's comfort zone."*

The heat didn't bother me. I prefer it 20 degrees above, instead of 20 degrees below the "comfort zone." Volunteers handed out paper cups of water at the aid stations every few miles, so I felt in no danger of dehydration. However, I was nervous about the unknown I would face when I reached the virgin distance past the mile 15 marker. How would my body handle those final 11 miles?

An estimated 1.8 million spectators lined the streets of the course. Crowds cheered, "You can do it. You're looking great!" At mile 5, I heard a joker, "It's all downhill from here!"

Every few miles, a singer or band played from an official

temporary stage set up along the side of the road. There was an even greater number of unofficial ad hoc musicians who stood curbside. They sang, strummed guitars, blew trumpets, and beat drums. I ran by one guy with raggedy clothes and long hair who preached the bible through a mega-phone, and warned me to repent of my sins.

I sensed the feeling of unity and community as I ran through diverse ethnic neighborhoods. Intolerances and racial prejudices magically disappeared for the day. The course wound through Little Tokyo, Chinatown, and the Hispanic neighborhood near historic Olvera Street, considered the birthplace of our great city.

I approached the famous Mann's Chinese Theatre in Hollywood at mile 13.1, the half-way mark. I ran side-by-side with a clean-cut, blue-eyed, blonde runner about my age. We struck up a conversation.

"Where are you from?"

"Chesterton, Indiana, a small town 45 miles east of Chicago. How about you?"

I pointed my arm toward the north to the hills above the Mann. "I live about two miles away, up there"

"Oh, so Los Angeles is your hometown marathon. How many times have you run this race?"

"This is my first marathon."

"Wow. Really? I'm impressed. We're doing a three-hour pace. Don't hit that wall! Most runners do in their first marathon."

"I am well aware," I responded.

We ran together the next few miles, then lost track of each other. I never saw him again.

This happens often in races. I met countless friendly people who came into my life for a few minutes on the road and then disappeared.

The homestretch of the Los Angeles Marathon was bleak. Gone were the street-lined spectators of the first twenty miles. It was like the party was over and everyone had gone home. Only a few straggling onlookers stood on the sidewalks the last five miles. A gospel choir performed upon a make-shift stage three miles before the finish line. They sang in perfect harmony. Their beautiful voices provided me a much-needed boost. I could use divine intervention as the marathon distance took its toll and I began to fade.

I played a mind game; I tried to think in only one-mile increments. At mile 23, I said to myself, "Just one more mile. Make it to mile 24."

I passed under the banner at mile 24. "Congratulations! You did it. Now get to mile 25."

The final mile of the race, I repeated my mantra, "Less than a mile, less than a mile, less than a mile."

Suddenly, there were crowds of people lining the road. The noise became deafening when the finish line came into view. I crossed over it. I ran my first marathon in 3 hours 5 minutes and 55 seconds. I was thrilled.

A volunteer draped the finisher's medal around my neck. I walked through the chute and grabbed a banana, a bottle of water, a few chocolate chip cookies, and a cinnamon raisin bagel. I found Gerry at our pre-arranged spot. We sat down to rest for a few hours while we waited for the other Flyers to finish the race and reconvene. *All* Flyers did finish. Our club record remained intact; 100% of the Flyers who start the Los Angeles Marathon finish the Los Angeles Marathon.

Eager to read the inside stories and reports of the marathon in the newspaper, I couldn't wait for the next day's *Los Angeles Times*. In 1989, we didn't have the Internet. We could not log in to our computer a few hours after a race to view results. TV stations covered the marathon on the evening news and showed footage of the victors. Camera crews captured some of the middle-of-the-pack runners at scenic points along the course. But it wasn't until we picked up the Monday morning newspaper that we could view the complete race results. I opened the sports page and learned I had finished 25th female.

Two weeks later, I arrived home from work to see a small brown paper package on my doorstep which UPS had delivered earlier. Inside was a beautiful plaque, 5 x 7 inches, made of walnut. Words were engraved:

1989 L.A. Marathon

Fastest in the Field: Accountant

Mary Button

3:05:55

The sponsor of the award was Reebok. An enclosed letter asked me to reply with my shoe size so they could ship me a pair of their running shoes.

When I had registered on March 3rd, I had written "accountant" on the application, in the field which asked my professional occupation. I had no idea about this "Fastest in the Field" contest sponsored by Reebok. It recognized and awarded the top female and male runners in twenty distinct job categories: the film industry, manufacturers, food and beverage, construction, banking, medical, and others.

I followed Gary's advice for marathon recovery. "Take one day easy for each mile raced." I took thirty days off from serious training and limited myself to five-mile jogs in the park three or four times a week. By early April, I felt fully recuperated, raring to go.

I talked with my friend Marie, who ran the marathon in the 1988 Olympic Games in Seoul, South Korea. She represented her native country, Ireland. She described her intense training schedule and her pre-race taper. "I cut my mileage in half two weeks prior to the race. I decrease it from 90 miles a week to 45. My legs feel fresh, rested and ready."

I thought, "40 miles is my peak mileage, and it's less than her taper mode?"

My mind flashed back to the spring of 1979 when I was a sophomore in college home on spring break. Dad had switched on the TV for the evening news. It was the third Monday in April, the day of the Boston Marathon. I saw the footage of petite Joan Benoit as she approached the finish line on Commonwealth Ave, a Red-Sox cap perched backwards upon her head. She broke the tape three minutes ahead of the second place female. She wore a huge smile. I kept that image in my mind. It inspired me!

CHAPTER SEVEN

My Sub-Three Quest

I KNEW I could go sub-three next year in the Los Angeles Marathon. I only had to shave off five minutes and 55 seconds. With a strategy of higher mileage and consistent track workouts, it would happen.

I added a hill run to my weekly routine. I ran from my backyard to the top of Mt. Hollywood and back, a grueling 6-miler (with an ascent of more than 1,300 feet). I grew stronger; I was focused and obsessed. Training became my number one priority. Passive hobbies faded into the background. At the annual Flyers award banquet in May, Coach Gary presented me with "The Flyer Least Likely To Miss a Workout" certificate, as voted on by my peers.

I raced every month: three 5Ks, five 10Ks, an 8-miler, a 10-miler, and two half marathons (all within the next year). I developed a keen sense of pace. I acquired proper race etiquette and learned how to make a beeline to the water stop without cutting off other runners. I became skilled at running in a pack, so as not to get elbowed or elbow others. I knew the polite manners to murmur, "Good Job" as I passed a runner mid-race. And I responded, "Thank You" when a runner whipped by me with words of encouragement and told me I was "Looking Good!"

I marked my calendar…March 4, 1990 – L.A. Marathon.

Gerry and I ran the Sweetheart Run 10K in Playa del Rey on Saturday, February 10. Playa del Rey is a beach town south of infamous Venice Beach. The flat and fast course was on the bike path along the beach. It brought back memories of when we had first moved to Los Angeles and lived in Marina del Rey.

Gerry and I were registered in the optional "Sweethearts Division" category. The winner was the couple who scored the fastest combined race time when the "his" and "her" times were added together. *(This was before same-sex partners were given equal consideration as "couples.")* Gerry ran his 10K in 44:19 and I ran mine in 37:41 for our Sweethearts time of 82 minutes even.

We jogged a short cooldown together. Then we stood in the paved parking lot at the beach near the finish line and awaited the official results. A guy in red shorts and a tie-dyed t-shirt approached us. Sweat dripped off his shoulder as he leaned toward Gerry and asked, "Doesn't it bother you that your wife is a faster runner than you?"

Gerry kept his cool and responded, "No, but it obviously bothers you."

Men dominated the long distance race scene in 1990. Participation ratios were often two to one, men versus women. Some guys with macho egos struggled to accept the fact a woman could outrun them.

Our 82-minute time won us first place! We were presented with a beautiful commemorative mahogany plaque at the awards ceremony. In the center was a red enamel heart engraved with the race date and the inscription, "Fastest Sweethearts."

Monday morning at the water cooler, I talked with my co-worker Joe, who was mild-mannered, personable, and a non-runner. Office gossip had spread, and Joe had heard about my Saturday race.

"Congratulations on your run. I heard you finished ahead of some of the men. That's great, but personally, I would never let a woman beat me in a race."

"What do you mean, 'You would never let a woman beat you?' "

"Well, I just wouldn't. I would run faster and stay ahead of her."

"Sorry, Joe. Especially when there is prize money involved, elite women will show up and finish ahead of 90 percent of the guys. Even without money at stake, some women run faster than men."

Joe just didn't get it.

L.A. Marathon was three weeks after Sweetheart Run. I was ready! I had survived two 18-mile training runs, had not succumbed to the flu, nor caught a cold. I felt strong and invincible, except for my on-again/off-again knee. It swelled after track practice, so I slept with an ice pack on my knee every Wednesday night.

I listened to coach Gary, but I did not heed his advice to do at least two 20-mile training runs. "No! 18 miles is far enough for me. I will save the 20-plus distance for race day."

I had upped my mileage to 50 to 55 miles per week for three months before my two-week taper, when I cut it in half. Taper mode made me nervous. I became anxious and clumsy. My mantra every day of the taper was DDSS (Don't Do Stupid Shit).

I walked to the movie theatre, my eyes fixated on the pavement and my footsteps. "DDSS! Watch out for those uneven cracks in the sidewalk. Do *NOT* trip!" I drove to and from work, the most defensive driver on the roads between my home and Beverly Hills. I avoided restaurants and cooked meals at home. I was paranoid about food poisoning; not worth the risk.

DDSS...DDSS...DDSS...

Marathon morning, Gerry was behind the wheel as we made our way downtown. I don't know which one of us was more nervous. He was about to run *his* first marathon.

We turned on the radio and listened to the weather forecast. "Ideal marathon running conditions expected today in Los Angeles. Temperatures should remain in the 60s, with overcast skies. The sun may not make an appearance until late afternoon." Perfect!

Gerry and I kissed goodbye and "good luck" before we began our respective marathon journeys.

The starting gun fired at 8:35 a.m. under a light drizzle. Barely enough moisture to dampen the pavement, it felt refreshing compared to the previous year's heat. I skipped the first few aid stations. No need to fight crowds to grab a cup of water from the table when I wasn't even thirsty! I waited until mile 5 for my first sip. By then, the crowd had thinned out enough that I could run at my pace without the worry of being tripped.

To crack three hours required a 6:52-minute-per-mile pace. During the first few miles, it was impossible because of the sheer madness of congestion. I clocked in my first two miles at an eight-minute pace. I was frustrated but didn't panic. I knew I could make up the lost time during the next 24 miles.

During the third mile, I hooked up with four runners who shared the same sub-three-hour time goal. We ran together at consistent 6:45 miles for the next 10 miles. So far, so good! I glanced at my watch as we reached the halfway marker at mile 13.1. "1:28:30." I was on target for a sub-three, and I did not feel fatigued.

I "lost" my running companions. I had a good sense of pace so I wasn't concerned about my time goal, but I missed the team spirit and camaraderie. I didn't know if these guys were ahead or behind me. I kept focused on my task at hand. I reached mile 22 and squinted to read my watch display, "2:30:30."

I was ecstatic. Four miles to go at a seven-minute pace!

Suddenly, my right calf muscle tightened. What was going on? I had never experienced muscle cramps. My solution was to shorten my stride. I tried to pick up the cadence to compensate.

I glanced at the large illuminated time clock as I hit the 23 mile mark. "2:38:30." I did a double-take to verify. *Yep. I had just run an eight-minute mile. This was not good.*

I gave myself a constant pep-talk as I ran the last stretch of the race.

"It's only another three miles."

"Pick it up."

"You can do this!"

"Focus!"

"Think of all the hard work and training you did for this."

"Don't give up."

"Run faster!"

It was to no avail. I couldn't pick up my pace. I crossed the finish line in 3:04:06. Damn.

I bowed my head as the volunteer draped the finisher's medal around my neck. "Congratulations! You did great!"

"Thank You!" I murmured, but I felt I had failed.

Gerry ran a 3:48 marathon, a respectable inaugural marathon. He was hurting when I saw him after the race; his face was chalky white, his legs wobbly. A volunteer handed him a bottle of Exceed, which was a Gatorade-type electrolyte drink popular in 1990. "Drink this. You'll feel better." Minutes later, Gerry bent forward, grabbed his knees and puked, spewing out a stream of bright orange.

"Why don't we sit down on the lawn and rest a bit?" I suggested. He didn't look so ghostly an hour later, so we ambled slowly to our car. On the drive home, Gerry leaned toward me, "I did two marathons today, Mary…my first and my last!"

History proved him a liar. Months later, we both registered for the March 3, 1991, L.A. Marathon.

———

I bumped up my training. Between March 1990 and March 1991, I raced seventeen times: three 5Ks, three 10Ks, a 15K, three 10-milers, five half marathons, and two other non-standard distance races – the 4.8-mile leg of a triathlon relay, and a 5.2-mile leg of the Jimmy Stewart Relay Marathon.

The ninth annual Jimmy Stewart race took place Sunday morning, April 1, 1990, in Griffith Park. The event raised money for the Child Study Center of St. John's Hospital in Santa Monica, a worthy cause. Over the past decade, the race had brought in more than a million dollars for St. John's Hospital.

Corporate teams paid $500 to register. Non-profits and running clubs were given a discount and donated $125 per team. More than 700 five-person teams (3,500 runners) participated in the 1990 event. Each runner ran a 5.2-mile loop and then handed off the relay baton to his/her teammate. The fifth runner completed the team's 26.2-mile marathon.

The Flyers fielded four teams and held our own "race within the race." Our goal was to make the teams as even as possible; we wanted to create an exciting neck-to-neck finish (with anyone's guess which one of the four teams would "win" and outrun the other three).

A stage was set up near the start line for race hosts Jimmy Stewart and Robert Wagner. Robert Wagner made a much-too-long speech. He thanked us all for being here and being part of a great cause. At 8:15 a.m., the elderly Jimmy Stewart fired the gun.

The loop course circled a large interior grassy area, which had scattered picnic tables and barbecue grills. Clubs had staked out their spots at dawn with pop-up tents and banners and had hauled in copious amounts of food and drink. The infield was covered with canopies, blankets, towels, beach chairs, grills, and coolers. This was a treasured Flyer tradition our club supported for over a decade.

(Jimmy Stewart passed away on July 2, 1997, at the age of 89. He appeared at the race every year until his death (although for the final three years, he was more or less "propped up" by Robert Wagner who held on to support him, placed the starting gun in Jimmy's hands, and then placed his hand atop Jimmy's to squeeze the trigger to start the race). It was kind of sad. Robert Wagner took over as official host of the race after Jimmy Stewart passed away. The final Jimmy Stewart Relay was April 23, 2006, the 25th anniversary of the race.

———

"Hallelujah!" I had tallied up my mileage the first week in October. The total was 56, and I was in virgin territory. I stayed at this new plateau several weeks.

I had a sub-three game plan. I intended to race well at the Alton 10-Miler on Thanksgiving Weekend, rest during the holidays, and then resume intense training after the first of the year.

Thanksgiving Saturday in Alton was unseasonably warm with temperatures in the mid-50s. I stretched under the bright blue skies and heard others grumble, "This is awful. It is too hot to run." I stood quietly, my lips sealed. This was my kind of day. I much preferred these conditions to the bitter cold.

I took an early lead in the race with my target pace of 6:15 miles. I picked it up the second half of the race and kicked in the homestretch. I won the race with my 1:01:53. It was a PR (personal record) for the distance, which was a true confidence booster. This 6:10-per-mile pace I ran was much faster than the 6:52-pace I needed to sustain in March to break three.

I was no longer a novice marathoner. I now understood the logic of doing long runs more than 20 miles in training. It is to build a tolerance for the distance, so the body is less likely to rebel on race day. Perhaps the reason I tanked in the 1990 L.A. Marathon was because my longest training run had been 18 miles. Maybe I should have listened to Gary when he advised a 20-mile training run. Things would be different this year. I planned three long runs: a 17-miler, a 20.5-miler, and a 22-miler. After the 22-miler I recorded in my journal, "I am too tired to do anything else productive today. I will take a nap this afternoon."

In mid-February, I peaked with a 64-mile week. I also trained my mind with my oft-repeated mantra, *"I will break three hours."* It was my first thought in the morning and the final thought at bedtime. A week before the race I obeyed my DDSS (Don't Do Stupid Shit) rule. I was antsy but ready for Sunday morning, March 3, 1991.

Finally, the day dawned. I followed my typical pre-race breakfast ritual of two cups of coffee, a bagel, and a PowerBar. But it left me with a gurgling stomach this morning. I swallowed a few Tums. Gerry drove us downtown. He was also eager to run again, despite his "Never Again" vow of a year ago.

When the starting gun fired at 8:35 a.m., I had a sense of déjà vu. The weather was similar to last year, the route was the same, spectators were out in full force; even some of the familiar bands, musicians, performers, and preachers returned. My race also felt like a repeat performance. I went out at the 6:45 pace I intended. I had pre-arranged for my good friend Bob to join me at the mile 20 marker. Bob was a tall, slender, talented runner who was twenty years older than I. He agreed to keep me on a sub-seven pace the final six miles. I did *not* want to repeat the eight-minute-per-mile slow-down of last year.

I ran toward the "Mile 20" banner strung across the street and saw Bob standing on the sidewalk ready to jump in and join me.

"How's it going?" You're looking good. You feel OK?"

"I'm great. This is the day."

"I think so too. Just stay with me, Mary. Don't let me get ahead of you."

"Don't worry, I won't."

Two miles later, Bob was inching ahead of me. I got angry.

"Bob, you are picking up the pace!"

"Ummm...I'm not, Mary. Come on. Hang in there. You're starting to slow down."

"No, I'm not!" I shouted.

"Just stay with me. We can do this."

The gap between us continued to widen. I became whiny and poor Bob suffered my verbal abuse. At mile 25 I told him to "Go to Hell" and shouted other obscenities. I've been both a pacer and a pacee in long distance events. As a pacer, you sign yourself up for abuse. The pacee becomes depleted physically, mentally, and emotionally (and isn't much fun to be around).

Bob stayed with me (slightly ahead) and kept up his pep talk and encouragement; and then he exited to go to the sidewalk at mile 26. I saw the clock as I approached the finish. My official time was 3 hours 4 minutes and 32 seconds. I had bumped up my training, and it was all for naught. This was *26 seconds slower* than the previous year. What was wrong with me?

"What could I have possibly done differently to achieve my goal?" I wallowed in self-pity. Until the middle of June, I was not inspired to run another 50-plus week.

Maybe I was jinxed with the Los Angeles Marathon course? Perhaps I should try a different marathon? I investigated my options.

I picked up race flyers which were readily available at The Sport Shoe and at local 5K and 10K races. This is how we heard about upcoming events in the pre-Internet days. I raced every few weeks and collected more than a dozen brochures and pamphlets.

In early summer, I looked at the stack of flyers I had stockpiled. Four marathons were scheduled in California before year end. I chose the inaugural Orange County Marathon, to be held November third. The OC Marathon, billed as fast and flat, also offered a prize purse for the top finishers, which meant it would draw a good field of elite runners. I registered; I was eager once again to train for a marathon.

Late June, I ran the "Run for the Halibut" 10K in Long Beach. It was sponsored by the Alaska Seafood Marketing Institute. The course ran along the beach. It was advertised as "guaranteed to give you a PR (personal record)." I was lured into the race by the prize to be awarded to the first place finishers, both male and female: an all-expense-paid, three-day weekend in Alaska, which included airfare, lodging, meals, and even an afternoon's deep sea fishing excursion for halibut. This potential prize had me hooked.

We arrived early on the morning of the race. I scanned the field and scoped out my competition. I raced often enough to know who the local competitive runners were. I did not know them all by name, but I definitely knew them by appearance.

At ten minutes before 8:00 a.m., with still only a few hundred runners ready to go, I did not recognize any elite women among them. Gerry stood next to me behind the starting line.

"I don't see anyone, Gerry."

"I don't either."

"Maybe I can win this. Maybe our next vacation will be Alaska."

"Go for it. Run like hell for the halibut!"

"I will. See you at the finish line."

I started off too fast and ran a 5:33 first mile instead of the 5:45 I had hoped. My eyes were focused on a female runner ahead of me by 10-15 seconds at the first mile marker. She didn't look like the typical elite runner; she was built more like a linebacker than a toothpick. "She can't sustain this pace. I'll be able to reel her in within the next mile."

Not so. With each successive mile, linebacker increased the gap. Both of us slowed down from the first-mile pace, especially me. She won the race in a time of 35:54. I finished second, running 37:05, more than a minute slower. I congratulated her and we introduced ourselves. Her name was Carrie.

An hour later at the awards ceremony, Carrie was presented with an envelope and her plane tickets to Anchorage. I went home with my second-place prize: three six-ounce tins of canned salmon (not even halibut!). At least, I left the race with my new PR 10K time of 37:05.

I kept consistent 55-to-60-mile weeks as I trained for OC. I started doing "doubles" two or three times a week. A "double workout" meant I ran twice a day, once in the morning and again in the evening. My typical doubles were an easy four miles in the morning, then five miles of faster-paced running several hours later.

I raced well in September and October, faster and stronger than ever before. I put in two 15-mile training runs and two 20-milers before my final two-week DDSS taper phase. I was rarin' to go.

A typical November day in Southern California is a high of 70 degrees, ideal running weather for me. On OC race day in 1991, the temperature soared to near 70 degrees before the 8:00 a.m. race start a few blocks from Disneyland in Anaheim. The sun beat down as we stretched pre-race. I overheard a fellow runner complain, "It's going to be brutal today. I'm just going to do 15 miles, then bail. I'll save my marathon for Sacramento next month." I was well-hydrated and well-trained and did not intend to drop out mid-race.

The start gun fired and we ran into pure sunshine. No canopies of trees, no tall office buildings, nothing to block out the bright rays. The flat point-to-point course started at Anaheim Stadium and finished at Irvine Marketplace, an outdoor mall near University of California, Irvine. We ran through the towns of Santa Ana, Orange, and Tustin.

This was a far cry from the hoopla of L.A. No excitement, no music, and few spectators. At mile 7, a handful of people clapped with little enthusiasm as I ran by. Ten minutes later, I spotted another bystander on the side of the road.

We were a group of 4,000 runners, minuscule compared to the field of L.A. Marathon with nearly 20,000 runners. I ran the entire race pretty much by myself, never able to lock into a pack of runners at my pace. Often elite runners form a tight pack the first half of a marathon. It is easier to keep the pace when you work together.

I looked at my watch at the halfway point: 1:28. "Good!" I was on target.

I didn't slow much the second half, except a brief pause every three miles as I grabbed a cup of Gatorade at the aid stations. Concerned about my electrolytes getting out of whack, I downed each drop of the liquid. I prayed, "Please, do not get cramps." It was 80 degrees when I reached mile 20, and I still had a 10K to go.

I tried to eat a piece of PowerBar at mile 22, but it stuck in my throat, and I couldn't swallow it. My mouth was too dry, and I spit it out. At the next aid station, I gulped down a chunk of banana. I looked at the life-size clock as I approached the finish line. The large blinking numbers displayed 2:57:50. I pumped my arms and ran through the finish line with a grin from ear to ear. Official time: **2:58:15.** I was finally a sub-three marathoner!

I bent down, hugged my knees, and took several deep breaths. When I stood up, a race official was by my side. "Congratulations. You are definitely one of our top ten finishers. We'll finalize the results within a half hour. I hope you can stick around for the Awards Ceremony." You bet I would!

Computer timing didn't exist in 1991. Timing was done the old-fashioned way. As the runner crossed the finish line, officials recorded the time as well as the number displayed on the racing bib, which was safety-pinned on the front of the racer's shirt. Later, they reviewed the registration roster to match and identify the runner's name according to his/her bib number.

We had passed through various Checkpoint Charlie stations on the course. Race officials stood curbside and jotted down our race numbers as we ran by. This was standard protocol, especially with prize money to be awarded.

Race directors hoped to avoid a "Rosie Ruiz." The famous Rosie Ruiz scandal helped to inspire the use of extensive video surveillance in long-distance road races.

Rosie Ruiz was the 32-year-old woman who appeared to be the winner of the April 21, 1980, Boston Marathon when she crossed the finish line first in a time of 2:31:56. She looked remarkably relaxed and sweat-free on the awards podium minutes later. Afterwards, officials reviewed countless photographs taken along the course. They could not find Ruiz in a single one. No official could remember seeing her at any time or place during the race. The next day, Boston officials received a phone call from Harvard University senior, John Faulkner. He and his friends had viewed the marathon at half a mile from the finish, along Commonwealth Avenue. He witnessed the ruse as he saw Rosie Ruiz jump from the sidewalk into the street entering the race at 25.5 miles.

Rosie Ruiz was disqualified the day after the race, and the rightful winner, Jacqueline Gareau of Canada, was recognized as the winner with her time of 2:34:22. But unfortunately, Gareau was gypped. She received very little of the pomp and circumstance she deserved for winning the Boston Marathon. The Rosie Ruiz scandal is one of the greatest sport cheats of all time. It marks one of the worst moments of the marathon.

An hour had passed since I was asked to hang around for the results and awards. What was taking so long? I grew impatient. I walked to the officials' table and learned there was some confusion. They couldn't figure out whether I was sixth or seventh female finisher. I didn't understand how they could not know. Maybe they suspected a Rosie Ruiz and were trying to get to the bottom of it? It didn't matter much to me whether I was sixth or seventh. I was happy either way. I had achieved my sub-three goal. The prize purse difference between sixth and seventh place was only $50.

Finally, after an eternity of two hours, the Awards Ceremony got underway. Goodyear Tires was the major sponsor of the OC Marathon. I went home with a very classy seventh-place plaque. It was a foot tall, with beautiful dark grey marble at the base. The OC Marathon logo, "November 3, 1991," and "Seventh Female" were etched in glass at the top of the plaque. None of the top ten finishers received prize money on the spot. We were promised our checks would be mailed to our home addresses within the next few weeks. It didn't happen.

Nearly three months later, at the end of January 1992, chairman and founder of the OC Marathon, Kent Bowen, went on public record and vowed to pay the race debts with the money the Marathon hoped to raise through corporate sponsorships of the upcoming November 1992 edition of the race. Race director, Michael Marckx, had resigned in December be-

RUNNING AND ME | THEN AND NOW

cause of "philosophical differences" with Bowen and also because he had not received the $20,000 commission owed him.
Marckx doubted there would be a 1992 event because the running community's trust in OC was so low.

OC owed the city of Santa Ana money for street closures
and police protection. They owed thousands of dollars to numerous consultants. Sports promoter Fred Lieberman filed suit
to try to collect $25,000 owed him for his promotional and
marketing services contract.

By June of 1992, athletes still awaited our prize money. I
called the race hotline number repeatedly, but I never could
get through to a live body. I left messages on voice mail, but
no one returned my calls. The June 27th *Los Angeles Times* reported Bowen admitted the race had overextended itself, but
"everyone would be paid as soon as possible."

I was to receive $200. The corresponding men's prize for
seventh place was $2,000. Second female Cindy James of
Homewood, Illinois, never received her $4,000, while third
male Rich McCandless of Hayward missed out on $6,000. This
payscale was typical of the era; top men were to receive the
significant portion of the total $40,000 prize purse.

None of us ever received any money. I thought, "Well,
I guess I'd rather be a woman and not get my $200 than be
a man and not get $2,000." It ended up being equal pay
after all.

CHAPTER EIGHT

A Tale of Two Races

"Relax! Rest on your laurels. Relish your sub-three," Gerry advised. "Take a break."

I listened, but my high-energy type-A personality does not like to take it easy, and I prefer to stay active. Plus, I still had a score to settle with Los Angeles Marathon; I wanted to break three in my hometown.

The next year, 1992, I ran more than 3,000 miles, 3,017 to be precise. *(Yes, I did count and record each and every mile.)* I ran 60-mile weeks, one after another, with plenty of doubles.

In March, I conquered the L.A. Marathon to my satisfaction with my 2:56:41 marathon. I recovered for two weeks and then set my focus on the granddaddy marathon of all, Boston, which took place in late April. I had registered months earlier in November, after Orange County Marathon.

On April 20, 1992, I ran my first Boston. I stayed in Arlington, Massachusetts, less than ten miles from Boston, with my relatives Emily and Bill Duserick. Emily, whom I hadn't seen since I was a kid, is my mom's first cousin. But when my mother informed them I planned to run Boston, they insisted that I be their guest. Emily's husband Bill, a gourmet cook, thought I looked way too skinny, and he did his best to help fatten me in the three days before the Monday race. He prepared dinners of lasagna, baked chicken with mashed potatoes, and pork roast with green beans. He served heaping portions and insisted I have seconds each meal.

My biggest fan on marathon day was Emily. She stood on a street corner at mile 25 and waved her handmade poster at me as I ran by. In bright, bold red letters it said, "Go Mary!" It motivated me for the final mile.

I wore bib #F73 (seeded 73rd female), ran faster than expected, and finished the inverse (37th woman, with a time of 2:54:57). In the evening, Emily surprised me after dinner when she presented me with a chocolate sheet cake with creamy mocha frosting. A runner was etched in the icing on top with the words, "Congratulations Mary."

I closed out my racing year on December 6, 1992, with a 2:51:02 marathon PR (personal record) in Culver City. The Culver City Western Hemisphere Marathon was the second longest continuous-run marathon in the United States, second only to Boston (which dates back to 1897). It was an honor to win the 45th annual Western Hemisphere Marathon in 1992.

Culver City, a small incorporated town surrounded by Los Angeles, covers fewer than 5.2 square miles. It has been a significant center for the motion picture and television industries since the 1920s. Selznick Studios, which later became MGM, was located in humble Culver City. Judy Garland and the cast of the Wizard of Oz were filmed here in 1938. The beloved movie *Gone with the Wind* was also filmed on the Selznick Studios lot in 1938.

Boston Marathon and Western Hemisphere Marathon were East Coast/West Coast opposites in many ways; both had fascinating histories and stories.

––––––

Boston Marathon is the "World's Greatest Marathon." It was a dream come true to run this race, which I am privileged to have done eight times. I ran WGM first in 1992 and the final time in 2001. I missed 1995 and 1999 due to issues with my right knee.

I believed the race took place upon sacred ground. I thought, "I will trace the footsteps and run the same hallowed path from Hopkinton to Boston as did the great legends of the sport for nearly a century." The Boston Marathon is my all-time favorite race. No place would I rather be on the third Monday in April, Patriots' Day, than upon the route from Hopkinton to Boston.

Patriots' Day, a Massachusetts civic holiday, commemorates the anniversary of the Battles of Lexington and Concord, the first battles of the American Revolutionary War. The holiday was originally observed April 19th. Boston Marathon was run every April 19th until 1969. The only exception was when the 19th fell on Sunday, the holy day. Then the race was postponed until Monday, the 20th.

In 1969, the Massachusetts state legislature voted to declare the third Monday in April an official state holiday, Patriots' Day. All state government offices are closed. Businesses shut their doors, and the residents of Massachusetts enjoy a long three-day weekend. Thousands flock to the marathon course on Monday to cheer the runners. If the third Monday happens to be April 15th, residents of Massachusetts get an automatic one-day extension for filing their income taxes.

Fifteen runners entered the inaugural Boston Marathon in 1897. They didn't pay a dime to enter the race, which was organized by the Boston Athletic Association (B.A.A.). Five runners dropped out mid-race, so only 10 of the original starters crossed the finish line. Each subsequent year, more and more runners found their way to Boston to embark on this 26.2-mile epic journey on Patriots' Day.

In 1969, the field reached the milestone of more than 1,000 starters for the first time when 1,152 runners lined up to run. The race had grown beyond the wildest dreams of the B.A.A.

The members of the B.A.A. Board met within weeks after the race for a strategy session. A heated discussion ensued as they discussed how to handle the dilemma of too many runners. Jock Semple, President of the B.A.A., was not bashful in having his say as they planned for the 1970 race. "We can't continue to put on a first-class event with this many people! We need to maintain our high standards, and it is impossible with these hordes of runners!" He proposed restrictive, qualifying time standards.

Semple was famous for his encounter with Kathrine Switzer two years earlier in 1967. A few miles into this legendary race, Semple, riding in the press truck, noticed registered runner, K. Switzer, a female. He jumped out, pulled on her shoulders and shouted, "Get the hell out of my race!" He tried to yank the number off her shirt. Switzer's linebacker boyfriend Tom Miller interfered and roughly shoved Semple. Images of this encounter appeared in Time-Life's *100 Photographs That Changed the World.* Switzer finished with a 4:20 marathon, which cracked the all-male institution of Boston and rocked the running world. Semple was an elitist, an arrogant man whose behavior and attitude helped spark the passage of Title IX.

Peter Stipe was also on the board of the B.A.A. in 1969. Stipe, a top finisher in the 1969 Boston Marathon, was anything but an elitist. He thought Boston should be all-inclusive. "There is a unique atmosphere surrounding an event where the worst can compete with the best. It is everyman's race." Stipe's friend and teammate, Phil Ryan, concurred. "Why limit it to people of above average running ability? Allow joggers to gain their own spot in the sun."

Jock Semple begged to differ. According to him, the 1969 race was mostly "idiots and prank runners. They are joggers and the Boston Marathon is no place for them. They disgrace Boston with their slow pace." Kathrine Switzer later verified, "I was with Jock plenty of times when he said he could 'walk' the speeds some of these jerks were running."

The final decision of the B.A.A. was ultimately up to Semple. In 1970, time standards were imposed for the first time. A four-hour qualifying time was required for the privilege of toeing the line in Boston. This weeded out the "jerks" since only serious well-trained runners (supposedly) could run at this marathon pace of slightly more than nine-minute miles. Yet despite this hurdle, a large field of 1,011 qualified and registered for the 1970 race. Semple was not happy because he did not want more than 1,000 runners in his race.

So Semple tightened the screws and lowered the qualifying time further, by a full thirty minutes, to three-and-a-half hours for the 1971 race. This was radical. Now a runner had to run more than a minute per mile faster to qualify. Only very talented runners who put in mega training miles can run a marathon at an eight-minute or faster pace.

Semple met his goal of reduced entrants. Participation dropped below 1,000 for the 1971 race, with only 887 starters. However, the lower time standard did not discourage runners; instead, it inspired them.

Marathoners stepped up their training regimens. In 1972, more than 1,000 runners once again took to the streets for the race. 1972 (the year of Title IX) also marked the first time women were officially allowed to run. Seven women entered. The champion, Nina Kuscsik, won with a finish time of 3:10:26. By 1975, a record number of 2,041 runners started the race, and the numbers continued to grow. In 1979, nearly 8,000 runners qualified for Boston.

The price tag also increased. In 1969, it cost $2 to run Boston. Race fees jumped 50 percent to $3 in 1970. Race fees crept up every few years, but it wasn't an issue. Few runners griped about the entry fee. I paid the reasonable price of $35 when I registered to run Boston in 1992.

The historic Centennial Celebration of Boston on April 15, 1996, drew a massive crowd of 38,000 registered runners, who paid $50 each. Not only did they have the once-in-a-lifetime experience, but they also received a commemorative long-sleeved T-shirt, a ticket to the pasta dinner the night before, and bus transportation race day from Boston to the race start in Hopkinton.

The quality heavy-weight white cotton T-shirt featured the badge-of-honor B.A.A. logo embellished on the front in colorful blue and gold. The pre-race dinner was a feast. Runners carbo-loaded with all-you-care-to-eat spaghetti with tomato sauce, sausage, salad, dinner rolls, baked potatoes with fixings, and a variety of cookies and pastries. People sat together on either side of long banquet tables while they ate and shared personal stories with one another of "How I Got to Boston." The road to Boston is often the result of years, if not decades, of running and training.

It was no simple task the B.A.A. faced to put on the 100th running. It took more than a year with countless hours of detailed planning and coordination. Before daybreak on race day, hundreds of buses began continuous back-and-forth trips from Boston to Hopkinton as they shuttled runners to the race start. The quiet tiny town of Hopkinton (population of 13,346, according to the 2000 census) exploded to more than quadruple its size as runners and their fans poured into town.

A temporary athletes' village, in the large grassy open square in the town center, served as a staging area for runners to rest, relax, and perhaps find a spot to stretch. Rows upon rows of tables were set up, stacked with paper cups of water and Gatorade. Hundreds of portable toilets lined the perimeter of the area. The "village" seemed surprisingly spacious and adequate for the 38,000 inhabitants.

The race lived up to its reputation of the World's Greatest Marathon. B.A.A. pulled it off without a hiccup. Thousands of volunteers were along the course and assisted the runners all the way to the finish line. On this gorgeous day, with crystal-clear blue skies and plenty of sunshine, screaming crowds lined the streets the entire 26 miles and cheered for hours. I ran a 2:48:40 and finished 32nd female, the 10th American woman. I was ecstatic to place so high in WGM and will always cherish this unforgettable race.

Weeks later, a rumor circulated in the running community: B.A.A. was going to raise the Boston Marathon entry fee to $75. Many became outraged at the idea of this proposed steep price increase of $25 and wrote furious editorials to magazines and newspapers. At the time, most big-city marathons cost between $35 and $50. A local small-town 5K costs as little as $10.

"How could they do this?"

"This is ludicrous."

"It is inexcusable. It is robbery!"

But the complaints fell upon deaf ears. In fall of 1996, the B.A.A. opened up registration for the 1997 race with the higher price tag of $75. More than 10,000 runners registered for the April 1997 marathon – the highest number of entrants ever for the race (except for the previous year's Centennial celebration).

Jack Fleming, the B.A.A. press liaison, was emphatic when he justified the price increase. He explained the huge costs associated with Boston. "Our race is unique in that we run through eight towns. It is a point-to-point race, and we offer the marathoner a wide range of services. It is a year-long operation for us, as it has to be in order to put on the best possible race we can."

"We had to do it," he said. He elaborated, "We held the cost down to a minimum the past two years. In order for us to ensure the future of the event as a going concern, we increased the fee to $75 this year. We have to plan three and five years down the road knowing that we will be able to work within our budget to continue to plan and put on the race in the future."

Road races skyrocketed in popularity in the late 1990s, as did their prices. They continue to soar. It cost $180 for USA residents to register for the 2016 Boston Marathon. International runners paid $240 to enter the race. Running is no longer the cheap sport it once was, especially when you add the costs of travel and lodging. I am glad I ran most of my marathons in the good old days when it didn't break the bank.

I don't know what it costs to put on a race the scale of the Boston Marathon, but it must be expensive when you figure the steep costs of insurance, traffic control, road closures, medical personnel, transportation, and much more. Still, the escalation of the registration fees of Boston seems extreme. Entry fees have more than tripled in two decades, rising much faster than the rate of inflation.

"If you build it, they will come." As races these days sell out months in advance, there is a corollary: "If you charge it, they will pay." Running has become a victim of its own success and has turned into Big Business.

———

My dad joined me for my second Boston race in 1993. He drove north from his home in Merchantville, New Jersey to spend Patriots' Day holiday weekend with me. We found inexpensive rooms in the small town of Westboro, 10 miles from Hopkinton. On Marathon weekend, it cost a fortune for a hotel in downtown Boston. I preferred to stay near the start anyway, where it was peaceful and quiet. My dad was a punctual person and an expert with logistics. He took charge on race morning. "I'll get you there in plenty of time. Don't worry." He did so; we arrived in Hopkinton two hours before noon.

The noon start was another quirky feature which made Boston "Boston." It added to the unique charm. No other marathon, of which I am aware, was run on a Monday at noon.

The start time presented a dietary dilemma. What should I eat for breakfast? I didn't want to stuff myself, but I also hoped to avoid hunger pangs midday when the gun fired. I tweaked my typical pre-race regimen (a PowerBar and a few pieces of toast with jam) which was based on the typical 8:00 a.m. race start. The morning of Boston, I tripled the calories of my usual breakfast. At 8:30 a.m., I ate two toasted bagels with grape jelly and a PowerBar. I washed it down with a glass of orange juice and a couple of cups of coffee. Yet, I felt a bit hungry as the noon hour approached. Maybe it was just nerves.

"I'll be in Boston by 3:00 p.m.," I predicted to my dad, as I gave him a hug and kiss goodbye and lined up for the 12:00 p.m. race start.

Dad and I had our plan. While I ran, he would "leap-frog" the course in his car and drive the side streets parallel to the route. He knew the pace I hoped to run; if all went well, he would arrive at a few of the towns along the course ahead of me so he could catch a glimpse of me as I ran by. He did this by his lonesome, in his trusty old Toyota, with no navigational device and no cell phone. He followed an old-fashioned detailed paper map upon which he had marked the course route with a bright pink highlighter.

I ran through Framingham at mile 5 and recognized my dad's voice when I heard a "Go, Mary!," though I couldn't spot him in the crowds which lined the streets. Twelve miles farther down the road, as I approached the town of Newton, I glanced to the right and saw my dad. I was thrilled that we made eye contact as I ran by. He gave me an enthusiastic "thumbs up," the motivation I needed as I approached the beginning of Heartbreak Hill. Heartbreak is a triad of three hilly climbs, the final and steepest is a climb of 91 feet between miles 20 and 21. The race has often been lost and won here, hence the name.

Patriots' Day cookouts were in full swing as I ran through the eight towns along the course: rural Hopkinton into Ashland, then Framingham, Natick, Wellesley, Newton, Brookline, and finally, Boston. The Red Sox game at Fenway Park ended just as the majority of runners headed through Kenmore Square, a few miles to the finish line. Red Sox fans, filled with peanuts and Cracker Jack, spilled from the ballpark into Kenmore Square and transformed into marathon fans. They were boisterous and added to the party atmosphere of the day.

Dad just barely beat me to the finish line. I squeaked in under three hours with a 2:59:26, which placed me 32nd female. My time was nearly five minutes slower than my first Boston the previous year, but at least I had kept my sub-three streak alive. I left the post-race area and walked a few blocks to the crowded street corner where dad and I had pre-arranged to meet. He spotted me first and rushed toward me with a huge grin on his face. He circled his arms around my sweaty shoulders, and then he planted a kiss on my right cheek as I snuggled into him. "Job well done, Mary! I am so proud of you!"

———

In 2007, Boston Marathon sacrificed one of its time-honored traditions when it let go of the 12:00 noon start time. After 110 years, the B.A.A. changed the start time to 10:00 a.m. They listed several reasons for the earlier time: runners would enjoy cooler temperatures, roads could re-open earlier to vehicular traffic, and most runners prefer to run in the morning. Sadly, marathons began to follow a "One-Size-Fits-All" formula as they became clones of one another with their large numbers, early-morning starts, high race fees, and aid stations each and every mile.

The B.A.A. opened the floodgates to online registration on October 18, 2010, at 9:00 a.m. for the April 18, 2011, race. By 5:03 p.m. that evening, they had accepted the first 26,000 entries and closed the registration. The race had sold out in a *record eight hours!* Those who had scurried fastest to their keyboards got in; everyone else was out of luck.

Was race director Dave McGillivray thrilled? "Thrilled? No, I was hiding under my bed," he recalled. A one-day sellout might be cause for celebration for a rock festival promoter; but it was not a celebration for a race director who had to field thousands of calls and e-mails from disappointed, confused, and angry runners who had busted their butts to qualify for the race and were denied entry simply because they weren't at their computers on October 18. Boston had become a bucket list ambition, while it became a headache for the B.A.A. which tried to cope with the consequences of its success. It is unfortunate so many runners experienced the heartbreak of Boston, not upon Heartbreak Hill, but with the heartbreak of not getting into the prestigious race.

April 15, 2013, Boston is proof the historic race is not immune to acts of terror. Two brothers conspired and detonated a pair of pressure cooker bombs which exploded at 2:49 p.m. near the finish line. Three innocent spectators were killed, and more than 270 others were injured.

"How could this happen?" I viewed the footage from my TV in faraway Los Angeles, and tears streamed down my face as I tried to grasp this tragedy.

"We are one Boston. We are one community. As always, we will come together to help those most in need. And in the end, we will all be better for it," vowed Boston Mayor Thomas Menino. He and Governor Deval Patrick formed The One Fund Boston to assist victims and families who were affected by the bombing. Individuals, foundations, and corporations gave generously in the following weeks. On June 28, 2013, the One Fund began distribution of over $60 million to more than 200 victims and families.

The B.A.A. expanded the field from 27,000 runners in 2013 to nearly 36,000 runners in 2014. Director Dave McGillivray invited back the 5,600 runners who were forced to stop mid-

A TALE OF TWO RACES

race the previous year. B.A.A. Executive Tom Grilk explained they enlarged the race to show that neither the community nor the sport give in to terror. Because of the high level of security, McGillivray and Grilk determined 36,000 was the maximum number B.A.A. could safely manage. "Meeting the high standards of all of the people whom we are privileged to serve remains our number one challenge," said Grilk.

The April 21, 2014, Boston Marathon was about redemption. After the horrors of 2013, the runners and spectators came back to honor the victims, salute the heroes, and own the finish line.

———

While Boston grew and thrived, the Culver City Western Hemisphere Marathon withered and died. The race was born May 21, 1948, and passed away on December 2, 2001, at the age of 54 years. It originally went by the name Culver City Marathon in 1948. Forty years later, in 1988, the race adapted the moniker Western Hemisphere Marathon.

When I ran the 45th Western Hemisphere Marathon, I was among a small group of 570 participants. On the cold overcast morning of December 6, 1992, I felt proud to participate in this historic race with a storied past.

On December 16, 1963, 20-year-old Mary Lepper showed up at the start line in Culver City along with another woman, her training partner Lyn Carman. The duo hid along the sidelines and then jumped into the race and joined the men just after the start.

A race official attempted to remove them from the course and Carman reportedly yelled, "I have the right to use public streets for running!" A sympathetic AAU (Amateur Athletic Union) gentleman agreed to time the women, though the race officials did not recognize them. Carman dropped out of the race at the mile 20 mark, but Lepper finished. Her 3:37:07 immediately became the female world record. Unfortunately, the course was later measured at 41.5 km, which is nearly a half mile short of the official 42.195 km marathon distance, so Lepper was denied her world record.

Culver City hosted the Olympic Trials Marathon the next year in July of 1964. Billy Mills finished second, which landed him a spot on the US Olympic Marathon team headed for the games in Tokyo that October.

Billy Mills is an Oglala Lakota (Sioux) Indian, born June 30, 1938, in South Dakota. He was raised on the impoverished Pine Ridge Indian Reservation. Other notable members of the Lakota tribe include Sitting Bull and Crazy Horse. Mills's given Lakota name is Makata Taka Hela, which translates to "love your country."

During his unhappy childhood, he faced prejudice and cultural discrimination. Mills, orphaned at the age of 12, took up running to help find a focus. He left the reservation when he won a track scholarship to the University of Kansas.

Mills also ran the 10,000-meter event in the Tokyo games, where the favorite was Ron Clarke of Australia. Mills was a virtual unknown; his time in the preliminaries was a full minute slower than Clarke's. Yet in the finals, Mills came from behind on the last lap and won the race in a time of 28:24, a time almost 50 seconds faster than he had ever run. He set a new Olympic record for the event, and his victory has often been described as one of the greatest upsets in Olympic history. Mills remains the only American ever to win a gold medal in the 10,000 meter. (His marathon wasn't as dramatic; he finished 14th with a time of 2:22:55.)

In 1983, Walt Disney Pictures released the major motion picture, *Running Brave*, which depicted the life of Billy Mills. The film honed in on the overt racism Mills faced at the University of Kansas.

I met Billy Mills on several occasions years later in Washington, D.C. at the Marine Corps Marathon Expo. He is the co-founder and national spokesperson for Running Strong for American Indian Youth, an organization committed to building the capacity of local Indian communities since 1986. RaceReady made the shirts for their team. Mills is passionate about his work; he is a gentle, humble man I greatly admire.

————

Culver City first officially recognized women in December 1971, months before Boston did in April 1972. Cheryl Bridges won the December 5, 1971, female race in 2:49:40, which shattered the previous world record of 2:55:22 set by Elizabeth Bonner three months earlier in the New York Marathon. Bridges held onto the record for two years until Michiko Gorman broke it with her 2:46:36 race on December 2, 1973, in

Culver City. Gorman's record stood until the following October when Chantal Langlace lowered the time to a 2:46:24 in Neuf-Brisach, France. On December 1, 1974, the world record came home for *the third time* to Culver City with Jacqueline Hansen's historic 2:43:55 marathon.

Gorman and Hansen were both coached by Laszlo Tabori, who was my coach for a brief stint in 1993. (Tabori was the third runner to break the four-minute mile back in 1955.)

In the 1950s and 1960s, Culver City drew more runners than nearly any other marathon in the country, but participants dwindled to a few hundred in the early 1980s. Race founders, Jeff Cooper and Syd Kronenthal, began to look into sponsorships to keep their race afloat. They declined to "go the corporate route" for their race, even though MGM Studios and Sony Studios, huge revenue giants in the popular film industry, were based in Culver City.

Kronenthal was offered a hefty financial sponsorship in 1983 but turned it down on principle. According to the *Los Angeles Times*, the deal required Culver City to forfeit their race name, "Culver City Western Hemisphere Marathon," and change it to "Los Angeles Western Hemisphere Marathon." Culver City held its pride; no deal was reached.

"I would be very opposed to any changes in the name of the marathon. It's a Culver City event. It always has been and it always will be," expressed Councilman Paul Jacobs.

"I wouldn't want it to be a race where you have 10,000 or 12,000 people and it just becomes a circus," voiced race director Jack Nakanishi in 1987. It is eerie, but Nakanishi had predicted the future of the modern-day marathon. A decade later in 1997, Kronenthal commented, "It's really always been a people's marathon. We never got into the hype. When everyone else turned toward marathons as exhibitions, we stayed focused on our marathon as a day for running."

The majority of runners supported big-time races and wanted to be part of the hoopla and rock-star party atmosphere. Small town races like Western Hemisphere didn't appeal to the masses. Despite its rich tradition and heritage, the race was overshadowed by its neighbor, the heavily-funded and much-publicized Los Angeles Marathon.

The L.A Marathon launched in March of 1986, nearly forty years after the inaugural Culver City race. It attracted over 10,000 participants, the largest inaugural marathon in the world. By contrast, the Western Hemisphere Marathon drew 1,500 runners during its heyday in the 1950s. Nine months after the initial L.A. Marathon, a measly 300 runners showed up to run Culver City.

The Western Hemisphere Marathon was doomed, unless it could raise money and draw more participants. Most years during the 1990s, 200 to 300 registered and ran. My year, 1992, was the exception, with the relatively large field of 570.

The city footed the bill for street closures and police overtime support until 1990 but then refused to do so. Race directors owed Culver City $12,000 for expenses doled out in 1991, but were unable to come up with the cash. The race struggled to survive its final decade and never got out of the red.

The 2002 Culver City Marathon was cancelled and the marathon died. It marked the end of an epic era.

CHAPTER NINE

Running into RaceReady

GERRY AND I became close friends with Gary, coach of the Los Feliz Flyers. We shared our passion for running, but we also met at pizza joints and other social events.

The three of us finished a 5-miler on a hot, humid Sunday morning in August 1992, and then we cooled down in our patio. We complained about the crappy shirts and shorts we wore (which chafed). We griped about the limited options in high-quality running apparel. The major shoe companies (such as Nike, Reebok, and Adidas) offered apparel. But their main focus was the product design of their shoes, which was their money-maker. Clothing took second fiddle.

A few small San Diego-based companies had ventured into the running apparel industry. DeSoto Sports, founded by tri-athletes Emilio De Soto and Dan Neyenhuis, appeared on the scene in 1990. Another company, Tri-Fit, was started in the late

1980s by a friend of Gary's named Victor. Victor was a vibrant and talented triathlete whose company offered a line of fluorescent shorts and shirts. His glow-in-the-dark shorts were all the rage for a few years, but the company folded in the early 1990s.

Gary was full of enthusiasm that morning and expressed his desire to enter the running apparel business. Gary is the most charismatic person I ever knew. He was also a dynamic salesman, who could easily sell a glass of water to a drowning man. By the end of our conversation, he had persuaded Gerry and me to form a partnership with him. He came up with an ideal name for the company, "RaceReady."

I'm the girl who couldn't master how to thread a bobbin in eighth-grade sewing class, though I was shown over and over again. I knew little about the apparel industry. But, I did understand runners and their clothing needs.

We signed legal documents with Gary in October 1992 and launched RaceReady. Our first product, Gary's invention, was a singlet (sleeveless tank shirt) with snap fasteners in the front for attaching a race bib. It eliminated the hassle and aggravation on race day. No more danger of poking your finger or chest with safety pins. No more worries of arriving at a race in a panic because you forgot to bring safety pins (and the registration table didn't provide them). We secured a patent on the product. Sales were decent, and we received positive feedback regarding the design and comfort of our singlets. Some thought the snap idea too gimmicky. The RaceReady singlet did not make us millionaires.

To pay the bills, I continued to work as a consultant with Button Accounting. I left it up to Gerry and Gary to figure out Race-Ready. Years ago, my dad once advised, "Never go into business with friends. It's likely to be the death of the friendship."

———

I became obsessed with my training. I ran 70 miles per week. Toward the end of January, I topped out at a personal high record (an 85-mile week). It was my build-up to the Los Angeles Marathon, my fifth consecutive LA.

Race day dawned sunny and bright. I was about to set off on a collision course with nature. It was 8:00 a.m. and already 70 degrees. I sweltered under the scorching sun. I stood at the 800th block of downtown Figueroa Street on March 7, 1993 and awaited the firing gun for the start of the eighth annual L.A. Marathon.

They say that "misery loves company," and I had plenty of company with more than 19,000 runners lined up. Most of them were behind me since I had earned the privilege to start ahead of the rope which separated the elite from the masses. I was among the 50 top seeded women and 500 top seeded men who were granted this honor of being at the front of the pack.

But I wasn't feeling the love (except maybe the love of my two comrades). Terry and Dave were my friends who also wore singlets with our club name written in eye-catching neon-pink on the front. We were much more than just running friends. You build up a relationship when running together stride-by-stride for hours. I had met Terry and Dave five years before when I first joined the Flyers.

I silently sang to myself the lyrics of a tune from our high school play, "Kiss Me Kate."

> According to the Kinsey Report
> Ev'ry average man you know
> Much prefers to play his favorite sport
> When the temperature is low,
> But when the thermometer goes 'way up
> And the weather is sizzling hot,
> Mister Adam, for his madam is not...
> Cause it's too, too, too darn hot.

Seconds later, I switched to the band Foreigner and their song, "Hot Blooded"

> Well, I'm hot blooded, check it and see
> I got a fever of a hundred and three
> Come on baby, do you do more than dance?
> I'm hot blooded, I'm hot blooded

I glanced at Terry on my left. He had an "Oh my God!" look of desperation. I swiveled my head to the right. Dave scowled and muttered, "I can't believe this weather."

Both Terry and Dave are six-feet tall competitive runners and capable of a sub-three marathon. We had a common goal of completion of the race in under three hours. Race director Bill Burke walked to the make-shift stage and podium minutes before the 8:45 start. He took the mike and proclaimed to the crowd, "It's a beautiful day for a marathon in the City of Angels."

I bent down to check for the seventeenth time in the last 30 minutes that my shoes were double-tied. It's a nervous habit of mine. Three years ago, I had a dream, or perhaps it was a nightmare.

I am in full stride about to cross the finish line and win "Boston" when my right shoe becomes unlaced. I lose the race as I retie my shoe and a dozen women whiz by.

Yep, the shoelaces were in secure double-knots. I felt a drop of water on my left shoulder as I resumed my upright stance. No way did it come from the cloudless sky.

"Sorry," Terry apologized. He was mortified, but his sweat continued to drip on me. He couldn't help it. He hails from Calgary and considers any day more than 50 degrees a heat wave. We stood squished together, more tightly packed than NYC subway commuters at rush hour.

Director Burke went on and on about our great city. Dave grumbled, "Cut to the chase, Bill. Can we stop praising this "Glory Be" weather and get this party started?"

Our trio had a strategy. *Run the first 10 miles together at a 6:50 pace. Kind of pretend we are doing our typical 12-mile weekend run in the Park.* Most Saturday mornings, we ran long runs together at a seven-minute clip. I could easily carry on a conversation at that pace. The miles go by more quickly when you are engaged in chit-chat. This mental strategy would lessen the pressure of the race. Once we reached the ten-mile mark, we would be free to break apart and run on our own for the final 16.2 miles of the marathon. We still believed we could break three, despite the wicked hot weather.

Finally, the starting gun fired at 8:50 a.m. It was 71 degrees, but the heat did not dampen the enthusiasm of the hordes that took off like a roiling sea along Exposition Boulevard. I lost Dave and Terry immediately as they disappeared in the tidal wave of runners. But the parade of runners had thinned out by the second mile, and I spotted them up ahead. Good! I was relieved. Now we could run together as planned.

We ran as a team up Sunset Boulevard and then onto Hollywood Boulevard. The spectators seemed sparse, unlike previous years. Perhaps they were soaking up rays at the beach or munching popcorn in an air-conditioned movie theater.

As we approached mile 10, I observed a couple of race officials on the sidelines. They were fairly easy to identify. They were dressed in suits and ties and held a clipboard and pen in their hands. I heard one say to the other, "Number Eight Female. Write her down - Bib # F108".

Terry beamed. "Mary, that's you! Wow! You're in eighth place!"

It revved me up and got me energized. If I kept it up, I would be in the money. The race paid out a prize purse 10 places deep. I picked up my pace, but no longer were Terry and Dave by my side. They fell behind. Maybe they'd catch up later.

I got into my runner's zone and my mind wandered dreamlike; all negative thoughts disappeared. I didn't pay attention to my surroundings at the half-way point near the infamous Grauman's Chinese Theatre on the Hollywood Walk of Fame. Perhaps it's because I live two miles north and it's my home turf. I've dined at the local Mexican and Thai restaurants. My gym is around the corner. I've driven this stretch of Hollywood Boulevard hundreds of times.

From that point on, it again became a blur. I was barely aware of anything except the mile banners as I approached them. I didn't notice the neighborhoods, the spectators, or other runners. I focused on my rhythm and my form. I coached myself, "Don't shorten your stride. Relax your breathing. Pump your arms."

At mile 18, the suits-and-ties again appeared. They informed me, "Runner F108, you are our seventh female." I didn't remember passing another woman, but I guess I did, or perhaps a runner ahead of me dropped out of the race. The heat radiated from the pavement and the soles of my feet were burning (like on a 100-degree day when you are at the beach and make a mad barefoot dash across the hot sand to jump in the ocean).

The aid stations couldn't come soon enough, though they were spaced every mile as usual. It took forever to reach them. I had my routine: Grab water in my left hand and pour it over my head. Grab a cup of Gatorade in my right hand and gulp it down. I screwed up at mile 18 and doused myself in Gatorade. My hair became a sticky beehive. I blinked my eyes. Good! I hadn't dislodged a contact lens!

The final eight miles dragged on. The sun had taken its toll, and I had a splitting headache. I passed the mile 26 banner. I managed a feeble wave to Gerry, whom I saw to my right among the curbside spectators. He gave me the "thumbs up" sign. I crossed the finish line; the illuminated three-foot-tall time clock blinked 2:57:24. It was my fifth consecutive sub-three marathon within the past 18 months.

A volunteer handed me an ice-cold bottle of water. Water never tasted so good. I was eager to get through the chute, find Gerry, and get out of there. I couldn't wait to get home and take a shower.

I walked a hundred yards, grabbed a banana from the refreshment table and felt a tap on my shoulder. It was a suit-and-tie official. "Congratulations! You are our sixth-place finisher! Are you OK?"

I assured him I was fine. He handed me a 16-ounce bottle of water. "Drink up. Then, we'll walk together to that building." He pointed to a one-story concrete structure on our right. "Once you pass the drug test, you'll be free to go."

"What are you talking about? What drug test?"

He explained the L.A. Marathon policy regarding drug testing. "The top three men and top three women are tested. Then, we randomly pick three other men and women who finish within the top 10 and test them. You've been chosen."

"OK. Let me find my husband and explain this to him. He'll be worried about me. We're supposed to meet immediately after the race. He saw me finish."

"Sorry. I cannot let you out of my sight. You are forbidden to leave this area until after your drug test." I realized there was no point arguing with this guy. I would obey the rules.

A friendly middle-aged woman with thin shoulder-length auburn hair met us at the doorway and ushered me into the building. I read her name badge, "Jean." She wore a white medical frock and handed me another bottle of water. I looked around the room and saw four other women and six men. Two minutes later, the sixth woman walked in. Each one of us dozen athletes was assigned our own "Jean," a personal medical assistant.

Jean told me, "Make yourself comfortable. Relax. Help yourself to pretzels, peanuts, donuts, or bananas. Drink some Gatorade. Let me know when you can pee, and I'll escort you to the bathroom. I need to watch you pee in this cup. I need to witness you seal the cup with the plastic top, and I need to see you write your name and date on the label."

I worried about Gerry's being worried about me and I wanted to get out of there *ASAP*. Not much titillating conversation was going on. The top two men were from Brazil; the third was from Mexico, and the fourth was from South Africa. Top female was from Ukraine, second placer was from Canada, and third was from Russia.

No one knew anyone, except maybe the two Brazilians. The guys sat around a big table in one corner. I noticed at least two dozen empty water bottles in the middle of their table, which made sense since they had been there awhile. The women sat on the opposite side of the room.

I never took performance-enhancing drugs. Until that day, I doubted other elite runners imbibed banned substances. Caffeine (via coffee), ibuprofen, and a multivitamin were the extents of my drug intake. But I got a bit panicky. How much caffeine is legal? I like strong, full-bodied French roast. Would the two soup-bowl-sized cups of coffee I drank at 6:30 a.m. cause me to test dirty?

Ten minutes after I entered this sterile clinic-like room with cold, uncomfortable metal folding chairs, I tapped Jean on the shoulder. "I think I can pee now."

We walked down the aisle to the bathroom. It is weird to crouch above a toilet and urinate (with knees bent and holding a plastic cup in your right hand) while a witness has her eyes glued on you. Jean was just doing her job, and I imagined she was as embarrassed as I was. I didn't envy her. I handed her my container of piss. She verified that I wrote on the label, "Mary Button, 6th Female, L.A. Marathon, 3/7/93." This was my first drug-test experience. I suffered through it again and again, and it never felt comfortable. I always felt humiliated.

I was the first one of us dehydrated dozen runners to piss and exit. As I walked out the door, I wondered, "How can I be the first one to pee? The guy who won the marathon finished 43 minutes ahead of me. Why is he still here?" He sat quietly in a corner, a bottle of water in his hand.

Several years later, I told my L.A. drug-test story to my friend Mark, a talented and competitive cyclist. Mark enlightened me. "Most top-notch bicyclists are on drugs. If they want to be competitive, they have to be (since everyone else is doing it). To even have a chance of victory, they need to be on 'a program.' The trick is to work with expert trainers who know which performance-enhancing drugs to take, how much and how often. Timing is everything. Do it right and you remain one step ahead of the curve and will always test 'clean.' "

Maybe I was naïve. Surely, long distance running was different from cycling. We were honorable athletes; we were purists. Marathoners don't do drugs!

Yet, if an athlete drinks enough water before he pees, the drugs become diluted and he will likely test clean. I believe that the athletes in the post L.A. Marathon testing room were "clean" and just severely dehydrated, and that's why I won the peeing contest. But, I'll never know.

The next day, Monday, the headline in the *LA Times* sports section read, "A Hot Time, Slow Times in the City." It listed the top 10 finishers, male and female. I saw my name and felt proud.

Little did I know, race director Bill Burke had revised the prize structure for this year's race. Top five men and top five women finishers were guaranteed prize money. These were the first tier winners. Second tier winners who placed sixth through tenth would only get paid if they broke a certain time standard. No money was distributed in 1993 to the second tier because of the relatively slow times that didn't make the cut. So I wasn't in the money after all.

Blame it on the weather. The temperatures soared to near-record highs and topped out at 87 degrees at 1 p.m. The heat produced the slowest times in the race's eight-year history. To win a prize purse would have been nice, but money wasn't the reason I ran.

———

In June 1993, nine months into RaceReady, Chuck called. "We have to talk. It's important and we can't do it over the phone. We need to meet in person. How about we meet at Palermo's this Friday?"

Chuck, Gerry, and I sat at a cozy table in the dimly-lit neighborhood Italian restaurant and drank cheap red wine, the kind that guaranteed a hangover the next morning. We ordered a large pizza with the works, and then Chuck dropped the bomb.

"Gary is opening a cappuccino bar in La Mirada. He's received the permits and has hired contractors. It's in a strip mall at a busy intersection. I think his grand opening is scheduled within a few weeks."

What in the world? I had noticed this past spring that Gerry seemed to be busting his butt with RaceReady while Gary did not pull his weight. Gerry and Gary worked from their home "offices" and divvied up the tasks and projects; but Gary was never on top of things. He seemed scattered and lacked focus. Now, it all began to make sense.

Gerry confronted Gary Monday morning. Gary came clean and fessed up that he saw dollar signs with gourmet java. He pointed out, "Look at all the Starbucks popping up everywhere!" I felt angry and betrayed. We disbanded our partnership and our friendship also dissolved. My husband Gerry became the sole proprietor of RaceReady in early July of 1993.

I cut back the hours at Button Accounting, and I worked late into the evening with Gerry as we tried to learn the running apparel business. We hired a pattern maker. We struggled with production issues. How much fabric should we order? How much inventory do we keep on hand? Which contractors are the best to cut and sew our products? How do we get stores to carry our line? The questions were endless, but we were determined to make a go of it.

It took over our house. Rolls of fabric were stored in the bathtub of our second bathroom. Boxes of shorts covered every square inch of our couch and were piled floor to ceiling on the living room floor. It was an obstacle course to walk from one room to another, though it was organized chaos. For example, I knew *exactly* where to find women's shorts by size and color. Or, I could locate immediately a man's large black singlet.

Once Gerry and Gary dissolved their partnership, it became awkward running with the Flyers. Gary was the founder and coach of the Los Feliz Flyers, and we respected that. Except for Chuck, our friends remained clueless about Gary's betrayal and the reason for the end of the RaceReady partnership. Gerry and I no longer attended the Flyers' Tuesday night fun-run or Wednesday-night track.

Perhaps now was the time to find a genuine coach. A friend suggested Laszlo Tabori, coach of the San Fernando Valley Track Club, (SFVTC.) I met with Laszlo at his Burbank running store, Tabori Sports, in July of 1993. We discussed my background and my dream to become a world-class runner. "I will be your coach. You don't pay me anything now. But in the future, you will pay me 25 percent of any prize monies you win in races." I signed the agreement and was eager to begin training with him. *He thought I had potential!*

Tabori is an Hungarian-American former Olympian, born in Kosice, Hungary on July 6, 1931. He clocked a 3:59:00 mile in London on May 28, 1955, and he became the third man to break the four-minute mile. Tabori also held the 1500-meter world record with his time of 3:40.8. In the 1956 Summer Olympics in Melbourne Australia, he ran the 1500 meter in 3:42, good for fourth place.

After the Olympics, Tabori defected to the United States. He settled in Los Angeles and began his successful coaching career. He helped individual runners, such as Miki Gorman and Jacqueline Hansen, achieve world-class status. Both Gorman and Hansen were world-record holders in the marathon. They set their records in Culver City (Gorman in 1973 and Hansen in 1974). Gorman is the only female to twice win both the esteemed Boston (1974, 1977) and the New York Marathon (1976, 1977). Hansen won 12 of her first 15 marathons, including the prestigious Boston Marathon in 1973 and Honolulu Marathon in 1975. It was an honor to follow in their footsteps and run under the tutelage of Tabori.

Tabori's coaching style was radical and unconventional in 1993. He was a true believer in the power of the track. He insisted that his athletes do track intervals at least twice a week. "REST" was a nasty four-letter word which he seldom advised.

SFVTC track practices Tuesday and Thursday evenings were brutal affairs, nothing at all like the fun-themed Flyer workouts. My first workout with Tabori was an evening in late July. It was 90 degrees when I arrived at 5:30 p.m. The sun was intense as we ran circles on the dusty dirt track. Coach Tabori didn't allow us even a sip of water. He thought liquid sloshing around in your body while you ran wasn't good. So I suffered, dehydrated.

After a few workouts, I caught on. Between intervals, I asked permission to go to the bathroom. I hurried into the facility (not to pee, but to go to the sink and gulp down as much water as I could in 30 seconds). I wasn't the only one with a small bladder who took bathroom (water) breaks. I wonder if Tabori ever knew.

Although I missed the Flyers, my running improved under the tough Tabori. I ran my track intervals faster than ever. But within a month, I came down injured. My problematic right knee swelled up after a tough Tuesday night on the track. I went home and wrapped a towel around a bag of frozen peas and placed it on my knee for hours. It didn't help. I talked to Tabori on Thursday. He excused me from practice.

"It's probably tendonitis from overuse. I want you to *rest*."

Did I hear him correctly? Did he actually say "rest" and prescribe "no running?" He further advised, "Ice your knee three times a day, and take Advil morning and night." I obeyed his orders, but, to my dismay, my knee remained status quo.

I panicked and I scheduled an appointment with an ortho-paedic specialist, Dr. Mikael Purne. Thank goodness, he fit me into his calendar within a week. He urged me to have an MRI test. MRI (Magnetic Resonance Imaging,) was the latest imag-ing technique used in radiology. It provided detailed visuals of internal structures, such as knee cartilage. Runners interpret MRI, as 'Maybe Really Injured.' The results of my MRI showed a loose cartilage 'flap' on the interior of the knee. Maybe it was the consequence of my knee surgery 20 years prior? Who knows.

I listened as Dr. Purne explained that the cartilage problem would not fix itself. (I had a flashback. This sounded eerily sim-ilar to the prognosis 20 years earlier when I was in eighth grade and met with the surgeon in Philadelphia.) Purne advised sur-gery as my only solution if I wanted to continue to run. It was a no-brainer for me.

Full of self-pity, I went under the knife Friday, August 20, 1993. "Why did this have to happen to me?" I set myself a goal and put it in writing to make it 'official.' "*I will* recover from this. *I will* train and *I will* qualify for the 1996 Olympic Marathon Trials." Time was on my side. I had more than two years to meet the criterion, a sub 2:50 marathon on a sanctioned certi-fied course prior to January of 1996.

I met with Dr. Purne two weeks post-surgery. I was angry and frustrated. "Why does my knee look like a balloon? It's twice the size of my left knee!" "Be patient," Purne advised. "Give it time. It looks like it should two weeks after surgery."

He gave me the green light to work out but not run. "Swim laps, ride the stationary bike, or get on the StairMaster machine at the gym. Build your aerobic capacity, but don't overdo it. Ice after every workout. Within two months, you will be able to run." Patience is a virtue I sorely lacked. But, I was forced to learn.

The Portland Marathon was the final weekend of September. RaceReady was one of the several dozen exhibitors at the two-day Friday and Saturday Expo. Gerry and I booked a room at the Mark Spencer Hotel, a quaint charming place in the downtown area. I set my alarm clock for 6:00 a.m. Saturday morning, so I could test my knee on a three-mile walk-run along the riverfront of downtown Portland before we went to work. It was September 25, my first run in five weeks. It didn't go as I had hoped. Being on my feet from 9:00 a.m. to 6:00 p.m. at the expo the day before probably didn't help. I could only tough it out for one mile running, two miles walking.

"Patience, patience, patience" became my mantra. By mid-October, I had built up to four short runs a week. I slapped the bag of frozen peas on my knee after every run. The knee hurt, but I was making progress toward my goal of making it to the Olympic Trials. It seemed far-fetched but possible.

I decided that Laszlo Tabori was probably not the best coach for me. My body wasn't cut out to do vigorous track workouts twice a week. By the fall of 1993, Gary had resigned, and a seasoned runner, Don, had taken over as coach. So I returned to the Flyers.

Mid-November, I logged a 50-mile week. We ventured back to Southern Illinois for our traditional Thanksgiving visit with Gerry's family. The Alton 10-Miler was my opportunity to test my knee and also test our latest RaceReady garment, our CoolMax long-sleeve shirt. RaceReady used CoolMax fabrics for all of the shirts we manufactured. CoolMax is a trademark for a series of moisture-wicking technical fabrics developed in 1986 by DuPont Textiles. Shirts made of CoolMax improve "breathability" compared to natural fibers like cotton, and the wearer stays dry and comfortable.

I shivered in 30-degree weather before the race start on Saturday morning. I had layered-up and I wore two long-sleeve CoolMax shirts beneath my singlet. My RaceReady shorts were worn atop Hind propylene tights. I had on gloves, but my fingers were numb.

We were blessed with a tailwind for the first half of this out-and-back race. I glanced down at my wrist to read my watch at the turnaround – '30:30.' This was good, much faster than I thought possible. But it didn't last. I got hammered by the headwind on the return five miles. I crouched down and leaned into the wind and pumped my arms. But it was impossible not to slow down. I finished in 1:03:43, completely spent. Seconds later, a reporter from the local newspaper, the *Alton Telegraph*, stood beside me.

"Congratulations! How does it feel to be the first female finisher?"

I was taken by surprise. I mumbled, "It feels great!"

Our CoolMax shirts were also a winner; the most comfortable running shirt I ever wore.

———

By now, I had quit Button Accounting and was full-time Race-Ready. We bumped up our trips to race expos to showcase and sell our clothing. We signed up for a dozen venues in 1994, including Minneapolis/St Paul, Chicago, Washington, D.C., Atlanta, Las Vegas, Philadelphia, Boston, and Sacramento. These extended-weekend trips were hectic but great fun. I loved to talk with runners, sell them the best running apparel on the market (made by RaceReady), and see them the next day on the race course.

I ran Boston Marathon on April 18, 1994, the fastest of my eight Boston races. The weather gave us "once-in-a-(marathon) lifetime" perfect conditions with cool temperatures and winds out of the southwest. I took advantage of the strong tailwinds and got caught up in a strong current as the winds pushed me toward Boston. At the halfway mark, an official called out my split, "1:22." The toughest part of the course was ahead, but I was full of confidence. I cried tears of joy when I finished the race. I had just run a 2:46:50 marathon (6:22 pace), finished 27th female, and I was the ninth American woman.

Records were set in both the men's and women's races. Cosmos Ndeti of Kenya slashed 36 seconds off the previous record with his 2:07:15 win. Uta Pippig of Germany finished her race in 2:21:45. She shattered the previous 2:22:43 course record set 11 years ago in 1983 by Joan Benoit. Aboard my flight from Boston to Los Angeles the next day, I was truly above the clouds. "Yes! My knee surgery was a success!" It had been a mere eight months since my August 1993 knee surgery.

But this April 1994 sub-2:50 would not gain me an entry into the Olympic Trials Marathon because of the timing. It was too early to count. The qualifying window for the Trials was from September 1994 until January 1996. I had to run the 2:50 within this time frame to make it to the Trials scheduled February 10, 1996, in Columbia, South Carolina.

The first few months of 1995, I barely raced because of knee pain. I swallowed fistfuls of Advil, and I gave up track workouts. I only ran easy workouts on my own; I ran on the soft surface of dirt trails, not pavement.

By spring of 1995, I felt ready to train for a sub-2:50 marathon race. Friends in the know urged me to run St. George Marathon in Utah in October. "It's a PR (personal record) course, Mary. Everyone runs their best times in St. George."

I made the commitment and registered. Then I put in consistent 70-mile weeks, even upped it to 80 at times. Most days I did double workouts. (My alarm was set for a 5:00 a.m. wake-up and an 11:00 p.m. go-to-sleep.)

St. George scored in the list of *Runner's World* magazine Top Ten Scenic Marathons. The start is in the Pine Valley Mountains at the almost mile-high elevation of 5,240 feet. Ancient bristlecone pine trees cover the area, their barks aglow with the green needles and the singular fragrance of pine. It's a world away from the desert town metropolis of St. George below. The course descends 2,600 feet as it winds through Snow Canyon, a striking area with the colorful pink and red sandstone formations. Light and shadow of early morning dance across the canyon walls. It's a unique view which changes in a subtle way every second. Blink your eyes or alter your gaze and you'll see a different majestic view. It's the only marathon, except for Boston, where I got slightly distracted from my task at hand.

Perhaps it was the sheer beauty, but it was the rare marathon that seemed almost effortless. I ran a negative split, with my first half in 1:25 and the second in 1:23. **2:48:53!** I did it. I earned my position on the starting line of the upcoming Olympic Marathon Trials, which was scheduled to be held in Columbia, South Carolina six months later.

Out of town trips were a good escape from the concerns of RaceReady on the home front. Our business had grown, and our house wasn't large enough to handle it. The bathtub could no longer contain the rolls of fabric. It was a constant up and down the stairs (from my office and computer on the first floor, to the "inventory" on the living room floor, to the couches on our second floor).

We looked at real estate and searched for a place to rent. We found a small industrial office park in the neighbor city of Glendale, fewer than five miles east of our home. We signed a three-year lease. RaceReady moved to Gardena Avenue in Glendale in January 1996, our corporate headquarters for the next 15 years.

CHAPTER TEN

Growing Pains and Gains

OUR HOUSE BECAME a home again; we could sit on our couch and walk from room to room without tripping over boxes of inventory.

RaceReady was more efficient with our Glendale office and warehouse. I tried to separate home from work. In Glendale, I aimed for RaceReady mode, strictly business. I tried not to think about work at home. We even pledged to not "talk shop" when we left the office. But it was impossible; my two worlds overlapped.

I awoke at 5:00 a.m. weekdays. By 5:20 a.m., I was out the door on my run. Gerry covered the early shift and arrived at RaceReady before 7:00 a.m. (10:00 a.m. New York time). Many of our vendors and customers were on the East Coast, so Gerry kept busy as he returned phone calls and planned production. He never complained. I arrived at the office by 8:30

a.m. with freshly baked bagels from the grocery store around the corner. We didn't "do lunch." Instead, I picked up a sandwich from the deli counter. We sat at our desks and quickly scarfed down turkey on rye; then it was back to work.

I ran mornings and evenings. Our office location was ideal, about a mile from Riverside Drive, an east entrance into Griffith Park. A paved lot provided ample parking (with access to a myriad of trails). Within minutes, I could be on an easy flat path or any number of steep trails. Most weeknights, we left RaceReady at 6:15 p.m. and then ran in the park five or six miles. It was close to 8:00 p.m. by the time we arrived back home, hungry for dinner.

I started a running journal in 1988 and kept it for more than 20 years. I scribbled in my daily mileage and a description of the run. I recorded the distance, rounded to the nearest half mile. I mentioned who joined me, the terrain, and my pace. I often jotted down random thoughts. In 1995, I ran my highest mileage ever; 3,155 miles. It was more mileage than I put on my car that year. In 1996, I ran 3,123 miles. Years later, I flipped through the pages and relived both joyful and painful workouts and races.

Hills were a critical element in my training, though I took my share of spills. My legs resembled those of a typical ten-year-old tomboy, covered with scrapes, scabs and bruises. I often walked out my back door and scrambled up the hillside into the Park. I ran on the steep and winding road which leads upward to the iconic Greek Observatory. From the Observatory, I took the dirt trail that ascends to the top of Mt. Hollywood. On a clear day, I could gaze to the west to view the Pacific Ocean (and even Catalina Island). If I turned toward the east, I saw the rugged San Bernardino Mountains, snow-capped in the winter.

It became a spiritual experience. My Mt. Hollywood run on Sunday Morning was my way of "going to church." I reflected upon my good fortune; grateful for my family and friends, the incredible gift of running, and my beautiful surroundings.

Running stimulated creative thinking and sparked the imagination. Gerry and I came up with some of our most original and successful RaceReady product ideas and designs when we brainstormed on a run.

———

My on-again and off-again knee was off-again on Christmas of 1995. Maybe 3,000-plus annual miles had taxed it. I took a break at the end of the year and hoped the rest would do me good. I couldn't wait for the upcoming Olympic Trials, February 10, 1996, in Columbia. What an honor to be among the top 200 female marathon runners in America! This race would be a special once-in-a-lifetime experience.

But as the New Year dawned, my right knee didn't cooperate. The Advil (ibuprofen) didn't kick in, and I suffered. Those tiny non-prescription pills were supposed to help reduce inflammation. Runners coined Ibuprofen "Vitamin I," as it was a daily vitamin for many long-distance runners. I swallowed an

800 mg dose of Vitamin I three times a day for a month, but it didn't help.

I received the official Olympic Trials Application from the USA Track & Field Association within two weeks after I qualified in St. George in October. Yet, I procrastinated and didn't complete it because I wanted to wait until I felt healthy and confident. In early January, I gave up my self-imposed stubborn waiting game and submitted the form.

Days later, I received written confirmation. Correspondence from politicians and other race officials also arrived in the mail.

Governor David M. Beasley warmly welcomed me to the great state of South Carolina. "We look forward to extending to you our special brand of Southern hospitality. I commend you for your years of dedication and commitment to physical fitness in preparation for this challenging event and offer you best wishes for a successful marathon."

Leroy T. Walker, President of the USA Olympic Committee, signed the *Certificate of Participation*. Dr. Russell R. Pate, President of the Carolina Marathon Association, wrote, "It gives us great pleasure to officially congratulate you on qualifying for the 1996 USA Women's Olympic Marathon Trials. Your accomplishment is every athlete's dream, the chance to go to the Olympic Games. Long after February 1996, we want you to look back and say you have never experienced anything like the Trials!"

I developed a relationship with Marsha Prytherch, the athlete liaison assigned to me by the Carolina Marathon Association. Marsha did not run, but her husband Ed was a competitive runner and the track coach at Heathwood Hall Episcopal School in Columbia. Marsha and I first spoke in mid-January. Our conversations were via the telephone. (Instant messaging didn't exist, and email was in its infancy in 1996.)

"Congratulations, Mary. You must be nervous and have a million questions about Columbia and the Trials. Please do not hesitate to call me collect anytime, day or night. I am here for you."

Marsha mailed me a lofty "Qualifier Handbook" binder. It was a well-organized, heavy document of more than 200 pages. The course was described in minute detail; included were blown-up sketches of the start area and finish area. The map showed every mile mark, kilometer mark, aid station, restroom, and an elevation profile. A full chapter on travel listed hotels, local attractions, and transportation options within Columbia. Weather conditions were addressed.

The Schedule of Events included a detailed itinerary which spelled out an hour-by-hour agenda for each day. This was all helpful information, but intimidating. As I leafed through this encyclopedic volume, I grew more and more nervous. *This was a big deal!* The top three finishers would become Olympians. I stood a snowball's chance in hell, but it was an honor to make it to The Trials!

Marcia phoned me each week to see how I was doing. I was less than honest with her as I faked cheerfulness. "I am fine. Bumping up the mileage. Gettin' ready for Columbia!"

A week before the Trials, I came clean and placed a call to her. I sniffled, "I won't make it to the Trials. My knee can't take it. I am heartbroken to miss out. I wanted this so much."

From 3,000 miles away, I felt a pat on my shoulder when Marsha responded, "I am very sorry. We'll miss you. If it's any consolation, you are not alone. At least 10 other women have cancelled."

Marsha mailed me a packet the week after the Trials. Her hand-written note read, "I'm sorry you were not able to come to Columbia, but you should be proud that you qualified for the U.S. Olympic Trials. I am sending you these mementos; you earned them. If you are ever are out this way, please come and see us."

Included were local newspaper articles which covered the race. Also enclosed were my Olympic Trials Race Number Bib, (#139), an Olympic Trials commemorative pin and a beautiful small, clear glass jewelry box. Upon the top of the box was engraved, "1996 Olympic Marathon Trials, Women's Marathon, Columbia SC." I cherish these mementos.

I was in Las Vegas the weekend of the Trials. The Vegas Marathon expo was a lucrative show for RaceReady. This was our third time there as exhibitors. We manned our booth 10 hours each day on Friday and Saturday. I concentrated on the business at hand, selling our shorts and shirts to runners. It kept my mind off the action in Columbia. I tried not to feel sorry for myself.

Dave, my friend who ran with me the first 10 miles of the sizzling 1993 L.A. Marathon, was in Vegas to run the half marathon on Sunday. We got together Friday evening for dinner.

Dave suggested, "Why don't we place a bet on Jenn?" Jenn

Latham was our mutual friend and training partner who was running the Trials. She had qualified with a 2:42 in St. George. She was seeded with bib #55, so it was a long shot she would make the top three.

I questioned that it was even possible to place a bet on a marathon event, a sport that at best reached the outer fringes. Dave assured me, "We're in Vegas. Trust me. We can bet on anything and everything." We plunked down a $50 bet that Jenn Latham would place in the top three.

Jenn won. But it wasn't *our* Jenn. The winner, Jenny Spangler of Gurnee, Illinois, wore bib #66. She was even more of a dark horse than Jenn Latham. She stunned the running community with her amazing victory in her win time of 2:29:51. Spangler was a virtual unknown to most of the competition going into the race, but the elite women sure knew of her by the end of the day.

Joan Benoit Samuelson (my heroine, and winner of the inaugural Olympic Marathon in 1984) remarked afterward, "It's great for the sport. It's always so cool when somebody unexpected finishes first. It's great to turn over new faces. Jenny Spangler gives hope to other runners." Samuelson herself raced well; she finished 13th with a 2:36 marathon. Jenn Latham ran a 2:58, 106th of the 129 women to cross the finish line.

––––––

On Sunday morning, I ran the Vegas half marathon with Dave. It's a fast downhill course. I felt well-rested and raring to go since I had cut back my mileage the past month. I breezed through the first 10K in 35:40. But then, my knee began to throb, which confirmed, "Yes, I made the wise decision. Running Columbia would have been a disaster." I finished the Vegas half in 1 hour 18 minutes, but it was not a pretty picture. I was in pain. No way could I have survived a full marathon. The knee hurt and remained swollen for days.

Twenty years later, thousands of runners flocked to Vegas to run "The Strip" on a Sunday evening in mid-November 2016. More than 22,000 finished the half marathon and nearly 2,600 completed the full. Portions of The Strip were closed to vehicular traffic, which seldom happens. Runners breathed in the glitz and glamour of fabulous Sin City as they ran by the palatial fancy schmancy resorts and hotels: Caesars Palace, the Bellagio, the Venetian, and the Mirage. Billboards larger than life sparkled with their million glittering lights.

This bore no resemblance to the 1996 race Dave and I ran, which wasn't even close to The Strip. Instead, we ran a boring point-to-point course out in the boonies. We were bussed to the start, 13.1 miles west of town, and dumped off in the middle of the barren desert at 2,900 feet elevation. The race upon the frontage road was a fast downhill course which descended 700 feet to the finish line at the now defunct casino, Vacation Village, on the outskirts of town. The course lacked scenery, but it lived up to its reputation as one of the fastest half marathon courses in the country. My PR (Personal Record) was set on this course when I ran a 1:16:27 a year later in February 1997, a 5:50-per-mile pace.

I ran my first Vegas half on February 5, 1994. RaceReady had a booth at the pre-race two-day expo. Gerry wasn't registered to run, but he offered to chauffeur me to the race start which meant I scored an extra hour sleep since I didn't have to board the pre-dawn bus at 5:00 a.m. He planned to hopscotch the course in his car on the main road (the only road) that paralleled the course. His idea was to stop at a couple of different spots and scurry over to the adjacent race course to yell, "Go, Mary!" as I ran by.

He stepped out of his car at mile 4, at what appeared to be an "aid station." Long wooden tables were set up with several gallon jugs of water on the ground underneath them. Unopened packages of paper cups were on top of the tables. *But there were no volunteers.* Gerry looked at his watch and did the calculations. He predicted the first runners would be coming by any minute.

Seconds later, a middle-aged guy in khakis walked over. He introduced himself to Gerry. "Hi. I'm Ron Wood from Arizona. I'm not a runner, but my wife Kathy is in this race. I'm here to cheer her on." Gerry and Ron got busy and set up the aid station. They poured the water into the cups as fast as they could and lined them up on the tables. They were pretty quick and missed only the first handful of guys who sped by.

I arrived at the aid station five minutes after the fast guys. My "volunteer" husband handed me a cup of water. He and Mr. Wood stayed and manned the station for the next 30 minutes. Finally, after hundreds of runners had passed, the official volunteers showed up and took over. Gerry returned to his car and drove to the finish line. He arrived before I did.

In a twist of fate, I happened to run most of the race alongside Kathy Wood. She pulled ahead of me the final few miles and finished third in a 1:16. I came in fourth, with a 1:17, good for prize money of $200.

———

We were swamped with business in the spring of 1996, in the months leading up to the Centennial Boston Marathon. It was a challenge to find time to train as we struggled to manage RaceReady production. We couldn't keep our shorts in stock and ship out the orders fast enough. It felt intoxicating, this heady feeling of success.

The word was out that "RaceReady LD shorts rocked!" We always believed in our slogan, "The Most Trusted Name in Pocketed Shorts." And now, store owners and fellow runners did too, in ever-growing numbers.

The Expo for the Centennial 1996 Boston was expanded to a three-day, Friday-Saturday-Sunday extravaganza for the first time in history. We anticipated the show and the valuable opportunity to introduce RaceReady to the 37,000 registered runners who were expected to attend the expo to pick up their race-packets.

Our LD Shorts had become our signature product and had put our company on the map. Stores called us daily. "I want to place an order for your pocketed shorts. How soon can you ship us a size run of two dozen?"

Retailers throughout the country faxed in their credit apps, and then asked, "When can we expect delivery of the LD Shorts?" They were our bread-and-butter, by far our best-seller, although the product had very humble beginnings...

Gerry ran the December 1994 California International Marathon (C.I.M.) in Sacramento. He had high hopes to run a sub 3:20 to qualify for the Centennial Boston. He trained with his friend Chris, a giant goofy guy who stood nearly 7-feet-tall. Chris tended to be loud and obnoxious, especially after a few beers, but he was harmless and fun to be around. Although blessed with a long stride (he could cover a city block in a dozen steps), he was perhaps the most clunky, ungraceful runner I ever saw. He was a Clydesdale runner, large and sturdy, built like its namesake horse. Clydesdale is a special division for heavyweight male runners who tip the scales at a minimum 200 pounds. It boggled my mind that Chris would even attempt to run a 3:20 marathon, but he stood a good shot at success. Chris's twin brother Fred, who lived in Reno, also registered for C.I.M. Fred, a few inches shorter than Chris, was the more coordinated of the two brothers.

I sat this race out, but I was along for support. RaceReady was an exhibitor at the two-day expo Friday and Saturday. I encouraged Gerry, "Stay off your feet and rest." It was a small enough show that I could handle it myself, except for a brief crunch period early Saturday afternoon when our booth got a bit crazy.

Sunday morning, I was the cabbie for the male trio. It was my job to get the guys to the race start in Folsom, California, 26.2 miles away from the finish line in downtown Sacramento. Shortly after sunrise, I sat behind the wheel of our white Ford Aerostar and glanced upward at the skies as I buckled my seatbelt. The clouds were gray, ominous, and threatening. They appeared churlish, nothing like the fluffy white cotton balls of the previous evening. "Oh God, please don't let it rain"! (I am not the best driver in the world, even with ideal weather.)

Soon, droplets splattered on the windshield and reduced the visibility. The wiper blades were on full force, but that didn't do the trick. I turned on the defroster, but the windows kept fogging up. I drove very slowly to avoid the deep puddles and to skirt the potholes. Finally, the rain began to let up and I paid attention to the conversation in the back seat.

Fred said, "I brought some GU. I have enough for all of us."

"What is GU?" Gerry inquired.

"It's like a pudding, easy to swallow and digest. I've taken it on long runs, and it works; it gives you a second wind."

Fred handed Gerry a small 2 x 4 inch foil packet. Then he reached into his gym bag and handed him a second one. "Maybe you'll need two GUs."

RaceReady shorts *did* feature a single outside key pocket, the size of a credit card. This exterior pocket on RaceReady shorts was innovative since other shorts on the market were pocketless, except for a pretty useless flimsy inner pocket. Gerry thanked Fred and stuffed the two GUs into his shorts pocket.

I thought, "What in the world is he doing? He is breaking one of the cardinal rules of the marathon! Never try something in the race you haven't tested in practice!" I didn't speak up. Perhaps Gerry had no intention of using the GUs and merely took them from Fred to be polite.

I dropped off the fellows in Folsom and returned to Sacramento in a torrential downpour. I felt sorry for their having to run in this cold rainstorm with fierce winds. I stayed cozy, warm, and dry as I made it safely back to Sacramento, but it was a slow drive and took me well over an hour.

I witnessed Gerry cross the finish line. He was soaked and looked miserable. Yet he ran a PR time of 3:21:18, just shy of the sub-3:20 time he needed for Boston. "I think the GU helped me. Too bad I couldn't carry more of them."

GU, made by GU Energy Labs of Berkeley, CA, appeared on the market in 1994. It was innovative and introduced athletes to a palatable, easy-to-swallow form of nutrition-on-the-run. It's far easier to squirt GU into the mouth than it is to chomp and choke on a PowerBar.

Our friend George Parrott, coach of the Buffalo Chips Club of Sacramento, was a big fan of GU. He planted the seed. "You guys should develop a multi-pocketed short so it is convenient for runners to carry half-a-dozen GUs with them on long training runs and races."

We came up with a prototype pocketed short six months later. The weekend of July 4, RaceReady was in Atlanta, Georgia, for the annual Peach Tree Road Race, the largest 10K in the country. A customer stopped by our booth to purchase a singlet. We chatted briefly and I asked his name.

"Larry Davis. But I go by L.D. – for Larry Davis." I heard "LD" and instantly thought "Long Distance."

LD = Long Distance… A perfect name for our new shorts!

We applied for and received a patent for our unique pocketed design. We introduced the LD short to the general public in September 1995 at the Philadelphia Distance Run expo. The PDR race is a scenic half marathon. Philly is only seven miles from my childhood home of Merchantville, New Jersey. In 1995, my parents still lived on Westminster Avenue, so we stayed with mom and dad while we were in town. Mom cooked up her Italian specialties while Dad stocked the refrigerator with beer.

At the expo, we offered customers a choice. For the same $20 price, they could purchase our standard short or the new fully-pocketed LD short. The overwhelming majority chose the standard version. They didn't see the need for this new funky-ass short with five mesh pockets across the back plus the two safe Velcro-enclosed, credit-card-sized side pockets. We sold a few hundred regular shorts and a mere 10 LD shorts over the course of the two-day expo. Clearly, our LDs had not yet caught on.

We stuck with our hunches and our belief that 'function trumps fashion.' We advertised in Ultra-Running magazine. Their readers were our perfect audience, the eccentric who runs distances of 26 miles and beyond. These folks needed to carry stuff and our LDs got their attention. Several called in to order our shorts

A few months later, the *Los Angeles Times* published an article titled "Blood, Sweat, and Pampering." The story began with the tagline, "Bruising While Cruising."

Staff writer Kathleen Doheny wrote, *"Is anything more aggravating than running a road race with your fanny pack bumping up and down on your behind? But where else do you stow energy bars, keys, loose change and other essentials? This dilemma inspired veteran runners Gerry Hans and Mary Button, the husband-and-wife team behind RaceReady sportswear of Glendale CA, to design and market the LD Shorts. In addition to a Velcro-fastened front pocket, there are five open pockets made of mesh along the back of the shorts. Vertical stitching between each section keeps these pockets in place. We tested these shorts on the run and found there was no pocket movement, even when the pockets were loaded with sports gel and loose change. Everything stayed put. And the shorts are comfortable, too."*

We received more favorable press. *Runner's Schedule*, a calendar publication focused on upcoming races along with editorials, reported, "RaceReady is a small Southern California company that originally built its brand on a singlet with sewn-on snaps for race numbers. Now, they are better known (and often imitated) for their running shorts loaded with pockets."

All of this media coverage occurred prior to the1996 Centennial Boston, by which time our LD shorts had become quite popular. We bumped up production to make as many LD shorts as possible in time for Boston.

This was prior to the terrorist attacks of September 11, in the days when it was pleasant to fly. Airlines didn't nickel-and-dime. We were allowed three free "pieces" of luggage. Our friend Terry J (who ran the hot-weather Los Angeles Marathon with me in 1993) traveled with us. The three of us checked a total of *nine 50-pound boxes* of clothes and set-up equipment. We packed our personal essentials (running shoes and tooth-brushes) into our carry-ons.

We talked with Fred of Reno in early April. Fred offered to help us for a few hours at the expo. He thought (rightly so) that we would be busy with 37,000 runners shopping the show. He was an original fan of our LD Shorts; they were the only shorts he wore. He advised us, "Think of how many shorts you can possibly sell at Boston. Then triple that number when you pack for the show." We thought Fred was crazily optimistic, but we did pack double the quantity we thought we could sell.

By Saturday evening (the end of the second day of the three-day show), we were sold out of all our LD shorts and most of our long-sleeve shirts and singlets. Damn. Why hadn't we listened to Fred? We "left money on the table" in Boston.

At least, we got a day of rest the day before the Centennial Marathon. It didn't take much effort to man a booth with no product to sell.

CHAPTER ELEVEN

Races on the Journey

WE FOLLOWED THE expo circuit in the 1990s and traveled to major running events throughout the country. I ran historic races and toed the line with heroes I had read about in *Runner's World*. It was an honor to be in the same race as Bill Rodgers, Jeff Galloway, Joan Benoit Saumelson, and other world class runners. Long distance running is a unique sport; elite and amateurs participate together and share the camaraderie of the race.

We visited Davenport, Iowa in July 1995 for "The Bix 7." The Bix Road Race was part of the Bix Memorial Jazz Festival, to commemorate Davenport native and jazz musician, Bix Beiderbecke. This multi-day event attracted crowds of music fans from all over the country.

The seven-mile race is the last Saturday in July. We worked the expo four hours on Thursday evening, then all day Friday from 9:00 a.m. to 9:00 p.m. I squeezed in a five-mile run Friday morning at 7:00 a.m., prior to my long work day.

The show took its toll on us as we stood on the concrete floor. Most expos are in hotel ballrooms or convention centers with carpeted aisles. We often paid an additional fee to have our booth carpeted, but it was money well spent. Concrete is an unforgiving surface, about 10 times as hard as asphalt. It's the worst surface to run (or stand) upon, except for brick. By Friday noon, all my joints ached, especially my right knee.

On Saturday morning, I awakened with weary, tired legs. We walked the mile from our hotel to the downtown race start at Brady Street. I lined up with the thousands, in what felt like a crowded outdoor steam room. The Bix was notorious for its heat, humidity, and hills that humble. At 8:00 a.m. gun time, the thermometer read 74 degrees with 78 percent humidity. I started near the front of the pack, just behind the elites. Ahead of me loomed a scary sight, a 400-meter faux mountain, the Brady Hill – a steep uphill climb of about a third of a mile with 8 percent grade. Not an easy way to start a race!

It was pretty much downhill for the next few miles until another climb. At the half-way mark, we made a 180-degree turn and retraced our steps. The return trip seemed just as brutal. This out-and-back course seemed more up than down *in both directions*.

A dozen bands were set up at various points on the course. I heard the full spectrum of musical styles: Dixieland, R&B, hip-hop, rock and roll, punk, and classical. Fifty thousand spectators lined the streets, and this party was just getting started. The celebration continued with live music from noon to midnight at the RiverCenter.

World class runner Olga Appell, on record-setting pace, dropped out near the 6-mile mark. She was rushed to the hospital and treated for heat exhaustion. When I finished my race, I walked past the medical tent which was located a block from the finish line. All of the 30 cots were occupied by tired, dehydrated runners.

The Bix was one tough course. A field of 16,761 runners persevered and finished the 21st annual Bix in 1995. I placed 35th among the 7,930 females, far shy of my goal of finishing in the top 20.

A mere 88 runners (85 men and 3 women) ran the inaugural Bix in 1975. The race grew over the years and exploded with over 5,000 runners in 1983, when my heroine Joan Benoit Samuelson won it. She was champion three more times in the 1980s, and she went on to win the master division (40-plus years old) several times.

I met Joan in 1995 at the expo on Friday, where she sold autographed copies of her recent book, *Running for Woman*. She was assisted at her booth by her cute seven-year-old daughter Abby. Abby beamed with pride as she handed out her mother's books to the fans who were lined up to purchase them. Joan signed my book with the inscription, *"Mary, may the many miles of life be good to you. I hope you are always RaceReady. May you always run with good health, happiness, and spunk!"*

I thanked her and wished her "Good Luck" in the next day's Bix.

———

My all-time favorite 10K is the Peachtree Road Race. I ran it 12 consecutive years until 2004. It takes place on the historic Peachtree Road in Atlanta Georgia every Fourth of July.

We first visited Atlanta in 1993. The race had met its cap of 45,000 registered runners, so it was bound to be a hectic show. Runners were given the option to pay $5 to have their race packets mailed to them in advance; thus they could avoid the expo on July 2nd and 3rd. But we were advised less than half would take this option, and we were told to expect 20,000 attendees during the long show hours from 9:00 a.m. to 9:00 p.m.

Ironic enough, the most critical item to pack for our trip to Atlanta in July was a sweatshirt. I nearly froze to death that first year, both at the expo and in the restaurants where the air was cranked up full throttle. The hotter it was outside, the colder it was indoors.

We always wore RaceReady at the expos. It helped sales when customers saw us model our apparel. I shivered in my skimpy red singlet and royal blue shorts as I stood in our booth in the ballroom at the upscale Hotel Nikko. Every few hours, I escaped the refrigeration for two minutes of relief by stepping outside where it felt like a sauna (90 degrees with 90 percent humidity). When we ate dinner al fresco at 10:00 p.m., it was a cool, comfortable 75 degrees.

The famed race started at 7:30 a.m. in the ritzy Buckhead area at Lenox Square on the wide four-lane Peachtree Road. We ran down this popular hip street which was lined with boutiques, shops, and restaurants that were tightly packed together block after block for miles. Live bands performed at numerous makeshift stages. Cafes were filled with customers who sat at sidewalk tables and sipped cups of coffee or imbibed a Bloody Mary. The whole city (runners, walkers, and more than 100,000 spectators) seemed to turn out. The road narrowed down to two lanes at mile 5 with the final mile in beautiful Piedmont Park

My hunch is I could have run Peachtree faster if the race started later than 7:30 a.m., which is 4:30 a.m. Los Angeles time. I felt out of sync as I did my warm-up. The caffeine from the two cups of coffee I drank earlier at 5:00 a.m. never kicked in. As I jogged my 15-minute warm-up and did a few wind sprints, the thought spun in my head, "It is 4:00 a.m. back home. I should be fast asleep, not running back and forth!"

I finished my first Peachtree, July 4, 1993, in a time of 36:47, the 21st female.

(Little did I know that, in less than two months, I would undergo arthroscopic knee surgery.) The next year, on the 25th anniversary of the race, I ran a 36:21 and finished 25th female.

The initial Peachtree Road Race in 1970 reported 110 finishers. The race grew in size and popularity with each subsequent year. The Atlanta Track Club, which puts on the event, caps the number of participants. In 2010, the cap was raised to

60,000; still the race filled quickly and many wannabes were turned away.

The first year I ran Peachtree, a tradition was begun to award the top 1,000 finishers a commemorative logo mug. A few seconds after I crossed the finish line, a volunteer handed me a postcard which congratulated me on being a "Top 1,000 Finisher." The flip side of the card gave the address of the Nike store where I was directed to pick up my mug within the next week. Nike was the sponsor that designed and paid for the mugs.

Gerry and I hurried to Nike's signature store, Niketown, to receive my logo glass mug before our late afternoon flight home. It was the first of my collection of a perfect dozen of the annual top-finisher Peachtree mugs.

***

Duluth, in eastern Minnesota, sits upon the northern shore of Lake Superior. It is the host city of Grandma's Marathon and the Garry Bjorklund Half Marathon. Grandma's was first run in 1977 with 150 participants. Newly-opened Grandma's Restaurant was the only local business that came aboard to sponsor the race. Race organizers in Duluth appreciated the sponsorship and named their marathon after the restaurant.

The course lived up to its reputation of being a PR (personal record) course. The pancake-flat course is along the shoreline of Lake Superior. Race day is often blessed with a powerful tailwind which pushes runners forward as they make their way on this point-to-point course from the town of Two Harbors to Duluth.

I never ran the full marathon, but I raced the Bjorklund Half three times (1996, 1997, and 1999) when we were in town for the expo. I placed amongst the top three women each time; most memorable was 1999 when I won the race one month after my vacation in Italia...

We traveled to Florence, Venice, and Lucca. I barely ran except for an occasional 30 to 40 minutes on my self-guided tours of the cities in the wee morning hours with Gerry.

I am proud of my Italian heritage. My maternal roots are from the region of Tuscany. My grandfather Michele was born in the mountainous village of Crasciana. He left his hometown in 1920 at the age of 15 and boarded a boat in search of a better life in America. He settled in Boston where he met his wife to be, an Italian named Maria. Maria became known as Marion when she was registered in school because her mother's language was not understood. Marion's ancestors were from Barga in Tuscany.

Marion was a woman who was very much ahead of her time. She was a consummate ecologist. (She recycled everything and never threw anything away.) She wanted to become a lawyer. (She had to drop out shortly after she entered law school because her father died and she had to go work to help support the family.) She was an excellent seamstress. (She could remake a man's wool overcoat into a winter coat for one of her daughters.) She was an excellent cook. (Her spinach/beef-filled ravioli took several days to make, and was made from scratch. She prepared delicious fried squash flowers.) In her senior years, she took up painting.

Michele struggled to find employment in Boston. He worked in plaster (making statures) and also in the restaurant industry as a busboy. He could not advance to be a waiter because he had a hearing problem due to a childhood ear infection. These jobs didn't pay very much, but at least they didn't require a good grasp of English. He taught himself many things. He had only a third-grade education; but, he learned to read and write Italian and English. He also could fix just about anything.

Marion and Michele raised three daughters: my mother Jane (born 1933), Ann (1937), and Norine (1942.) Together, Michele and Marion worked and scrimped and saved enough to send all three of their daughters to college. In those days, low-income was not a qualification for scholarships.

My mother and father, my aunts Ann and Norine, and my brother Paul and his wife Corinne all joined us on our 1999 vacation in Italia.

The highlight of our trip was the day in Crasciana with my mother's first cousins, Pina and Lucia and their husbands. They gave us a personal tour of the ancient village. I saw the humble house where my grandfather Michele was born and drank water from the infamous well which Michele had described it as "the most delicious water in the world." The "humble house" in Crasciana was sold by Michele to a Belgium doctor in 1950 for $2,000. It looks like a grand palace now, one of the finest in the village.

In the evening, we drove to a special ristorante in the hill town of Montecarlo, just outside of Lucca. It wasn't a restaurant per se, but a renovated ancient building whose owners specialized in *private party gatherings. We gathered on the outdoor patio and viewed the spectacular sunset over the Tuscan hillside, and then we moved indoors to the dining room where our scrumptious marathon feast began. It remains etched in my mind.*

We sat down at a long banquet table. Waiters clad in pressed white linen shirts and black pants put before us baskets of freshly baked bread and platters of prosciutto accompanied by specialty olives from the region. Next, they graced our table with crostini ("little toast" topped with mushroom, tomato and liver). Then, came zuppa di panne ("bread soup," a Tuscan specialty). All of this was served before the main event.

The multi-course dinner featured ravioli, fillet au poivre (steak with a caper sauce), roasted potatoes with rosemary, tagliata beef, (thin slivers of beef, barely cooked, sprinkled with pepper), and grilled rabbit. We drank special reserves of vino Montecarlo.

Pastries and gourmet cheeses were presented for dessert. The waiter opened a bottle of Vin Santo, a sweet desert wine. I loved every minute of this four-hour-long dinner/feast. We drank, we dined, we laughed, and we talked. With famiglia, there was no language barrier.

When I won the June 1999 Bjorklund Half Marathon in 1:20:53, my fastest half marathon in two years, I attributed it to the fact I was well-rested and rejuvenated post-Italia.

———

We ventured to Spokane Washington in May of 1994 for the annual Bloomsday Run, a 12K race. This expo was a disaster.

Attendees walked the show floor and picked up all the free food and drink samples that were offered. They whizzed right by booths like RaceReady which were selling products and not just giving away freebies.

The race was far better than the show. The scenic, hilly Bloomsday course featured the Doomsday Hill, a steep ascent at mile 5. I raced well, with a time of 45:15, just over a six-minute-per-mile pace. It placed me 280th of the 55,193 finishers, sixth of the 3,104 females, ages 30 to 34.

After the race, I had the pleasure and the honor to meet the Bloomsday Run founder and race director, Don Kardong. Kardong is an Olympian and author of several running books. He ran the marathon in the 1976 Games in Montreal, and finished fourth, just shy of the awards podium.

Two years later, in May of 1996, I met up again with Don in Knoxville, Tennessee at the 39th annual RRCA (Road Runners Club of America) Convention. Kardong was the president of the RRCA, a position he held from 1996 until 2000.

The first evening of the RRCA Convention, Thursday, May 9th, the Knoxville Track Club led a run tour of historic downtown. Hundreds of us took to the pavement. A poolside picnic followed and I chatted with the very personable and witty Don Kardong. I saw him the next day at a seminar and purchased his new book *Hills, Hawgs and Ho Chi Minh*. He autographed it for me, "To Mary Button, a kindred spirit. Don Kardong." I added another book by the heroes of our sport to my ever-growing collection.

On Saturday, we ran the RRCA National Championship 10K Race, a challenging course through the streets of Knoxville. This was less than a month after the 100th Boston and I wasn't fully recovered. I felt I had no fast-twitch muscles. I was disappointed with my 10K time of 38:46, though it was good enough for a fifth-place finish and a $100 check.

The final day of the RRCA Convention on Sunday, we were treated to a spectacular run on the 11-mile loop in Cades Cove, a lush verdant valley in the Great Smoky Mountains National Park.

———

In May 1997, Gerry and I took a mini-vacation to Cabo San Lucas, located at the far southern tip of the 1,000-mile-long Baja Peninsula in Mexico. This was the rare exception when we traveled to a race with no RaceReady business or expo. It was a genuine four-day vacation!

The Los Cabos Half Marathon, described as "a beautiful coastal race on the Baja," took place Saturday, May 17. A prize purse was offered: $1,500 for first place, $800 for second, and $300 for third. The race was not heavily advertised, at least not in Southern California. I doubted many of the elite Los Angeles runners would make the trip to Cabo.

The race started at 7:30 a.m. upon the cobblestoned avenue at the main square in San Jose del Cabo, Plaza Mijares. It was a gorgeous traditional square with a kiosk, fountains, and an open air theater which was directly across from City Hall and the iconic church. As we ran on the narrow streets, we went past dozens of art galleries, jewelry shops, handicraft stores, upscale restaurants, and bars. Within two miles, we were on the outskirts of town with no buildings and no shade. By the time I was in mid-race, the temperature soared to 80 degrees under the bright blue sky.

It was an out-and-back hilly course. Most of the uphill was in the first half of the race. Three aid stations were set up along the route for the 500 runners. Instead of paper cups of water, the volunteers handed us plastic baggies filled with water. At the aid station at mile 7, I grabbed the bag and popped a hole in it with my thumb. I aimed it toward my mouth and missed. The water splashed my face and dripped down my chin instead.

I heard several locals chant "Tercera" (third place) as I ran by them. Near mile 10, I caught sight of the second place female up ahead. I was gaining on her. Her pace slowed to almost a walk when I passed her. The heat had taken its toll. I recognized her – Carmen Martinez from Los Angeles. I often saw her take the awards podium back home. She always finished ahead of me.

Within 15 minutes of crossing the finish line, an official handed me an envelope. He said, "Felicidades!" "La Segunda Mujer!" (the second woman.) I opened it and expected to see pesos. What a pleasant surprise to see eight crisp one-hundred dollar bills!

An elaborate post-race fiesta was held that evening at the Hotel Finisterra, a luxury resort dubbed the "Heart and Soul of Cabo." It took hours to create the festive atmosphere in the courtyard. Lights were strung on the trees. Colorful handmade linens covered the tables. Beautiful flower arrangements were everywhere you looked: orchids, roses, calla lilies, gerbera daisies, and birds of paradise. Balloons were tied to the railings.

A mariachi band serenaded us. We walked the lengthy buffet line and loaded our plates with ceviche, fish tacos, chile rellenos, chicken enchiladas, tamales, fluffy seasoned rice, black beans, pickled vegetables, homemade tortillas, guacamole, and fresh salsas. It was scrumptious. Plates were cleared and we were instructed to "Please sit back and enjoy the entertainment." The local ladies and gentlemen appeared in native costumes and put on a show of folk dancing and singing which lasted until nearly midnight.

———

Six months later, in November 1997, I embarked on another vacation to a foreign country. I traveled to Ibigawa, Japan, courtesy of the St. George Marathon.

There is a special place in my heart for the St. George Marathon. In 1995, I ran my 2:48 here to qualify for the 1996 Olympic Trials. In 1996, I finished second with my 2:42:11 marathon PR. I returned in 1997, with the hope of a sub-2:42. I even ran more than 90 miles in a training week, the highest mileage week in my life.

Although I ran a smart race in St. George, I fell shy of my goal. I never felt quite right, and can't explain it. Some days you have it, and some days you don't. The long one-mile ascent uphill at Vejo, mile 7 on the course, took it out of me. I felt depleted by mile 8, which is way too early to feel "heavy legs" and fatigue in a marathon. I was disappointed with my 2:45:40 marathon, but it was good enough to finish the third female.

St. George has a sister-city relationship with Ibigawa, Japan. Each October, Ibigawa sends a select group of politicians and runners to the St. George Marathon. St. George reciprocates the next month in November and sends representatives to Ibigawa for their marathon and half marathon races. The St. George delegates include a handful of city officials as well as four athletes: the top male and female in the open division (39 years and younger) and top male and female in the master division (40 years and older).

I have no idea how Ibigawa determines which athletes they send to St. George in October. But in 1997, Ibigawa did send at least one very fast runner, Kayoka Nomura, to St. George. She won the women's marathon with a blistering fast time of 2:39:31. The prize of a trip back home to Japan didn't make sense since she already had her return-flight tickets. The officials came up with an alternative award for Kayoka: beautiful native pottery and a sandstone clock.

They offered the Ibigawa trip to the second place finisher, Cheryl Harper, who ran a speedy 2:40:18, less than a minute behind Nomura. Cheryl and her husband owned a running store, The Runner's Corner, in their hometown of Orem, Utah. They stocked RaceReady shorts in the fall marathon season. Cheryl became the mother of a baby girl in the summer of 1997. How she managed to run a 2:40 marathon within months of giving birth is beyond me. Cheryl turned down the offer to go to Ibigawa.

Next, they offered the trip to the third-place finisher. I received a phone call from race director Kent Perkins a week after the marathon. "Would you like to go to Japan for six days and run in Ibigawa? We will cover all your expenses." I thought about it for maybe 10 seconds before I gave him my enthusiastic, "Yes!"

Kent explained that I could bring a guest, at a cost of $1,150. I wrote the check to the City of St. George to include Gerry on this adventure. Neither of us had passports and we killed an entire day waiting at the local federal office in west Los Angeles to obtain them. The next month was hectic at RaceReady as we prepared to be away from our business for six days in Japan.

We flew from Portland, Oregon to Nagoya, Japan on November 12. I didn't sleep a wink on the long 11-hour flight. Then, we boarded a luxury tour bus for the two-hour ride to Ibigawa. The scenery quickly changed from bustling city to rural countryside. The landscape was dotted with rice paddies and lush grassy meadows. We arrived at the Community Hall in the center of Ibigawa and met our host families.

Gerry and I were assigned Kenichi and Yoko Iwama. They were a delightful couple in their early thirties with two young children, a seven-year-old son, Kazuki, and a three-year-old daughter, Risa. Grandma Chiyomi, Kenichi's 57-year-old mother, also lived with them.

Kenichi was a strong, bulky guy about my height, who looked like he could have been a sumo wrestler. Yoko was 5 feet 2 inches tall. She was a slender, very petite, beautiful woman. She had smooth porcelain-like skin and shoulder-length dark hair. Her lips curved upward in an almost perpetual smile.

The Iwamas considered us their honored guests and outdid themselves with their kind and generous hospitality. Yoko cooked us fabulous feasts, mostly seafood. (I had been given a questionnaire to fill out prior to the trip and had stated my preference for fish.) We were served shrimp, crab, sea urchins, snails, cod, and other fish I didn't recognize. Pickled vegetables and steamed rice accompanied every dinner. Breakfast was warmed-up leftovers from the previous night's feast.

Kenichi and Yoko insisted we not "help," though I offered every day. Before meals, I wandered into their kitchen. Yoko always shooed me away, saying "It's OK. It's OK," as she gestured me back into the living room. We replayed this scene four or five times before I finally gave up and learned to accept my fate of being the pampered guest.

Yoko spoke about as much English as I spoke Japanese, but Kenichi had a good grasp of our language. He had studied fundamental English in school and became fascinated with America. After high school, he enrolled in adult education and took English Conversation class for four years. He knew thousands of English words and phrases. We were able to communicate quite well, though we both constantly held our Japanese-English dictionaries in our hands.

I learned early on not to be too vocal in my admiration for their home décor and possessions. The first night, I marveled at a wooden clock that graced the living room wall. Kenichi replied, "I'm happy you like it. Please take it home with you." I insisted I could not.

The next night, I pointed to a framed picture and remarked, "This is very nice. What beautiful scenery!" Kenichi replied, "I think it will fit into your suitcase. You can put it on your wall in Los Angeles!" Again, I declined.

I whispered to Gerry, "We need to be careful about what we say, or we'll wind up taking all their furnishings back to Los Angeles!"

I ran the half marathon in Ibigawa on Saturday morning. The race started at 11:00 a.m. on an unseasonably warm day. The thermometer had soared to 70 degrees by noon. It was the 10th anniversary of the race, which drew a record number of participants. Nearly 5,000 runners ran the full, while 4,000 joined me in the half. The course began at the town square; within a mile we were on narrow winding roads. We passed rice fields and headed into a gorgeous canyon. The vibrant colors of the leaves reminded me of the fall foliage in New England. We passed by gurgling streams and waterfalls. I regret that I didn't carry a camera with me. It was a photographer's paradise. (This was in 1997, long before smartphones existed.) The course certainly had its share of hills, but nothing too steep.

Unlike most races of this size in the U.S., the spectators were quiet. They didn't jump up and down and scream encouragement. Instead, they stood along the side of the road and waved small flags, and softly murmured, "Gambaru" as runners passed by. Gambaru is a motivational word, which roughly translates to "Do your best until the end." I heeded their advice.

My knee had been problematic the five weeks since St. George. In fact, I had serious doubts about even being able to compete in Ibigawa. As the race date approached, I became nervous. Race director Kent Perkins had assured me on the phone a month earlier, "You don't even have to run the race! The trip to Ibigawa is an experience of a lifetime. You'll experience a unique culture, but running the race is not required." Yet I felt compelled to run the race when I accepted the honor of visiting Ibigawa as a delegate of St. George.

The first miles of the race were OK, but by the fourth mile, my knee felt like it was buckling under me with each step. I was in third place at the turn-around point, half-way through the race, but two women passed me in the later half. I finished the fifth female, in a 1:28:45. It was my slowest half marathon race ever, but I had done my best. When I crossed the line, an official handed me a card with a message on it. I quickly found Kenichi, who translated it for me. "Congratulations. You are among the top ten finishers. Please proceed to the stage where the Awards Ceremony will occur at 1:00 p.m."

I approached the stage a half-hour later as instructed. The 10 award winners, male and female, were lined up according to finish order, first to tenth. Women were on the left side of the long stage and men on the right. Town dignitaries gave a few short speeches. Of course, I had no idea what they said. Then, they handed out the awards. First place winners received a huge sack of rice. Maybe it was a bushel? It looked like it weighed 40 pounds. The top three also received running shoes. The rest of us were each handed two beautiful medals, a plaque, and three separate certificates signed by the race sponsors. I can't decipher a word on any of these documents, but they remain treasured items.

I stood out during the Awards Ceremony. Four Japanese runners, average height of five feet, were on my right. Likewise, five petite Japanese runners flanked my left. I towered over *all* of these women; I was fully aware of every inch of my five-foot, ten-inch height. I was also the only person on stage, and perhaps even in the audience of a thousand, with blonde hair. I felt awkward, but in a good sort of way.

Mary on her tricycle

The Button kids:
Mary, Paul, Eileen, Anne

Flying high on the
swing my grandfather built

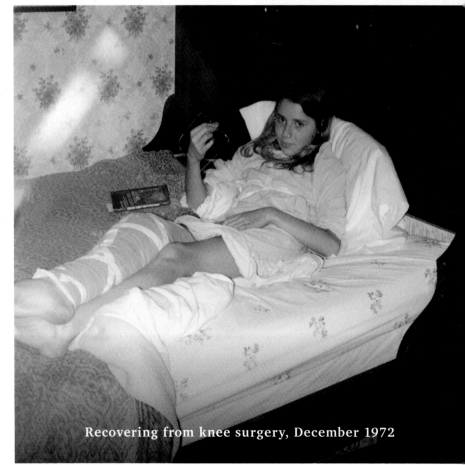

Recovering from knee surgery, December 1972

My determined look

High school
graduation, 1977

At the Grand Canyon, 1981

My first marathon,
L.A., 1989

Winning the Culver City
marathon, 1992

With Gerry in Rosarito, Mexico

With dad after the
Boston marathon, 1993

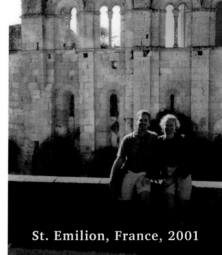

St. Emilion, France, 2001

Strutting our stuff and the RaceReady booth

谷口幸治	00.48	
岡 喜一	46.75	
原口雄	32.42	
北原彦	4.50	
中垣	7.83	
谷川		
ブランドン	2	

ハーフマラソン女子入賞者

1	大谷はづみ	1:22:11.02
2	原田圭子	1:27:00.52
3	宮脇多見子	1:27:46.60
4	佐々木春子	1:28:06.57
5	メアリーバトン	1:28:40.00
6	前田 望	1:29:05.52
7	森 友紀	1:29:47.35
8		1:30:53.92

Ibigawa, Japan, 1997

My two sisters and me, all in RaceReady

In training

Olympic Trials
2000 with dad

A dozen "Top 1000" Peachtree mugs

RaceReady 2006

RaceReady
Exclusive...

LONG DISTANCE SHORTS
RaceReady Catalog, 2006
The most trusted on the marathon course Page 2

709

Competitive mode

CHAPTER TWELVE

Olympic Trials 2000

"**S**TAY INSIDE THE Bubble."
This was my thought when I toed the line on a hot sunny morning, February 26, for the Women's Olympic Marathon Trials in Columbia, SC. I repeated the phrase over and over again to myself, "Stay Inside the Bubble."

The Bubble was an imaginary balloon. Every woman who ran at a sub-3-hour marathon pace was within this bubble. If you ran slower, you were outside of the bubble, and your finish time wouldn't count. Official Race Results were to list all finishers who ran under 3 hours within this stupid Bubble, and no one slower.

We were the cream of the crop of American marathon runners. All of us had cranked out a sub-2:50 marathon within the qualifying window of the past sixteen months, which granted us the privilege and honor to be here at the Trials.

The top three finishers today would represent the USA at the Summer Olympics in Sydney, Australia. All of us had trained countless hours and had run mega miles to make it this far. It was our dream come true to be here. Most of us stood little chance of placing among the top three and becoming Olympians. It wouldn't happen short of a miracle. But this didn't concern me. The honor to participate in the Olympic Trials was what mattered, and it was its own reward.

I took a deep stretch and reached down to touch my toes. I stood up and glanced over my left shoulder and saw Joan Benoit Samuelson. I glanced to the right and saw the strong, lean Anne Marie Lauck, a favorite from New Jersey.

I wore bib # 91, which indicated I had posted the 91st fastest qualifying time. My friends and running partners, Jenn and Bev, stood nearby. We waved to one another, mouthed the words "good luck," and gave a "thumbs up" sign.

Two evenings ago, on Thursday night, we had been briefed. Officials described in detail the rules and regulations of the race. Yes, there would be official aid stations every few miles. Yes, we could plant our personal bottles of our preferred sanctioned energy drink concoctions upon the tables. But, we had to attach labels to the bottles with our race numbers written in bold black lettering to make it obvious which bottle was "ours" to grab as we raced by. We were warned not to accept a cup of water from a bystander along the course. To do so put us at risk of disqualification. Perhaps the beverage which appeared innocent contained a banned drug substance, and not plain old H2O.

I felt the pressure to run fast and stay within the Bubble. On this day in South Carolina, friends and family had come from far and wide to be here with me, to support me, and to celebrate and share the experience. I didn't want to disappoint them. Also, I craved the official recognition of my name in the Official Race Results.

A few years ago, our good friend Chuck had a hunch that the three of us, (Jenn, Bev and Mary) were capable of running a 2:50 marathon time to qualify for the Trials.

He pledged his support, "If all three of you qualify, I am going to Columbia. I will be there for the race." As other Los Feliz Flyers promised the same, it almost became a challenge. After Jenn, Bev, and I all qualified for the Trials, our friends, Skip and Diane, and another couple, Dave and Sylvia, booked flights from LAX. Gerry's parents and Uncle Mike flew out from Illinois. So did Gerry's sister Ginny, whose daughter Maggie was a college student at Winthrop University in Rock Hill, South Carolina. Maggie drove to Columbia for the weekend. My parents and my very pregnant sister Anne flew in from Denver. Talk about great support! *And talk about pressure!*

Jenn, Beverly, and I had met in the early 1990s. We were training partners for nearly a decade. We shared laughs and jokes, but we shared also the serious dedication to the sport of long-distance running. The three of us were obsessive-compulsive, a common trait of endurance athletes. We trained for months like maniacs and ran six days a week with high mileage.

Jenn quit her job six months before the Trials and headed to Lake Arrowhead, California. She shacked up there for two months in Skip's and Diane's mountain vacation home so as to reap the benefits of training at 5,100 feet. (Scores of world class runners train at high elevations. It's like legal blood doping because it boosts the oxygen-carrying capacity of red blood cells when the athlete returns to sea level to race.) Jenn ran 100-mile weeks at the high altitude to get in the best shape of her life.

I managed to squeeze in 70-mile weeks while I worked 50 hours each week at RaceReady. I didn't do much else but eat and sleep. I pulled plenty of "doubles," got up before sunrise to run five miles, and then I did another six miles in the evening.

My typical week a few months prior to the Trials included a seven-mile hill run, a weekend long run of 15 to 20 miles, a few days of doubles, and a killer track workout. The track workouts were the toughest. I ran short intervals, between ¼ mile and a full mile, as fast as possible with little recovery between the intervals. I topped out at my anaerobic threshold pace and gasped for breath after each interval, sometimes on the verge of puking. But it was worth it. I became stronger and faster, though I still had nagging injuries and knee problems that flared up from time to time.

I grew excited as the Columbia date drew close. I had missed out on the Trials in 1996, so my participation in 2000 was to be my redemption and my last chance. I was 40 years old and the odds of making the Trials again in 2004 were slim to nil.

Chuck brought up how remarkable it was that three of us from a small low-key running club, the Los Feliz Flyers, made it to the Olympic Trials. Jenn was the first of us to qualify, followed by Bev, and then finally me. I struck out twice, with a 2:51:25 in Boston of April 1998 and a 2:51:52 in Rock N Roll San Diego in June of 1999, before I finally went sub-2:50 in Las Vegas in February of 1999 with my 2:47:37.

What a grand celebration The Trials turned out to be! I was a bit undertrained, having lost valuable quality training time in December and January when I succumbed to two bouts of a nasty flu. It is impossible to train hard and power up a hill when you suffer a raging fever of 101. I lacked confidence in the final days before I flew to Columbia.

My faithful support crew of family and friends reassured me. "We don't care how fast or slow you run the race. We are just so proud you made it to the Olympic Trials and we're thrilled that we will be there with you!"

On Wednesday, February 23, Gerry and I flew from Los Angeles to Atlanta, then we caught the short commuter flight into Columbia. We had reservations at the host hotel, the Adam's Mark on Main Street downtown. It was fully booked with female marathon runners and their families. Fortunately, plenty of nearby hotels were available to handle the overflow of friends and fans who were in town for race weekend.

We were given keys to a spacious, quiet room on the sixth floor of the Adam's Mark. Old photographs with tranquil scenes of Columbia from a century ago adorned the walls. A king-size plush bed took center stage. I couldn't wait to test the bed. I wanted to stretch out upon it and squish the plump pillows in the crook of my neck and open a book and try to relax for an hour. A sliding glass door opened to the balcony with a view of Main Street below, the start line of Saturday's race.

We dined that evening at an Italian café down the block; then we returned to our hotel to unwind. Despite the luxurious suite, I barely slept Wednesday night. I was too nervous, and I tossed and turned upon the 500-thread-count sheets.

Early Thursday morning, I got out of bed and walked into the elegant marble bathroom. I gazed at myself in the mirror, not at all happy with my reflection. Staring back at me was a face with blood-shot puffy eyes, obvious proof of my lack of sleep.

I slipped into my running shorts and shirt and walked down the six flights of stairs to the lobby to meet Bev at 7:00 a.m. Bev had also flown into Columbia the previous day, but on a different flight. We had planned to go out together for a 40-minute easy run. Bev sipped her coffee while we exchanged pleasantries, each of us glad the other didn't experience a snafu with travel plans getting to Columbia.

"You look really tired," Bev told me. I returned the compliment, "Well, so do you."

She hadn't slept much the previous night either. Minutes later we headed out the door for an easy run, our tour by foot of downtown. Bev and I shared a terrible sense of direction, but we kept our wits about us and didn't get lost. We talked non-stop about how excited we felt being in Columbia amongst the top female marathoners in the country.

The Carolina Marathon Association provided a course tour available to the athletes and the media at 10:00 a.m. Jenn, Bev, and I boarded the filled-to-capacity bus. The driver navigated the route along the "blue line." A sky-blue, foot-wide stripe had been painted on the pavement in the middle of the road the entire 26.2 miles of the course. When we ran on Saturday, we would have no worries about getting lost and veering off course. All we had to do was act like Dorothy. Just as she had followed the yellow brick road to Oz, we would follow the blue-striped road to the finish line on Main Street.

The bus tour lasted 1 ½ hours, though it seemed to take forever. I thought, "God help me. If it seems this long seated on a bus, how long will it seem on foot?" The course ran by scenic areas on the outskirts of the city. I tried to take it all in on the ride since I was well aware I wouldn't "see" any of the scenery on Saturday when my focus would be on the race itself and the terrain of the uphills and downhills. The course didn't seem too intimidating from my perspective in the bus. The high point of the course was at 322 feet elevation, and the low point was at 148 feet; but very few portions of the course were as flat as a pancake.

It was a nerve-wracking ride. I squirmed in my seat and thought about my race strategy. The toughest challenges would be the hills between mile 8 and mile 10 and then the ascent between miles 20 and 22. My plan of attack was to start the race at a moderate clip, no faster than seven-minute miles. I knew I had to psyche myself and conserve my energy for the hills. It was crucial that I stay well-hydrated throughout the race in order to keep my pace and not fade at mile 20.

On Thursday evening, the Columbia Museum of Art hosted an athlete reception between 5:00 p.m. and 9:00 p.m. in their interior Garden Terrace. Family and friends were welcome, but we were encouraged to be respectful of the limited space and bring only one or two guests. I brought Gerry.

The place was packed when we got there at 7:00 p.m. White linen tablecloths covered the lengthy banquet tables which were piled with a variety of delicious hors d'oeuvres. We stood in small groups and mingled with other athletes. Waiters roamed the room with trays and offered guests glasses of white wine and sparkling Perrier. We saw the press as they honed in on the top-seeded runners to "get a few words." Sound bites were on the late-night television news and in the next day's paper, the *Columbia Star*.

Friday morning, Gerry drove Jenn and me to Forest Lake Elementary School so we could meet our "class." Three months previously, the Carolina Marathon Association had assigned all 210 Olympic qualifiers a third-grade or fourth-grade class. They paired us up, two athletes to one class. By sheer coincidence, Jenn and I were both assigned Mrs. Halford's third-grade class at Forest Lake. We became pen pals with the kids and wrote letters back and forth.

The kids learned all about the Olympic Games from Mrs. Halford before the December holiday season. She bragged about

Jenn and me and we became their heroes. I received a dozen Christmas cards and letters from her third-graders.

Alex M. wrote me, "Dear Ms. Button, I hope you can come and visit us. I hope you win the race. You have to have a lot of guts to win."

Kyle B. said, "I hope you do good in the race and win it and go to the Olympicks and do well."

Matthew W. offered his help, "Dear Ms Button. I am excited you will visit our school. Do you know where it is? If not, mail me and I will send you a map."

Sandra asked, "Do you have any pets? Please send a good picture of your pets in your next letter."

Jeanna A. inquired about my holiday, "How was your New Year? I just can't wait for you to visit our school. You look like a beautiful lady."

A few weeks before the Trials, Jenn and I talked on the phone. We decided to hand out medals to the class when we visited. Both of us had shoeboxes full of medals that we had won over the years. We were happy to unload them in Columbia to our 30 young fans.

The kids were thrilled when we walked into their classroom. Bless their naïve little hearts! They thought we were Olympians, not mere qualifiers for the Trials. We visited with them for nearly an hour. We told them about Los Angeles, our families, and our running careers. Mostly, we talked values. I think they got our message, "To pursue your dreams and never give up, and to work very hard to achieve your goals."

At the end of our conversation, we distributed our medals. Their eyes sparkled and they grinned as we draped the gold medals around their necks. I was touched to be their hero. It was difficult to keep my composure and not cry. I did tear up on the ride back to the hotel. The Forest Lake school visit is one of my fondest memories of the Trials.

I hoped to take a nap that afternoon, but couldn't fall asleep. At least, I was able to lie down and read my book, *Mama Flora's Family*, the 1997 historical novel by Alex Haley, the famous author of *Roots*. The theme of *Mama Flora's Family* is the powerful love of family which gets one through difficult and desperate times. It resonated with me. Here I was in Columbia, South Carolina, at the Olympic Trials. I would not be here if not for the love and support of my family and friends.

We made dinner reservations in the evening at Villa Tronco, Columbia's oldest Italian restaurant, which dates back to 1970. Our party of seven included Gerry's parents, my parents, my sister Anne, Gerry, and me.

We walked to the restaurant, down a street lined with stately mansions, theaters, ancient banks, and shops. I felt like I was in a previous era. The restaurant was in an old brick building, formerly a 19th-century firehouse. It was declared a historical landmark in the early 1980s and given a significant facelift in 1983. Extensive renovation had been done to return the building to its former glory, with particular attention paid to preserve the oak wooden floors and the red brick walls.

When we arrived at this family-owned restaurant promptly at 7:00, we were immediately seated. I pored over the menu and selected their pasta primavera, a "light" entrée, or so I thought. Our waiter brought us baskets of homemade, steaming garlic-parmesan bread, which we devoured. Twenty minutes later, I tucked into a huge platter of sautéed zucchini, broccoli, onions, and tomatoes atop a bed of angel hair pasta. I did the meal justice and cleaned my plate. We all did. None of us exited with a doggy bag of leftovers.

Saturday morning, February 26, I pulled open the blinds and looked down below. Spectators were already gathered near the start line under the bright blue skies at 7:00 a.m. I turned on the TV for the weather report, "A beautiful day is in store for us in Columbia. It is currently almost 70 degrees and the thermometer is expected to climb above 80 degrees by mid-afternoon. This is a great opportunity to go outside and enjoy this unusually warm summer-like weather!"

I walked down to the lobby for coffee and toast and gave myself a pep talk. "This is good, Mary. You run well in heat." I practiced visualization, and pictured the choo-choo train from one of my favorite childhood books, *The Little Engine That Could*. This illustrated book, published in 1930, depicts a blue engine that struggles up a steep rail. He repeats the mantra, "I think I can, I think I can," as he overcomes the seemingly impossible task and conquers the hill. The final page of the book shows the smiling engine at the top of the hill. He did it. He conquered, and so would I.

At 8:30 a.m., I stood in the center of Main Street with the 180 or so other athletes very anxious for the 9:00 a.m. start. I paced back and worth. I spotted my family and friends on the sidewalk, behind the roped-off street. I rushed over to them for final "good luck" kisses and hugs. My dear dad squeezed me tight. "Go show them what you can do!" I left his embrace and I returned to the start line, more determined than ever to do him proud. I took deep breaths and stayed calm and focused, while I awaited the firing gun.

We were off and running. The first few miles circled downtown. We ran past the Capitol and then through the communities of West Columbia and Cayce. I concentrated on the painted blue line in the middle of the road and didn't see much else. But every few miles I heard, "Go, Mary," and my eyes veered away from the pavement in front of me as I tried to spot my fan and give him or her a wave of acknowledgement, or at least a smile.

Gerry drove his parents and navigated the perimeter of the course quite well. They saw me at five different points. I spotted them at four of the five. My dad, mom, and Anne, who were in a separate car, stopped at four other locations to cheer me. They blew kisses as I ran by them. Jenn's husband Mike and our friend Skip were on their bikes, which was the best way to view the action of the race. They popped up unexpectedly eight times. I heard Skip shout, "We're so proud of you! This is the Olympic Trials and you are here!" I have fond memories of my personal entourage and their cheers.

The race itself felt strange. With fewer than 200 runners, I ran "by myself" pretty much the entire way. A few minutes here or there, another woman and I were together stride-by-stride, but not for very long. I did catch up with Bev at mile 16 and we ran together for four miles. We shared the same goal to break three and be in the bubble!

The weather was not our friend that day as the temperature soared into the 80s. Gerry later described a conversation with his dad:

"Can you please turn on the air conditioner? It's pretty hot here in the back seat!"

"Sure dad, let me cool it down a bit for you."

I had been running for less than an hour.

Chris Clark, age 37, from Anchorage, Alaska, took control of the race at mile 20 when she passed leader Ann Marie Lauck. Chris was unchallenged the final six miles and ran alone to break the tape and win the race with a time of 2:33:31. It was ironic that the woman from Anchorage won the race on this beastly hot day. I later learned that, because it was so bitter cold in Anchorage, Chris did most of her training indoors, on a treadmill, in a gym with poor circulation. She had learned to master the heat. Clark would be the sole representative of the USA in Sydney since she was the only woman who met the required Olympic "A" standard of a 2:33 marathon. Second-place finisher Kristy Johnston ran a 2:35:36, followed by Ann Marie Lauck, with her 2:36:05.

I learned all of this after I finished the race more than 20 minutes later. I placed 87th with my time of 2:58:13. Bev was fewer than two minutes behind me, and finished 101st, with a 2:59:53. Jenn finished far ahead of the two of us with her speedy time of 2:51:02, the 49th fastest time of the day.

The three of us friends burst that three-hour bubble, which as it turns out didn't exist after all. Race directors had come to their senses and chose to recognize each and every finisher. The Official Results listed all 141 finishers of the race, including the 40 who ran slower than "three."

The top 20 finishers were acknowledged and awarded their prize money at the 1:30 p.m. Awards Luncheon in the banquet room of the Adam's Mark. Chris Clark took the podium. "My expectations were top 20, and a great day would be top 10. Winning, I never thought about. I stayed focused on what I needed to do. I never thought I'd run this fast. The crowd was unbelievable and I'm in shock." She was handed a $45,000 check. Johnston was awarded $30,000, and Lauck received $25,000. The payscale diminished for the rest of the "slower of the fast" top 20. Tenth-place prize was $10,000; the twentieth finisher went home with $1,000.

Craig Masback, executive director of USATF (USA Track & Field), spoke to the press. He defended the choice of Columbia as the site for the Trials. "In February, this city's typical weather approximates the conditions marathoners would expect to face at Sydney in September. Eighty-six degrees today turned out to be about 25 degrees warmer than we expected."

At the end of the luncheon, a photographer from the USATF took a picture of just the master runners, the 17 of us over the age of 40. I never saw the photo, and I've tried to track it down, but to no avail. At least I have the pride of being the twelfth master to finish the Olympic Trials.

I stepped into the elevator with Joan Benoit Samuelson, whom I greatly admire. Joan, at the age of 42, ran a remarkable, 2:39:59, finished ninth place overall, and was the first master. I towered over her at my 5-foot, 10-inch height. She is 5 foot 2, perhaps all of 100 pounds. I looked down at the woman to whom I have "looked up to" for decades. "Congratulations, Joan, you ran a fantastic race."

Her gracious response; "Thank you. As did you and all the women today."

We celebrated in style on Saturday evening. It could not have been better. Gerry pretty much organized the whole affair. It was at the Faculty House, a private dining club located on the Horseshoe which is the original campus of the University of South Carolina. The three-story brick building, built in 1813, was named the McCutchen House, in honor of George McCutchen, a professor of history and economics. During the Civil War, most of the buildings on the Horseshoe were converted to hospitals and military offices, but the McCutchen house remained a faculty residence.

A massive restoration of the historic buildings on the Horseshoe began in 1971, which took six years to complete. The original frame of hand-hewn timber was retained, the original window glass was put in place, and the graceful double stairways and entrance halls were returned to their former glory. When the McCutchen residence reopened in 1977, it was christened Faculty House.

Gerry had reserved one of the small, private, beautifully-appointed rooms on the third floor. It was ours from 6:00 p.m. until midnight. RaceReady hosted the party. We mailed invitations weeks in advance to our family and friends. We also invited Bev, Jenn, and their families. Nearly 30 joined us for this memorable evening.

We convened at 6:30 p.m. in The Cellar, the classy bar on the basement floor. It was a dimly-lit room with dark wood-paneled walls, quite the cozy atmosphere. We sat on burgundy-colored leather seats and couches. The bartender stood behind the stunning mahogany counter. We toasted one another with locally-brewed bottles of Palmetto Pale Ale and rehashed stories of the race for the next hour.

We then climbed the wooden staircase three flights to our dining room. The stairwell walls were lined with old stately photos of former officers and dignitaries of the South.

Faculty House prides itself on tradition, charm, and understated elegance. As we entered the room, I noticed the waiters dressed in black linen trousers with freshly pressed white shirts and jackets. They wore white silk gloves, which added a certain sense of dignity and glamour. Colorful flower centerpieces were atop the eight round dinner tables, which were draped with white linen and set with polished silver. South Carolina's state flower, the Carolina Jasmine, was the star of the bouquet amongst the clusters of purple and white asters and clumps of baby's breath.

We sat down, four to six at a table, for an exquisite dinner. The waiters served us piping hot bowls of their famous she-crab soup, a rich creamy bisque made of crab meat, seasoned fish stock, cream, sherry, celery, onions, and intricate spices. Next, we tucked into a simple mixed-green salad with toasted pecans, goat cheese, dried cranberries, and a honey mustard vinaigrette.

We were offered our choice of the following four gourmet entrée selections:

Fillet of Salmon with Chef's signature sauce

Chicken Montrachet (with Montrachet, Ricotta, pine nuts and basil)

Veal Cordon Bleu

Tagliatelle with marinated Grilled Vegetables

I selected the salmon, which had a sweet-sour glaze and was grilled to perfection. It had a delicate pink color and was very flaky and moist. I tasted honey, lime, garlic, and a hint of rosemary. A side of lemony asparagus and roasted potatoes complemented the entrée. Everyone raved about the food and the setting of Faculty House.

A podium with a mike was set up in the corner of the room. We took turns and told family stories, running tales, fables, and jokes. Waiters served our dessert - triple mousse torte, a buttery sponge cake with alternating layers of vanilla cream, chocolate mousse, and raspberry mouse topped with fresh whipped cream. Coffee was brewed and poured. We stayed until nearly midnight, and it was truly a night to remember. I'll never forget those four days at the Olympic Marathon Trials.

CHAPTER THIRTEEN

An Extended Vacation

IT WAS CHUCK'S idea. He lifted his glass with his toast, "Let's run the Medoc Marathon." Chuck was at our house in Los Angeles for dinner on a Sunday evening in March of 2000, a month after the Olympic Marathon Trials.

We were sitting in the patio of our hillside home which is located a few miles east of the famed Hollywood sign. We uncorked a bottle of wine. Whenever Chuck joins us for dinner we tend to uncork more than one bottle of wine. We share an infatuation for running as well as a fondness for wine.

Chuck continued his toast. "It's too late for this year's Medoc. The race fills up months in advance. But let's make a pact to run it together in 2001."

Medoc Marathon is run in the Bordeaux region of France in early September. Aid stations feature wine tastings, and the participants dress in costume. There could not possibly be another marathon more the polar opposite of the Olympic Trials.

Over the previous dozen years, I had run 24 marathons, *all* of them were competitive. I was always focused on my running time, hoping to lower and improve it. It would be a welcome change of pace to focus on my time running instead.

Our friend Ed lived in Paris and was fluent in French. Ed ran Medoc in 1999, and he couldn't stop raving about the event. "It is like no other marathon in the world!" He helped us complete the registration which was written in French, "Organisation le Marathon du Medoc." A few months later, we received written confirmations for the September 8, 2001, race; seven of us from Los Angeles plus Ed were officially in.

Gerry and I planned an itinerary to include six nights in Bordeaux and three nights in St. Jean de Luz, a quaint coastal town in the Basque region, 130 miles to the south. We booked our return flight home from Bordeaux for September 15, 2001.

Ed insisted we run the race in costume. "7,500 of the 8,000 runners will be wearing a disguise. It is a faux pas not to do so, like showing up at a nude beach wearing a bathing suit."

We came up with the idea to dress as Playboy Bunnies. The guys resisted. At first, Gerry, Chuck, and Ed proclaimed, "No way!" But we wore them down eventually. They finally consented. We did cheat a little (base layer of black singlets and shorts isn't exactly a costume), but we adorned it quite well: floppy bunny ears, a fluffy white tail attached to our in-shape asses, cuff links of silky-white fabric with gold-colored enamel studs, and shiny white collars with velvet black bows upon our necks. Veritable sexpots we would be!

We left it in the hands of Marathon Tours to work out the details for our six days in Bordeaux. Marathon Tours, based in Boston, specialized in running-related travel. It was founded in 1979 by Thom Gilligan, a veteran of more than 60 marathons. Thom's company provided package deals for destination marathons worldwide. By signing up with Thom's company, we would be spared the planning headaches of our trip. Marathon Tours covered the logistics of hotels, meals, sightseeing, city transportation, guided tours, language translation, and more.

In the spring and summer of 2001, we trained for Medoc, focused on long walks and jogs, and imbibed wine. We had yet to *combine* drinking and running in a workout. How would that unfold?

We tested it one Tuesday evening. Chuck placed a card table on a corner of the track and put upon it a few opened bottles of wine. After each mile (four laps on the track), we stopped at our improvised aid station to sip some wine. Five miles later, we staggered off the track. Our designated drivers drove us home. It was a prelude to what awaited us the following month. Marathon du Medoc featured 23 wine stops along the 26.2-mile course.

———

Vacation time at last! Thom greeted us when we landed at the airport in Bordeaux. He was in his mid-fifties and possessed a runner's physique, a gaunt appearance to the layman's eye. I noticed his skinny legs with well-defined calf muscles and the lack of the typical stomach gut you see on middle-aged men. Except for the fine crinkles on his face and his graying hair, he could have passed for a man half his age.

"Welcome to Bordeaux, a paradise for runners and wine connoisseurs. We'll be visiting several of the famous vineyards over the next several days. Better pace yourselves! But you're runners; you know all about pacing."

The courtesy shuttle van dropped us off in front of our hotel, Chateau Chartrons, in the Old Wine Trade District located a few blocks from the city center of Bordeaux. I gazed in fascination at the stone gargoyles etched above the curved archway of this Victorian-style building. Inside, I was immediately disappointed because it was a modern American-style hotel, similar to what could be found in any major city in the USA. The receptionist boasted, "Your air-conditioned rooms will have a TV with remote control, and the channels include CNN in English!"

Dinner that evening was in the restaurant of the Chartrons. We eight Flyers mingled with 50 other runners who had also signed up with Marathon Tours. By 10:00 p.m., the evening was winding down. Thom took the microphone, "Get a good night's sleep. Load up at the breakfast buffet, 7:00 a.m. – 9:00 a.m. and meet in front of the hotel at 9:30 sharp."

I don't sleep well when I travel, but I managed a few hours of shut-eye before I heard the beep-beep-beep of my alarm at

7:30 a.m. The best part of breakfast was the croissants (flaky, rich layers of pastry perfectly baked to a golden brown). They tasted buttery and had a slight saltiness, not so salty that I couldn't resist topping them off with jam. Petite jars of apricot and berry jams, tiny pitchers of honey, and pats of butter adorned each of the small breakfast tables which seated four. With these croissants as an option, I wasn't even tempted to fill my plate with the typical American fare of eggs, potatoes, and bacon.

At 9:30 a.m., we boarded the two deluxe tour buses parked in front of the hotel. I don't remember many of the people on our tour, but I will never forget Frank, a balding older man in his 60s; there were a few straggly gray hairs fighting for survival. Red capillaries zigzagged across his face which was already a rosy tone even before we started drinking. He had a pronounced bulbous nose, a perfect complement to the protruding stomach on his very rotund body. Given his physique, I was puzzled. "How can he possibly run a marathon?"

Franks' voice was thunderous. He shouted when he spoke. I doubt he was even capable of whispering. Gerry and I were seated a few rows ahead of him. I was tempted to stick my fingers in my ears whenever he talked, which was often.

Frank was a highfalutin' lawyer from New York City. At 3:00 p.m., he pulled the cell phone from his pocket and placed a call to New York, New York, where it was 9:00 a.m. Frank yelled into the phone to, I assume, his secretary. "Anne, tell him I'll call him back tomorrow." A few minutes later, he dialed another number. "Stan, hold tight. Keep your financial position. It will all work out." Moments later, I heard him say, "Joe, don't sign anything. I'll help you with the will next week when I get back to New York." Frank apparently was in high demand in New York. He let all of us aboard the bus know it.

Two glorious days touring wineries and estates throughout the picturesque region of Bordeaux! Our bus rumbled up and down narrow gravelly roads. Little villages dotted the country-side. It is gorgeous farmland with blooming sunflowers, bucol-ic vineyards, and ancient medieval castles.

We visited half a dozen chateaux daily; each one had its unique charm, such as the Chateau Pontet which was con-tained within an ancient 18th-century castle. We took in the sweet aroma of the wine with every breath.

I drank more and better wine during those two days than I normally do in a month back home. We stopped by the quaint town of Cognac for a tour of Remy Martin. I did know Bor-deaux was from Bordeaux, but it was news to me Cognac was indeed from Cognac. I thought it was just a fancy-schmancy name for expensive brandy.

Friday evening, we gathered at Fort Medoc, a 15th-century stone fortress built on the marshy banks of the Gironde River. A huge white tent, large enough to accommodate a sit-down dinner for a crowd of 1,500, had been temporarily set up for the pre-race "Soiree Mille Pates" ("Thousand Pasta Party").

Wine hour began at 7:30 p.m. Copious amounts of wine were poured from the makeshift bar on the lawn. We drank glass after glass of the rich and earthy Medoc wines as we sat atop the waist-high stone walls of the fort. Ninety minutes later, the flaps of the tents were opened. Row upon row of tables, covered with elegant white linen tablecloths, were set up. Colorful floral centerpieces and bottles of wine graced the tabletops. In the center of the tent was a wooden platform stage, large enough for 200 to shake their booties after dinner.

It was impossible for our entire Marathon Tours group of 60 to sit together. At least, the eight of us Flyers secured seats across from one another at a table near the stage. A band played pretty much nonstop from 9:00 p.m. until past midnight.

"Mille Pates" was a four-course dinner served family style. Dozens of waiters started us off with platters of a cold vegetable corkscrew pasta salad and baskets of crusty bread. Thirty minutes later, heaping bowls of hot linguini were placed on the table with nearly overflowing plates of chicken tenders in a béchamel sauce (a rich white, creamy sauce made with butter, milk, flour and a touch of onion). Wine glasses were topped off again and again and again. For our third course, we got a break from the pasta when we were served a fresh green salad with juicy local tomatoes. Stuffed as I felt, there was no way I was going to pass on the grand finale dessert, which was chocolate linguini doused with chocolate custard and topped with flakes of shaved chocolate. It was the most decadent dessert imaginable, sinfully sweet melt-in-your-mouth chocolate. Pure bliss!

Plates were cleared. People headed to the dance floor. When it was filled, people danced in the aisles to American pop songs. After midnight, Thom came over to us. "It's time to leave. We have a marathon to run tomorrow morning."

The race, officially titled "Les Marathon des Chateaux du Medoc," lived up to its reputation. The 26.2-mile journey began in the village of Pauillac. We stepped out of the bus, weary-eyed and hung-over from the night before. I struck up conversations with cloven-footed devils, winged angels, transvestites, cowboys, and Indians. I can't say for sure, but I suspect the loud and pudgy Bozo the Clown was Frank. I walked by Batman and other comic book heroes, pirates, nuns, ballerinas, a herd of zebras, a herd of cows, a school of jumbo shrimp, Cleopatra, Beauty and the Beast - all before the firing of the 9:30 a.m. start gun.

The course was a stunning, beautiful circuit which cut through vineyards of famous wineries. We passed by or through more than 50 chateaux while we ran on country roads through small villages. Townsfolk cheered us as they waved small French flags and chanted enthusiastically, "Allez! Allez!" (Go! Go!) The 23 gastronomic support stops along the course offered specialties such as tender cubes of grilled beef, local Arcachon oysters, a variety of cheeses, fruits, salty crackers and chips, even ice cream at mile 25. I approached each station and was asked, "Blanc ou rouge, madame?"

Of course, we had to pee. There were no porta potties. *Everyone* pees multiple times in the vineyards along the course. I veered a few feet off course, dropped my drawers behind some taller vines of grapes for privacy, and thought, *"Maybe this is the secret to the region's great wine. Rich muddy soil fortified by runners' pee."*

Gerry and I crossed the finish line together at 4:00 p.m., six-and-a-half hours after the race start. He gave me a big smooch and said, "I'm so glad we did this!" It was double the time of any previous marathon I had run...It was also more than twice as much fun!

The next day was even better. September 9 is my birthday. What better way to celebrate my 42nd birthday than to do the post-marathon ballade with friends! The ballade was an eight-mile recuperation stroll over rural roads. Everyone walked the ballade, dressed in normal casual attire. The course wound through four grand chateaux, each with live music and bottomless glasses of wine. The idea was to relax, kick back, and stay at each chateau for a half hour or so. At two of the chateaux, the bands played standard rock and roll. At a third chateau, we listened to rhythm and blues and jazz. My favorite was the fourth and final elegant chateau where we were treated to a fine orchestral performance of classical music. At the end of the ballade, we entered a big top tent for a luncheon of quiche, chili, salads, crusty bread, and soft cheeses.

I took a much-deserved afternoon nap. Later in the evening, Gerry said "Wear your nice dress tonight. I'm taking you to the Dolce Vita restaurant." We feasted on mussels steamed in a light broth, grilled spicy calamari, steak with Marsala sauce, and crème brulee for dessert. I thought it *truly is* dolce vita (the sweet life.)

On September 11, Tuesday, we boarded our deluxe tour buses. The destination was St. Emilion, an ancient medieval town forty minutes east of Bordeaux. When we arrived, we were shooed off the bus. "Explore! Enjoy the cafes and shops. Browse about on your own. We'll meet back here in four hours at 3:30 p.m."

Gerry and I escaped our tour group for a romantic afternoon together. We walked hand-in-hand along the narrow cobblestoned streets. "Let's see if we can visit every single shop in town before we have to board the bus," I suggested. "Only if restaurants and cafes are included in your definition of 'shop,'" was his response.

We came pretty darned close to our goal. We laughed at ourselves as we attempted conversations with the shopkeepers. My two years of high school French were hardly adequate.

We took dozens of pictures of each other and of this delightful medieval village. At every jewelry boutique, Gerry insisted, "At least try it on. I want to buy you a necklace or a pair of earrings." I settled on a pair of pearl teardrop earrings.

"Good. Now when you wear these back home, you'll remember this glorious day."

The afternoon went by far too quickly.

We boarded the bus. Damn, once again we were sitting two rows in front of Bozo the Clown, AKA Frank. I had been trying to avoid him ever since the first day of the bus tour.

Minutes after we boarded, his phone buzzed. "What do you mean, 'They hit the World Trade Center?' Make certain, and call me back." He hung up.

Seconds later, his phone rang again. "OK, you *are* sure. A plane flew into the World Trade Center. And then a second plane flew into the World Trade Center? Find out more, and call me back." He hung up again.

I looked at Gerry, "This can't possibly be true. It's just Frank being Frank. Right?"

It was the world's longest bus ride back to Bordeaux. I sprang from the bus, sprinted into my hotel room and turned on the TV, for the first time grateful to be in this Americanized hotel with CNN Worldwide in English. My eyes were glued to the TV as I watched over and over again a jet plane crash into the World Trade Center. I was in agony. I cried. I wished I could be Dorothy and simply click my heels together three times, and then, like magic, be back home in Los Angeles. I felt confusion, anger, and fear. Why did this happen? For several hours, I tortured myself and watched the relentless coverage with the wrenching images and tried to understand this. I simply could not comprehend. I didn't want to be in a foreign country anymore. I wanted to be in the same country as my fellow Americans. I craved the sense of security of familiar surroundings and a language I could speak, a newspaper I could read.

We carried on half-heartedly, and drove to St. Jean de Luz the next morning as scheduled. I went through the motions of being on vacation, but I no longer was. The beautiful sandy beaches didn't register. I can't remember what the famous Basque cuisine tasted like, though surely I ate it. Those three days remain a blur. I came down with a cold which developed into the full-blown flu by the final night. I passed on dinner and lay in bed alternately shivering and sweating as I suffered with a fever.

We returned to Bordeaux. Chateau Chartrons welcomed us back kindly. "You poor Americans!" They offered us half-priced rooms and threw in free breakfast buffets for as long as we were their guests. September 15, our scheduled departure date, came and went. I was no longer physically sick, but was emotionally drained.

I called our airline, USAir, and got a busy signal. I dialed my parents and asked them to try to contact USAir and speak on my behalf. Surely they would have better luck reaching the airline calling from their home in Fort Collins, Colorado. My dad got through to USAir the next morning. The airline representative assured my dad she would call him as soon as they could book us a flight home.

Dad gave us advice. "You are in Bordeaux! There are worse places to be stranded. Buy yourselves a bottle of wine each evening. Drink it and talk to us in the morning. We'll give you the update. If you don't have a flight booked, go out and sightsee and buy another bottle of wine. Bordeaux will not run out of wine." *Yes Dad, but we might run out of cash.*

We walked up and down the streets of Bordeaux for five days. I memorized the merchandise of every aisle in every store and recognized the faces of the shopkeepers. We drank wine each evening, but it didn't taste as good as it had the week before. On September 19, my dad gave us the good news that he was able to book us a flight home to Los Angeles on September 20.

Our final night in Bordeaux, we were seated at an outdoor café. I watched couples stroll by, hand in hand. They looked happy. I became irrational and angry. It wasn't fair. How could they be smiling and laughing?

September 20, early evening, our plane touched down at LAX. Tears streamed down my face as the pilot announced, "Ladies and Gentleman, Welcome to Los Angeles."

CHAPTER FOURTEEN

The Modern-Day Race

IT AIN'T LIKE it used to be. Races in the new millennium hardly resemble the races of the 1980s and early 1990s. The changes have not all been for the better. Promoters and marketers cashed in on the running boom. Races became rock star events that drew huge crowds and often sold out months in advance. Local races simply disappeared. The few that survived lost their small-town charm and appeal as they caved to corporate sponsors with their one-size-fits-all formula. Gone were the mom and pop race directors of yesteryear.

Road races formerly focused solely on running turned into multi-sport events. Participants were now offered a myriad of options. People signed up to run, bike, or even roller-blade the 26.2-mile marathon course. These events brought in valued revenue, but also added much chaos. Running lost some of its glory.

My good friend Ric Munoz had run each annual Los Angeles Marathon, starting with the inaugural race in March of 1986. The March L.A. Marathon was a highlight on his calendar. He had no gripes with the event for nine years.

Ric tested positive for HIV the year after he ran his first L.A. His friends were shocked when he told them the news. They begged him, "Please, stop running!" He appreciated their concern but was adamant about his decision. "No. I will not give it up. The marathon is my passion!"

Ric was a survivor. He had suffered childhood molestation, poverty, bigotry, and physical and emotional abuse. HIV was just another hurdle for him to conquer. Why would he stop running? It was the one thing that gave him inner peace and comfort.

He ran the first nine L.A. Marathons (1986 through 1994) when it was nothing more than a foot race. The event drew thousands of participants, mostly from local running clubs and communities, though a small number of "destination runners" did travel to Los Angeles. The March race offered an ideal spring break escape and a welcome respite from the shivers of the East and Midwest.

I am proud of my hometown marathon and happy to have run it five consecutive years (1989 through 1993). The L.A. Marathon put on a good show in its early years. The first Sunday in March brought our city together. The Marathon took runners on a journey through various ethnic neighborhoods. We sniffed the smoke of Korean BBQ from make-shift sidewalk grills and breathed in the aroma of sizzling curbside fajitas.

Ric became slightly distressed in 1995 when the cycling event was added. He griped, "Why can't the *RUNNING* of the L.A. Marathon be sufficient? Why do we need bikes on the course? It strips our beloved Marathon of its dignity!"

The L.A. Marathon added insult to injury when the event was expanded *even further* in 1996 with inline skating as an option. Ric became frustrated and furious. At this point, he declared, "Enough!" "Mary, they have turned our beloved Marathon into a circus!"

Ric had pre-registered months in advance for the 1996 race. Two weeks before the race, he decided to bail. He no longer wanted to run or support the event. He called the L.A. Marathon office and asked for a refund. He was informed of their "No Refund" policy.

"Why don't you go to the expo the day before the race and try to sell your number?" the person in the office suggested.

This response was preposterous and only stirred up his disgust for the race. He couldn't believe that the office person actually proposed that he scalp his number! It confirmed his belief the race had truly lost its integrity.

Ric and I were not alone. Quite a few running purists were disappointed with the twisted turn the L.A. Marathon had taken. Clearly, the race had become overly profit-driven and damn the runner. The directors' prime focus was on the financial bottom line, not the runners' experience. I imagined their boardroom discussion. I pictured the suits seated in leather chairs around the long, polished, rectangular oak table on the 20th floor of a downtown skyscraper. I heard them brainstorm how to "milk this baby for all it's worth."

It made no sense to me. Sporting events *are* specific. You don't attend a golf tournament and expect to view a tennis match at the same time. They are two separate, distinct athletic events. Why should running be any different? Especially the marathon, which is the granddaddy of the long distance! It deserves respect and should stand alone.

L.A. Marathon finally dropped the bike ride in 2009 when the route was changed to a point-to-point course from Dodger Stadium to the sea (for fear the thousands of cyclists wouldn't be able to get their bikes home).

————

The Cherry Blossom 10 Mile Run takes place in our nation's capital the first weekend in April. Runners flock to Washington, D.C., to take in the sights and the scenery. The fast course winds by famous landmarks on streets lined with fragrant cherry blossom trees. The route passes by the Jefferson Memorial, the Franklin Delano Roosevelt Memorial, the Washington Monument, Arlington National Cemetery, the Lincoln Memorial, and the Watergate complex. It's the perfect tour of the city by foot. The race fills up five months in advance via its two-week December lottery, which quickly reaches the 15,000 cap. The fee is reasonable, a price tag of $43 for the 2017 race.

Few realize that the inaugural Cherry Blossom in 1973 was a free event. Perrier, the mineral water from France, sponsored the race. Perrier's goal was to introduce their product to the USA. What better audience than thirsty runners? They put on a low-key race which had only 141 finishers. Back in the 1970s, it was common to run a race and pay next to nothing, perhaps a $10 nominal charge. By the mid-1990s, race fees had skyrocketed to an average of $50, often higher.

I never ran Cherry Blossom, but I did run what I consider its West Coast equivalent, the Valley of the Flowers Half Marathon in Lompoc California. It too had humble beginnings. The first Valley of the Flowers in June of 1977 listed 247 finishers. The race managed to survive, though it never drew the crowds of Cherry Blossom.

Lompoc is 150 miles north of Los Angeles. The quiet town is situated slightly north and inland of coastal Santa Barbara. Cool temperatures combined with the perennial overcast morning skies make Lompoc a heavenly place to run in the summer. Beautiful flower fields dominate the outskirts of this charming community. Long, narrow roads weave back and forth through a colorful showcase of blossoms. Acres are planted with varieties of cut flowers and those grown for seed, which include poppies, sweet peas, larkspur, stock, marigolds, sunflowers, Queen Anne's lace, bachelor buttons, and delphinium.

Vegetables also dot the landscape. Fields have dedicated patches of celery, lettuce, beans, artichokes, cauliflower, broccoli, and cabbage. It's a vegetarian's picture book.

I first ran Valley of the Flowers on Father's Day, June 16, 1991, the fifteenth year of the race. I placed second female with a 1:22:28. We returned to Lompoc four years later for the race on Sunday, June 11, 1995. Gerry and I had pre-registered in March when I mailed in our $60 check which covered our $25 entry fee and the $5 pre-race pasta dinner. La Purisima Concepcion, the Catholic Church, hosted the Saturday evening feast.

The local women of the church certainly knew what they were doing in the kitchen! They cooked up gallons of delicious, authentic, made-from-scratch tomato sauce.

We entered the church Saturday evening and I inhaled deeply as I tried to breathe in this tantalizing aroma. I followed my nose down the steps to the banquet room in the church basement. Dozens of long rectangular tables were set, draped with red and white checkered tablecloths. The place was packed. Many runners had come early and were dipping into their spumoni ice cream by the time we walked into the room at 6:00 p.m. The dinner had begun at 4:30 p.m. and would continue until 7:30 p.m.

It was buffet style. I loaded my plate with a generous portion of spaghetti and meatballs, salad, and warm garlic bread. The Italian woman on the serving side of the buffet exclaimed, "You must come back for seconds and thirds. You are too skinny. Mangia! Mangia!" (Eat! Eat!) It was the dinner bargain of the decade – five bucks for this delicious authentic Italian dinner, non-alcoholic beverage and dessert included.

The race started and finished at Lompoc High School. After a lap on the track, we ran up and down the flat-as-a-pancake streets of town for four miles. Then, we embarked on a hilly, gravelly dirt road which passed by La Purisima Mission. I loved this part of the course. (La Purisima is my favorite of the 21 Californian missions established between 1769 and 1823 by the Spanish religious order of the Franciscans whose goal was to spread the Christian Faith among the Native Americans.)

There were fewer than 650 participants in 1995. Most ran the half; only 260 held tough for the full marathon. A cool breeze prevailed for the 380 of us in the half, but the brave souls who ran the full struggled with gnarly headwinds that battered them as they ran their final 13 miles through the flower fields.

I took the lead from defending champion Keena Carstensen at about mile marker 9 as we headed out of La Purisima Mission and began a long, gradual downhill stretch back toward town. The next day's paper, the *Lompoc Record*, quoted Carstensen, "All I saw was long legs and big strides as the 6 foot 2 Button went by me. I knew I was in for a tough go ahead." *(For the record, I'm only 5 foot 10, but I admit I am 'all legs.')* I won the race with a 1:22:26 and was ecstatic.

That spring, I had been in serious training mode with my sights on a fall marathon under 2:50, in order to qualify for the Olympic Marathon Trials. My confidence took a boost after I won the Valley of the Flowers Half. I hadn't tapered for this race and had just come off a month of consecutive 70-mile weeks. I knew I could have raced faster if I had been well-rested instead of running with dead-tired, heavy legs.

The Awards Ceremony took place in the early afternoon on the well-manicured football field at the high school. I was crowned with a beautiful fresh wreath made of flowers from the local fields and handed a gorgeous bouquet and a trophy, the Valley Victory Cup. I felt like a queen for the day. I saved the next day's *Lompoc Record* which featured my picture on the front page of the Sports section. The photo was snapped right after I was awarded my wreath. I am decked out in a Race-Ready logo t-shirt and warm-up pants. There's a happy, dorky grin on my face.

Ten years later in 2005, we took a getaway weekend to Lompoc. The course had been completely revamped and moved away from downtown and La Purisima to the Vandenberg Air Force Base on the outer fringes of town. This was post 9/11 and tight security measures were in place. We were required to show proper IDs, which were scrutinized by Check-point Charlie before we were admitted into the base. The course was pretty much nondescript, except for the midway part when we ran near the rugged coast. My time was 1:34:22, 12 minutes slower than I had run in 1995. I was surprised that was fast enough for first place. I received the Lompoc Victory Cup once again, but they had done away with the floral wreath and bouquet.

In 2006, after five years at Vandenberg Air Force Base, the Lompoc race returned once again to the grounds of La Purisima State Park. More than 75 percent of the course was on dirt trail, the remainder upon a gravel road. They had cancelled the full marathon, but the half marathon drew nearly 200 runners.

Race fees had crept up over the years in modest $5 increments. In 2007, it cost $50 to register, still quite the bargain. The price included not only the typical post-race water, bagels, and bananas, but also a barbeque lunch. After the race, we gathered at picnic tables in the shady grove and filled our plates with grilled chicken, salad, beans, bread, corn on the cob, and chocolate chip cookies.

We were given a free day pass to tour the historic La Purisima Mission. But best of all, we received a beautiful RaceReady long sleeve CoolMax shirt, which featured a three-color artsy design on the front, with no advertising.

I have run hundreds of races in two decades. The Lompoc Half Marathon remains among my favorites. It was fun in the good old days of the Italian ladies pre-race dinner, as well as its current format with the post-race chicken barbecue at La Purisima.

Cherry Blossom and Lompoc were the exceptions with their inexpensive registration fees. As half marathons became quite popular in the new millennium, the entry fees have gone through the roof. By 2011, the majority of half marathons charged between $80 and $100 and gave runners very little swag. You received support on the course, post-race snacks, a t-shirt and perhaps a finisher's medal, but not much else. The shirts were often cheap-looking, covered with sponsor logos and ads. Even the so-called "technical" shirts which race directors started to promote were cheaply made.

America's Finest City Half Marathon, (AFC) of San Diego charged $90 for early bird registration in 2011; late signups paid $100. The event sold out and reached its capacity of 7,000 months in advance of the August 21 race date. Runners were required to visit the Expo Friday or Saturday to pick up their bib numbers, t-shirts, and goody-bag. The venue of the AFC Expo was the ballroom of the Sheraton Hotel, which charged $10 to park in their lot.

You could avoid the expo hassle, but it came at a price. For an add-on fee of $20, AFC would mail your race materials to you. Many took this option. For frequent racers, expos all began to look alike. You saw the same vendors and products over and over again. There were a few mom and pop companies (like RaceReady) that made the circuit, but for the most part, the big guns dominated the shows. Nike, Brooks, Asics, and Reebok set up elaborate booths with their shoes and clothing on display and available for purchase. Clif and PowerBar battled to see which one could give away the most of their free samples to runners who walked up and down the aisles.

It's a far cry from the way it was in the 1990s when race expos featured smaller innovative companies. Our friend Lillian from Portland worked the expo circuit and sold her custom-designed, one-of-a-kind runner gym bags. Lois of Huntington Beach sold jewelry. She made beautiful necklaces consisting of a simple gold chain with a pendant of a running goddess. An artisan from Atlanta offered her hand-crafted ceramic mugs for sale; they were etched with a runner or an inspirational quote. Another lady promoted her "runners' quilts." She made quilts from those old race shirts you had stashed away in your bureau drawers. If you mailed her 20 t-shirts she would convert them into a beautiful quilt. You could spell out where you wanted each shirt to be positioned, or leave the artistic design up to her. She was highly experienced and her lucrative business kept her busy. The average turnaround for her quilts was six to eight weeks.

AFC was a scenic point-to-point course. Runners started at Cabrillo National Monument on the Point Loma peninsula. They ran the streets of scenic Harbor Island through downtown, and then climbed a steep uphill final two miles to the finish in historic Balboa Park.

The $90 to $100 race fee included bus transportation to the start at Cabrillo National Monument. It also covered the added security which was in full force at the National Monument. Road closures, police protection, medical tents, and aid stations along the course were legitimate expenses that added up. AFC was a pricey race to enter but it was for an excellent cause. The proceeds benefitted the American Lung Association.

The Long Beach Half was a different story. They charged $100 for their race two months later in October 2011. Buses weren't required since it was a loop course and you finished right where you started. The race was sponsored by International City Bank, which paid the standard costs for permits and city street closures, medical personnel and police protection. But ICB didn't give the runners anything special – just an ugly t-shirt and a medal. With more than 11,000 runners in the half, plus another 3,000 in the full marathon, the ICB easily took in more than $1,200,000. My guess is they made a huge profit.

Surf City Half Marathon, a Super Bowl Sunday tradition in sunny Huntington Beach, charged $90 for their 2011 race. Fourteen thousand signed up for the run and the famous post-race Michelob Ultra Beer Garden Beach Party. It also did not raise money for charity. Three years later, in 2014, 15,000 runners forked over $115 to run Surf City.

Sold-out races are a somewhat recent phenomenon. In the 1990s, I ran a dozen races each year and did not pay more than $50 per race. The possibility of being turned away because a race had reached its limit was unheard of. Often, I decided on a Friday afternoon which 10K or half marathon to race that very weekend.

I understand race directors' desire to have an idea of registration numbers in advance so they can properly plan. They need to have sufficient aid stations, plenty of volunteers, medical personnel, t-shirts, and enough porta potties. An often-used calculation is one porta potty per 100 runners. Countless times, races were delayed in the 1990s as a courtesy to the long line of runners in front of the porta potties who were still waiting to "go" at the time the start gun was to be fired. It turned into a race director's nightmare when double the runners they expected showed up on race morning.

It seems outrageous that runners are forced to sign up for races far in advance, sometimes six months ahead of time. Since races seldom issue refunds, runners take a chance when they pre-register and pay. They can only hope a wedding, a funeral, work responsibility, or family obligation doesn't come up and conflict with race day, not to mention the ever-present possibility of illness or injury.

I know several race directors of the more popular races in the country. They have been straightforward and told me they are well aware that "life happens." They factor into their equation and calculations that 20 percent of registered runners will be "no shows."

If the race capacity is 5,000 runners, the director allows 6,000 people to pre-register. It is a safe bet he'll be okay come race day and that fewer than 5,000 runners will show up to run. The race fee of the 1,000 no-shows is free money.

In late 2008, my right knee ached, but I remained optimistic and pre-registered for two half marathons on the calendar for spring of 2009. I didn't want to risk being shut out of these events.

The inaugural Illinois Marathon and Half Marathon, scheduled the Saturday before Easter, took place in Champaign, Illinois, hometown of the University of Illinois, Gerry's alma mater. I had never seen the campus or town. Gerry's brother and his wife lived close by in Decatur and we had planned to spend the holiday weekend with them. We committed to the Half, and RaceReady to the pre-race expo.

I also pre-registered for Destination Races Wine Country Half Marathon, a May race in the beautiful Santa Ynez valley near Santa Barbara. I ran the Wine Country Half its inaugural year in 2007, and also in 2008. It is run upon rural back roads that wind through vineyards and bucolic farmland with grazing cattle and horses. The race also passes through downtown Los Olivos, a tiny artist community in the region. Fabulous running combined with superb wine tasting and dining makes a perfect weekend get-away. I didn't want to miss out.

By early April, a 30-minute run left me with severe knee pain. We traveled to the Midwest for Easter, and I walked the Illinois Half Marathon on Saturday. Gerry could have run, but he walked with me instead. He reminisced about his days in the early 70s (*University of Illinois Class of 1973*). The campus was a hotbed during the Vietnam War, on par with Kent State. We walked along the main street where historic protest marches had occurred more than 30 years earlier.

The following month, stride by stride, we walked the Wine Country Half-Marathon. We were not alone. Until that spring, I had no idea of the masses that walk these events. It was unheard of twenty years ago to "walk a race." Now, it was not only accepted but encouraged.

"Sold Out" events seem to be here to stay. At least, the multi-sport circuses of the mid-1990s have disappeared. Ric and I need not worry now about bicyclists and skaters on the course. It is all about the pedestrian once again.

CHAPTER FIFTEEN

"All for a Good Cause"

I RACED IN the days before the Internet when we did not go online to research and register for races. Instead, we connected via a visit to our local running store where we picked up pamphlets and flyers of upcoming races. Most weekends in Southern California, we had a dozen race options. They were low-key affairs with only a few hundred runners.

I always caught a glimpse of familiar faces at the start line. We hard-core runners who raced often got to know one another after a while. We mingled after the 5K/10K and either bragged or griped about how we had run that day. I knew five to ten percent of the athletes at any given race. The experience felt personable, unlike the current days of the mega races when you don't recognize anyone in the field.

Races in and around Los Angeles in the 1980s and 1990s raised money for local charities. There were numerous worthwhile causes. We ran to benefit schools, churches, women's shelters, rape victims, the hungry, and victims of domestic violence. We helped injured animals and helped heal the Bay (Santa Monica Bay). We brought in dollars to fund the Los Angeles Philharmonic. We raised money to fight tragic diseases such as AIDS. It was a win-win situation for the runners and the causes. The races exuded small-town charm and brought the community together.

In the 21st century, the race director is likely to be a huge corporation. Competitor Group, a privately-held, for-profit sports marketing and management company based in San Diego, owns and operates races on a massive scale, such as the famous Rock 'n' Roll Marathons. It's the world's largest running series and includes races in more than 25 cities worldwide, which sell out weeks in advance. More than 500,000 participate in Rock 'n' Roll events each year. Rock 'n' Roll continues to expand and add new destinations each year.

The inaugural Rock 'n' Roll Marathon took place on the streets of San Diego on June 21, 1998. Elite Racing (the company later acquired by Competitor Group) put on the race. I saw Elite Racing's pamphlets more than two years in advance of the debut race. Their personnel, dressed as Elvis Presley, attended the major marathon expos. Rock and roll blared from the booth. In April 1996, at the Expo for the 100th Boston Marathon, I walked by the Elite Racing Booth and "Elvis" handed me a flyer. In bold letters, it stated, *"You missed the first Boston Marathon. You don't want to miss out on the first*

Rock 'n' Roll!" It advertised a fast and flat course. Olympian marathoner Frank Shorter had come on board to help draft the course.

San Diego is only a few hours drive from Los Angeles, and the promise of a non-hilly course caught my attention. I registered early, with the lofty goal to run sub-2:50 to qualify for the 2000 Olympic Marathon Trials. I was given a seeded number for the race since I was ranked among the top 25 women who had signed up. This special bib number granted me the privilege to start at the front of the pack with the other elite men and women. It was a valuable perk since it would allow me a clean start ahead of the crowds. In large races, it often takes more than 10 minutes for mid-pack runners to reach the start line after the gun is fired.

I awoke race morning at 6:00 a.m. and cranked open the blinds in my room on the third floor at the Holiday Inn. My heart sank as I gazed upward to the bright blue skies with nary a cloud in sight. The weather god had played a nasty joke on us. He had stripped us of the typical June Gloom. June Gloom is a Southern Californian term for a weather pattern that results in cloudy, overcast skies with cool temperatures. It is often accompanied by dense fog and a light drizzle. It tends to dissipate by noon when the clouds give way to afternoon sunshine.

I arrived downtown at 7:00 a.m., an hour prior to the 8:00 a.m. start. I grew nervous as the temperature rose with each passing minute. I scouted for a shady spot to hang out and relax, but no such luck. Instead, I walked toward the start line, showed the official my elite bib number, and stepped in front of the rope that separated the handful of elites from the masses. I nursed a bottle of water while I waited.

At 7:50 a.m., the race announcer stepped up to the mike. "Ladies and gentlemen, can I please have your attention? I have been informed that automobiles are still parked illegally on the course. For your safety, we need to tow these cars before we can start the race. I appreciate your patience and apologize for the delay. We'll handle this just as quickly as we can."

A collective moan was heard from our antsy crowd. I became unstrung because I really had to pee. But I feared a visit to the porta potty might cause me to miss the start of the race. The announcer offered no clue as to how long it would take for this car issue to be resolved.

It was iffy at best that I could run my 2:50. If the gun went off while I was in the john, it wasn't going to happen since I had little margin to spare. Special porta potties were set up for the exclusive use of the elite athletes, so at least I wouldn't have to wait in a long line if I took the risk and decided to "go."

Every five minutes, the announcer gave an update. "We should be underway any minute now." He repeated a version of this optimistic spiel for the next half hour. Finally, I could no longer hold it. I made the mad dash to the toilet. I took care of my business and made it back to the start line with 10 minutes to spare. The start gun finally fired at 8:45 a.m.

The pre-race hoopla promoted live bands and entertainment each mile of this 26.2-mile musical tour, which was a first-time concept in the world of marathons. One blurb boasted of 40 live bands. A primary reason I chose Rock 'n' Roll for my Olympic qualifier *was because of the music.* I am a fan of rock and roll, and I thought the music along the way would distract me from my body's aches and pains.

I kept my eyes peeled and my ears perked the first few miles, but I saw no bands and heard no music. There were loud cheers from the crowds that lined the course. I appreciated the support (their claps, and shouts), but I craved the real live music we had been promised. As I approached a right turn at mile 5, I hoped, "Maybe a band will appear beyond that bend in the road." It didn't happen.

So I improvised and played a soundtrack in my head. I "listened" to Bruce Springsteen belt out "Born To Run." I heard Neil Young encourage me with "Long May You Run." I zoned into the lyrics of "Eye of the Tiger" and inspired myself with Diana Ross's "Ain't No Mountain High Enough." It helped, but I still wondered where the real musicians were. *Perhaps they thought they were scheduled for 9:00 p.m. instead of 9:00 a.m.?*

My split at the halfway point clocked in at 1:23:30, right on target for a sub-2:50 but with not much of a cushion. I focused and grew determined. I would not let the heat and my frustration with Rock 'n' Roll get the better of me.

I ran by myself the next several miles. The runner in front of me was at least 200 yards ahead. As I neared mile 20, I heard a loud truck behind me; a few seconds later, I saw a car drive towards me. *What the hell? This can't be right!* I realized I had veered off course!

I retraced my steps to the previous intersection, livid that a volunteer hadn't been stationed there to direct the runners. My error caused me to sacrifice close to a minute, time that I could ill afford to lose. I tried to pick up the pace the final six miles but to no avail. Furious and frustrated, I approached the finish line and viewed the large official time clock. A brightly lit **2:51** time teased me. I stepped over the finish line, exhausted, with an official time of 2:51:52.

It placed me 68th runner overall and ninth female. The race awarded prize money to the top 10 finishers, male and female. Two weeks later, I received a $700 check and a beautiful framed gold LP record with the colorful Rock 'n' Roll logo inscribed in the center.

San Diego Rock 'n' Roll Marathon was recognized as the largest inaugural marathon in U.S. history, with 19,979 entrants in the 1998 debut race. I graded the race an "F" because it failed on multiple counts.

They ran out of water on this brutally hot day. Only the first few thousand runners were able to grab a cup of H2O. Mid-pack and back-of-the-pack runners and walkers passed by aid stations where the tables had empty water jugs.

My good friend Mark ran a 3:39 marathon that day and finished 1,422nd. It placed him well within the top 10 percent. He confided, "Mary, I became severely dehydrated. This is the worst race I have ever run."

He was outraged and vented his complaints in a lengthy letter he wrote to the directors at Elite Racing. He was not alone. For weeks, runners blogged about their personal horror stories. They chimed in and tried to trump one another as they described their Rock n' Roll nightmare experiences. None of them dreamed the race would evolve into the successful lucrative money making machine it later became.

Rock n' Roll was my 19th marathon, but my first experience to run a race engulfed by the sea of charity runners. You couldn't help but notice them; they were clad in their official shirts with the eye-catching colors of bright purple and deep green. They ran to benefit the Leukemia Society. Their program was called TNT (Team in Training). Supporters of TNT lined the race course. They stood curbside, held signs, and waved posters. They screamed "Go, TNT!" as runners and walkers passed by.

Mid-race, I noticed a spectator, a short, thin woman with grey hair who was perhaps in her fifties. Her hands were raised high in the air as she displayed her poster. The message was written in a bold, black Sharpie and read, **"If you think running a marathon is hard, try chemotherapy."** It inspired me to push on.

Elite Racing heavily promoted TNT. When the race sold out in April, Elite vowed to expand the field to include each and every TNT runner who raised enough money to meet his/

her individual pledge amount which was typically $1,000. Six thousand TNT individuals raised a record $15 million dollars for lifesaving cancer research when they hit the pavement that hot, scorching day in June of 1998. It was a commendable achievement.

In 2009, 11 years after the disastrous inaugural race, an investigative report by the *San Diego Union-Tribune* uncovered some disturbing facts. The *Tribune*'s May 15, 2009, article reported results of an independent audit by the law firm, Sheppard, Mullin, Richter & Hampton. The gist was that the charity, Elite Racing Foundation for Children, Education & Medical Research, had improperly comingled funds with the for-profit company, Elite Racing, to the tune of $340,000.

"The Foundation was operating inappropriately, in many instances, for the benefit of the for-profit," admitted Scott Dickey, chief operating officer of Competitor Group, the parent company of Elite Racing. Dickey declared he was unaware of the unusual setup between the for-profit and the Foundation until the *Union-Tribune* broke the news.

Competitor Group agreed to abide by the recommendations of the audit. They paid $190,500 to San Diego County and $153,676 to the city, for a grand total of $344,176. Then, they dissolved the Foundation, but not the race. "We're excited to put this chapter behind us and clean up the past history of the event here in San Diego," said Dickey.

The financial scandal quickly became yesterday's news, with no further press coverage. Great enthusiasm to run Rock 'n' Roll remained. The 2009 race drew 16,312 participants. In 2010, a Half Marathon was added. 15,915 runners registered for the Half, while 12,771 signed up for the Full. The race sold out two months in advance with the crowd of more than 28,000 who paid the hefty $115 price to participate in this now-famous musical race.

———

TNT is the largest endurance sports training charity in the world. The Team In Training website (teamintraining.org) provides a wealth of information about its training program and the Leukemia & Lymphoma Society (LLS.) The site boasts of TNT's successful fundraising. In 2014, the 25th anniversary of TNT, the charity proudly proclaimed that 600,000 runners and walkers had raised more than $1.4 billion to help find cures for blood cancer patients.

Individuals who registered as TNT for the 2014 San Diego Rock 'n' Roll Marathon were asked to meet a personal fundraising goal of $2,200. They were assured the required fundraising "will be easy with our staff support." Participants were given a personal fundraising page on the TNT website. Family and friends could click on the page to donate and also to view the runner's current status to track how close he or she was to his/her goal.

Even people who had never run a step in their lives were encouraged to join. "No prior athletic experience is required." mentors reassured, "With proper training, you can progress from zero exercise to a marathon in six months." TNT provided the weekly training schedule which included long weekend runs with qualified coaches. The charity also hosted clinics on nutrition, injury prevention, and motivation.

Race weekend was promised to be an unforgettable experience of a lifetime for those who met the $2,200 challenge. TNT footed the bill for the two-night stay in an upscale hotel in downtown San Diego. The charity hosted an exclusive Inspiration Dinner for team TNT on Saturday evening, the night prior to the race. Thousands of runners from TNT chapters throughout the country gathered for a buffet-style dinner in a large fancy ballroom of the host hotel for an evening of fine food, inspirational speeches, and camaraderie. This spectacular dinner has been described as almost as memorable as the race itself.

It is difficult to argue with the financial success of TNT. More than $1.4 billion is an enormous sum of money raised for the Leukemia & Lymphoma Society. However, the TNT program and participants are not always transparent.

During the years of RaceReady, I was hit up hundreds of times by TNT runners who asked for donations. Usually, it was via an email request which linked me to the individual's personal TNT webpage. These solicitations came from friends and acquaintances, but mostly RaceReady customers. One request read, "I plan to wear RaceReady shorts next month in Honolulu when I run the marathon to fight leukemia. With your generous support, we can fight cancer." It was implied that I should support her cause since she "supported" RaceReady.

Another letter informed me, "Over 75 percent of your donation goes directly to cancer research." I became curious and did some fact checking. I didn't have to dig deep to find the annual reports and tax filings on the Leukemia & Lymphoma Society website.

Below is the Report of Expense Details of LLS for the year ended June 30, 2013 (in thousands of dollars).

Research
$ 79,234   24.1 percent
Patient and community service
$117,769   35.1 percent
Public Health education
$ 47,875   14.6 percent
Professional education
$ 9,330   2.8 percent
TOTAL PROGRAM SERVICES
$254,208   77.4 percent
Management and general
$ 27,258   8.3 percent
Fundraising
$46,140   14.3 percent
TOTAL SUPPORTING SERVICES
$73,398   22.6 percent

Cancer Research was, in fact, only 24.1 percent, but it was included in "Program Services", which was 77.4 percent of the money spent. It was a "minor" mistake in the letter's wording and terminology.

The LLS Revenue numbers were even more revealing. The financial reports of the Society listed the various fundraising events and the dollar amounts they generated.

For the year 2011, the San Diego Rock 'n' Roll showed gross receipts of $6,943,611. LLS deducted $2,119,732 (roughly 30 percent) for "direct expenses" and reported $4,823,819 as net revenue on the tax filing, which is 70 percent of the monies raised.

For every dollar TNT raises, only 70 cents is considered income. In the dozens of solicitations I received, not once was I informed that 30 percent of my donation would be applied to Direct Expenses, which are the funds that paid for the TNT vacation weekend. TNT runners should be more upfront about this fact. They should fully disclose to prospective donors that more than 25 percent of the money raised is used for their (the runner's) personal benefit.

Is it fair that race directors give preferential treatment to charity runners, such as TNT? Should charity runners be allowed entry into otherwise sold out races? Should a regular runner be shut out of a race to allow room for a team TNT runner? These questions are highly debatable.

———

Races often take credit for the thousands of dollars given to charities when the race itself does not "raise urgent funds" as they suggest on their pamphlets and literature. It is the *individual* who does the footwork and gets the pledges. However, race directors seldom make this clear.

In May 2009, RaceReady was an exhibitor at the expo for a half marathon in the Santa Ynez Valley of Central California, one of Destination Races Wine Country Half Marathon Series. In June 2009, RaceReady received a letter of appreciation from Destination Races.

I quote from the letter:

"We are pleased to report as a result of this event over $50,000 was raised for our non-profit beneficiaries and training partners who include The Breast Cancer Fund, Moms in Motion, Multiple Myeloma Research Foundation, Chances for Children, Hirschberg Foundation, and Team Believe."

No further explanation was given. The letter implied Destination Races raised monies for these charities. Although Destination Races hosted the event, it was the individual participants, *on their own*, who brought in the coveted charity dollars.

It is an excellent sales pitch for race directors to take the credit, which encourages runners and walkers to register. People feel good about participating in a race where the money goes to charity.

———

My neighbor and friend Caroline is athletic an avid tennis player, but she was not a runner until the summer of 2012. She is a few years younger than I am and was in her late forties when we talked one evening in June.

Caroline sounded excited as she gushed, "I signed up to run the Las Vegas Half Marathon in December!" I was surprised and responded, "But you hate running." (Years earlier she had questioned me, "Why do you run? It seems so boring.")

"I feel I need to do this. I am running for Team Challenge, and the funds I raise will help fight Crohn's Disease." Her college-age daughter Margo was afflicted with the disease, so it was a personal cause for her. Team Challenge is the Crohn's and Colitis Foundation's endurance training program. It is similar to TNT; registrants raise funds, train, and then participate in the race.

I was unfamiliar with Crohn's, a chronic inflammatory condition of the gastrointestinal tract. I learned that the disease afflicts both men and women equally. It can occur at any age, though is more common among the younger crowd between 15 and 35 years of age. The illness can cause severe abdominal pain and discomfort. In worst case scenarios, it is debilitating. There is no known cure for the disease, though drug therapies exist to reduce the painful symptoms and bring about long-term remission. With proper treatment, many people afflicted with the disease are able to function well.

Caroline asked us for a personal donation. We were glad to contribute and help our friend, now a charity runner passionate about the cause.

She embraced her training and became fanatical. I witnessed her transformation, which warmed my heart. I softened my stance against "Charity Runners." Even if 25 percent of our donation went to fund her weekend in Las Vegas, so be it. She deserved it after all the time and work she spent both training and fundraising.

We traveled to Las Vegas in December to support her and be there for her race. Gerry paced Caroline the final five miles of the race on a cold Sunday evening. I stood in front of the Mirage Hotel near the finish line and cheered them on. When she crossed the finish line, we all felt like winners.

CHAPTER SIXTEEN

Fashion vs. Function

RUNNING IS A simple sport. The only necessary equipment is a decent pair of running shoes.

In the late 1980s, good-quality running shoes might set you back $50. They lasted 300 to 500 miles on average. A skinny runner like me was able to squeak by with higher mileage. I often logged 600 miles before I retired a pair of shoes. Twenty-five years later, runners are still advised to replace their shoes after 500 miles, but the price tag has doubled to roughly $100.

Terrain is a key factor in determining shoe life. A runner who ran upon soft surfaces, (such as trails, sand, and grass) got more mileage from his shoes than someone who pounded the pavement day in and day out. The recreational runner who topped out with 30 miles per week purchased three or four pairs of shoes per year, which cost around $200. Quite the bargain compared to the price one paid for gear to ski, snowboard, cycle, golf, or play tennis!

Thirty years ago, I didn't give much thought to the clothing I wore. It took me two minutes to throw on a t-shirt and shorts and lace up my shoes before heading out the door for my exercise fix. The phrase "running apparel" didn't even exist. In the summer, I opened my dresser drawer and pulled out the lightest-weight shorts and shirt I could find. Often, it was a t-shirt that had been through multiple washings to the point of being risqué and see-through, but I didn't care. In the winter, I dressed in layers and put on heavy-weight cotton sweatpants and sweatshirts. I wore thicker socks to keep my toes warm.

I live in Southern California, which meant my decisions were pretty simple. I didn't face the dilemmas of those in the Midwest or on the East Coast who dealt with frigid winter conditions and hot, humid summer days. As a New Jersey native, I had a special appreciation for our ideal Los Angeles weather.

I raced most weekends and noticed that everyone else also wore cotton t-shirts, which became sweat-drenched within minutes after the start gun fired. My royal blue shirt at the start of the race turned into a darker navy hue by the time I finished because it was so soaked.

Guys often finished with streaks of blood on the front of their shirts. The culprit was nipples which bled, rubbed raw from the friction of the wet shirt against their sensitive skin as they ran.

Women also suffered. I wore an "exercise bra," which was minus the hooks and fasteners of my standard everyday bra, but it wasn't comfortable. The fabric was a non-moisture-wicking blend of cotton and spandex. The seams dug into my underarms and caused nasty rashes.

Since our clothes were anything but quick-drying, any part of the body was fair game to painful irritation and chaffing. Technical running apparel had yet to make its debut. It was a godsend when it finally did. The timing was perfect for me as a soon-to-be-serious competitive runner and the owner of RaceReady. Sophisticated sports fabrics appeared on the scene in 1992, the year we started our business.

Arguably, the greatest advance in technical fabrics was the advent of CoolMax by DuPont Textiles (now marketed by Invista). CoolMax is a trademark and brand name for moisture-wicking technical fabrics. It was developed in 1986, but didn't become popular until the 1990s. The fabrics employ special polyester fibers to improve "breathability."

CoolMax fabric aids thermoregulation, which is the process that keeps your body at its optimal temperature. When you exercise, 70 percent of the energy used by your muscles is lost as heat. Your body then struggles to keep itself at the proper temperature. Blood transfers heat from the muscles to the skin; your veins dilate to allow more blood to pass through them, and your heart pumps faster to transfer the heat. When the heat gets to the skin, it is released through sweat. This evaporation of moisture from the skin results in a cooling effect.

CoolMax took the exercise world by storm in 1992. Runners quickly saw the benefits of the fabric. Running in a cotton t-shirt became a thing of the past. Why suffer in cold wet clothes when you had the option of CoolMax?

RaceReady introduced thousands of runners to CoolMax, the only fabric we used for our shirts. Singlets and short sleeves were a lightweight version, and our long sleeves were of a slightly heavier grade. We employed a thin CoolMax crepe for the lining of our shorts. We swore by this DuPont product!

In addition to its breathability, advantages of CoolMax include resistance to fading, shrinking, and wrinkling. The fabric is durable, lightweight, soft, and super comfortable. It dries within a few hours after a washing. Other fabric manufacturers, in addition to DuPont, developed their own brands of high-performance evaporative fabrics. But CoolMax set the industry standard and remained my fabric of choice.

Our original RaceReady CoolMax mesh shirts were a hit. Fans wore the CoolMax mesh once and then were forever hooked (myself included). But we received a few complaints; the gripe was that the fabric was susceptible to "pilling." After multiple washings, loose fibers began to push out from the fabric and formed tiny fuzz balls on the surface of the shirt. The fabric also easily snagged. Even a rough fingernail could cause a snag.

Twenty-five years later, in 2017, I still prefer the CoolMax mesh when I go for a hike, bicycle ride, or gym workout. I am glad I have my personal stockpile since the mesh shirts are no longer readily available in running stores or online.

Sports apparel manufacturers converted from CoolMax mesh to its later-generation cousin, CoolMax Alta, which Dupont introduced in 1999. It was their solution to the pilling problem posed by the mesh. CoolMax Alta combined new patented low-pilling DuPont technology with the fast-drying properties of CoolMax. The Alta shirt looked brand new after multiple washings, unlike the mesh with its fuzz balls. It wasn't as comfy as the mesh, but by the new millennium, looks trumped comfort in most runners' minds. Alta and similar versions dominate the market today.

RaceReady always focused upon function, and not fashion. Our goal was to design and produce the best comfortable running apparel possible. We used superior fabrics and kept it simple. We paid little attention to the trendy colors and patterns which varied from season to season. We didn't embellish our shirts with decorative trim. In fact, we did the opposite and constructed our garments with as few seams as possible. Fewer seams meant a lesser likelihood of chaffing.

Our best-selling product, the patented LD (Long Distance) short, was the first pocketed running short to hit the market. We enjoyed a monopoly at first, and couldn't make our LD shorts fast enough to keep up with the demand. It took a few years before the big apparel companies, such as Asics, Nike, Pearl Izumi, and others, stepped into the arena with their versions of pocketed running shorts. Even lesser-known smaller companies wanted a piece of the action and came up with RaceReady "knock-offs." The pocket design on all these other brands was far inferior to the RaceReady design, but these newer copycat shorts were flashier than ours. They featured spiffy prints and patterns, often with accented color side panels. They were offered in an array of bright eye-catching colors, not the boring basic solid colors of black, royal blue, navy blue, and red of RaceReady shorts.

We used Supplex nylon for our shorts in the early 1990s. It was DuPont's state-of-the-art fabric. The individual polymer fibers in Supplex nylon were finer and more numerous than in standard nylon, which resulted in a short that was softer and more hydrophobic (water-hating).

Initially, we made only one style of LD, the split-cut style. They were very brief and a far cry from the to-the-knee shorts that became popular a decade later. In the 1990s, I never dreamed a runner would prefer a long and baggy short. Our philosophy was "the shorter, the better." Less fabric meant less constriction. The split-cut short allowed the runner to take advantage of his/her maximum stride. And why would a runner want to wear bulky clothing, especially on a hot, humid day?

Runners weren't the only athletes who wore skimpy shorts. NBA basketball stars in the 1990s were scantily clad in singlets and shorts. Tattoos had yet to go mainstream. Plenty of unadorned bare arms and legs is what you see when you view the ancient footage. The hotshots dressed nothing like 20 years later when shorts dropped below the knee.

By the late 1990s, skimpy shorts were no longer in vogue. RaceReady adjusted to the times and began to offer our LD shorts in four different lengths. The longest, called "the Sixer" (for its six-inch inseam), became our best seller. Fashions tend to be cyclical, and what is old becomes new again. Maybe the next generation of athletes will show more leg.

On the cusp of the 21st century, a superior fabric was introduced to the sports apparel industry, Microfiber. Microfiber was even more breathable and water-repellent than Supplex. It was feather-light with a silky feel and a luxurious touch, like that of fine lingerie. Runners quickly became fans of Microfiber, though some old-school rebels were sorry to see Supplex shorts go by the wayside. They didn't appreciate the clinginess and flimsy-look of the Microfiber and questioned the longevity. I was asked, "Will these shorts survive multiple rounds of laundry and not fall apart?" The truthful answer was, "Yes, although Microfiber doesn't appear to be a sturdy fabric, it is nearly as durable as Supplex."

RaceReady did its homework before we made the transition to Microfiber. We did a small-production run of a few hundred Microfiber shorts. We asked our friends for their help as test-wearers. "Try these. Wear them often for the next month. Let us know what you think and be honest." We received a unanimous "thumbs up" from our dozen test-wearers and became convinced Microfiber was the way to go. For the next dozen years that we owned and operated RaceReady, all our shorts were made of Microfiber. We sold them by the thousands.

Bright colors were popular in the 1990s, when neon-colored shorts and shirts were all the rage. Today, in 2018, fluorescent colors are once again back in style. The apparel is flashy and joggers are decked out in color-coordinated outfits. Even their shoes and laces match to fully capture "the look." Vibrant clothing in colors that dazzle makes sense in modern-day society with a crisis of distracted drivers. It is wise to be as visible as possible. Reflective piping on clothing is now common, a welcome feature for early morning and evening runners.

———

Female tennis players have competed in skirts for decades, but you rarely saw an athletic skirt outside of a tennis court. Running skirts were obscure until the 1990s, although they do have an interesting history.

In July of 1870, Mary Martha Maun and Julia Monroe of Cleveland wore white gabardine dresses when they competed in a foot race, which Monroe won. (She was awarded $50.)

Nearly 100 years later, 19-year-old Julia Chase ran the November 1961 Manchester Road Race in a dress that resembled a school uniform. The 4.748-mile race in Connecticut was a very prestigious race in New England at the time. Julia finished 128th among the field of 157 men (though she was not recognized as an official runner).

Kathrine Switzer ran the 1973 Boston Marathon decked out in what she described as a "red nylon dance tunic." She declared it to be one of her favorite running outfits. (Kathrine Switzer is notorious for her initial 1967 Boston Marathon when she registered as K Switzer in order to sneak into the race as a female.)

Twenty years later, during the New York City Marathon in 1993, Pamela Kezios of Chicago married her husband Thomas Young at the Mile 8 marker. The 31-year-old wore a short white skirt atop a stretchy white leotard as she exchanged her wedding vows. The couple finished the race in a fast time of 3 hours and 41 minutes. They approached the finish line hand in hand, but then Tom was shooed to the right and Pam was steered to the left since the race back then had separate finish chutes for the men and women.

More significant in the saga of running skirts, is the story of triathlete Nicole DeBoom, the winner of the September 2004 Ironman Wisconsin. Nicole wore a skirt of her own design and received plenty of attention. She launched her company, Skirt Sports, the following year in 2005.

It wasn't long before running skirts became all the rage and their popularity surged. The skirt phenomenon appealed to all ages and body types. Younger women in their twenties, as well as older women in their fifties, became fans. I was skeptical of running skirts at first and not eager to convert. I had worn shorts for two decades and they worked fine for me. We resisted adding skirts to our Race-Ready product line. Then I listened to all the reasons women listed for why they preferred running skirts to the traditional shorts.

"I like to look like a girl and look feminine."

"Skirts are fun. Funky patterns and prints in running shorts are dorky, but look cute on a skirt."

"Skirts are flattering. They hide your butt and are more forgiving of a less than perfect figure."

"Skirts are super comfortable and sexy."

The demand for a RaceReady skirt grew. At every expo, I was asked multiple times, "Do you carry skirts?" Or, "Why doesn't RaceReady make skirts?" We were losing sales. We finally decided that, if women were going to run in skirts, they might as well be ours.

We went to the drawing board. Our idea was to incorporate our patented LD pocket-design, for which we are famous, into the skirt. I handed off samples to my girl friends to try. It took months for us to come up with a skirt which met our high standards. We finally did in 2008, when we joined more than a dozen other athletic clothing manufacturers who were in the skirt business.

Even I became a fan of the skirt. I felt stylish when I wore it. I cringe with embarrassment when I think of the early 1990s when I wore skimpy shorts, not just on my run, but out in public on the post-run trip to the grocery store or library. The running skirt is far more modest.

––––––

I was out of the apparel business before running sleeves, also known as arm warmers, hit the scene. I don't grasp this latest 21st-century fad. If it is cold enough to justify arm warmers, wouldn't you simply wear a long sleeve shirt? On colder mornings, I often put on a long sleeve CoolMax shirt; as I got warm mid-run, I rolled up the sleeves above my elbows. It worked like a charm, and I did this for more than two decades.

Apparently, many runners saw the benefits of arm warmers. As of 2016, at least a dozen successful sportswear companies featured running sleeves in their product line. They often came with a hefty price tag and could set you back more than if you bought an entire shirt.

One company (sleeves priced at $40), touted its product and boasted about the sleeves; their sleeves "keep the runner's arms warm and protected from the elements during a run, without the bulk of a jacket." A wear-tester praised the product and testified, "I find the sleeves durable, light, breathable, and easy to put on and take off."

Another company (sleeves priced at $30), made a compression sleeve. The sleeve was a seamless design with an ergonomic fit which supposedly increased blood circulation and helped prevent DOMS (Delayed Onset Muscle Soreness). The product's literature suggested that the circulation-improving benefits of the sleeve's compression would enhance running performance. I personally didn't buy the logic.

A different twist on running sleeves came from a company that promoted them, not for warmth but for sun protection. Runners were urged to wear their sleeves during the hot summer months. The sleeves (priced at $30) were rated UPF 40 and were lined with CoolMax. The wearer reaped the benefit of the moisture wicking fabric and reduced the risk of sun damage to the arms.

Running sock styles have also come and gone since 1987. I was a fan of thin CoolMax socks, which were very short and barely covered my ankles. They were super-comfy and light-weight. My philosophy was, "the thinner the better."

Since 2001, runners have sported socks that are anything but minimal. These compression socks are lengthy and extend almost as high as the knee. Paula Radcliffe legitimized them when she wore them April 13, 2003, in the London Marathon, which she won with a world-record time of 2:15:25. The record still stands more than 14 years later.

Paula is a great poster child for compression socks. If they worked for her, most likely they would work for athletes who aren't quite of her caliber. By 2015, sales of compression socks had soared. They were heavily marketed to the masses, not just the handful of elite runners.

Yet, the reviews are a mixed bag whether these socks can enhance performance and recovery. The theory is that compression of the lower leg will increase blood flow. With this increased blood flow during exercise, the by-products that cause fatigue are flushed out of the muscles and tissues faster. Running performance is improved because we can run at a faster pace for a longer period of time with less fatigue.

Compression socks first appeared in the late 1990s, when they were worn to help prevent deep vein thrombosis. Initial wearers were not athletes but people who were bedridden or who faced forced inactivity. Physicians recommended the socks for those who had to sit still for a long period of time, such as airline passengers on plane trips to the other side of the world. It wasn't until the 21st century that they were seen on the legs of marathon runners.

Enough time has elapsed to review the results of the scientific researches and studies. Most professionals and experts in the field of sports medicine seem to agree that compression socks are helpful in speeding the recovery process after a long run or race.

In May 2007, the American College of Sports Medicine wrote an article in the organization's flagship monthly journal, *Medicine & Science in Sports & Exercise*, titled, "The Effect of Graded Compression Socks on Maximal Exercise Capacity and Recovery in Runner." It concluded that the socks did aid in recovery, but there was no proof compression socks helped a person run faster. John Smith, assistant professor of kinesiology at Texas A & M University, explained, "Compression socks hold the muscles together so to speak, minimizing the vibrations and contractions so you won't be as sore afterward and you can return to running faster."

The quicker you recover from a previous workout, the sooner you can do your next workout. A friend of mine, who suffers from chronic tight calf muscles, is a fan of compression socks. She recently explained, "I paid $30 for them. I consider it a cheap price to pay for a calf massage every time I run!"

———

When I competed in the 1990s, I never saw a "fashionista". A "fashionista" is a person (usually female), who follows trends in the fashion industry. She is obsessive and stays ahead of the curve to adopt the current fashions. Fashionistas are also sometimes called "stunners" (combination of "stylish + runners"). It's become big business to cater to stunners.

According to Running USA, the non-profit organization formed in 1999 with the mission to advance the growth and success of the running industry, women in 2010 made up more than half the participants in 5Ks, 10Ks, and Half Marathon races.

Sports apparel companies have taken note. They focus more of their budget and attention on females and cater to the fashionistas. Sales of women's running-specific apparel grew from $275 million in 2008 to $350 million in 2010, according to the research and analysis firm, SportsONESource. This is a huge 25 percent jump in sales.

The attention has clearly shifted from function to fashion. This isn't so bad. If being stylish motivates a person to exercise and embrace a healthy lifestyle, who can argue?

CHAPTER SEVENTEEN

Training Philosophy

RUNNING IS SIMPLE. Just put one foot in front of the other and move forward; that is all it takes. Some of us train to increase our pace and run faster. However, many runners could care less about their speed. They run for the sheer pleasure of the sport. Their goal is to participate and stay injury-free.

When I was a competitive long-distance runner in the 1990s, I was often asked, "What are your training secrets? Any tips you can give me?" I offered advice and shared my training journals with other athletes. Yet, we are each an Experiment of One, with our own unique formula for success. My fellow competitor, another Mary, who lived in San Diego, remarked to me, "I can't believe you can run a sub-three-hour marathon on only 60 miles per week." I responded, "I can't believe you can survive 100-mile weeks and not come up lame!"

A slew of articles have been written on the optimal way to train. Training theories change as rapidly as fad diets. The current issue of *Runner's World* offers tips on how to run pain-free, how to increase endurance, and "How to Run Your Fastest Race."

Runner's World has advised runners for more than 50 years, ever since their first issue hit the stands in 1966. They have mastered the formula for selling their popular monthly magazine. When I compare one issue with the previous year's issue, the gist of the articles is similar. Much is recycled information; training ideas are rehashed with fresh words and new photos. The April 2012 and April 2013 issues of *Runners's World* were both "Weight-Loss Specials." The April 2012 issue included, "Nutrition Plans for Dropping 5...10...15...20 lbs or More." The April 2013 magazine featured the article, "Lose Five Pounds the Right Way."

I did not cross-train in the late 1980s and early 1990s. (Neither did many of my friends in our club, the Los Feliz Flyers.) Instead, we ran as much as we could. We thought high mileage was the key to faster times. I was consistent and logged at least 50 miles per week. For 17 years straight, starting in 1991, I ran more than 2,000 miles each year. My highest mileage year was 1995, when I peaked at 3,155 miles. 1996 was slightly less, with the tally of 3,123 miles. It is not a coincidence that, toward the end of 1996, I set my Personal Records for a 10-mile race (1:00:07), half marathon (1:16:27), and marathon (2:42:11). My high mileage paid off.

Since the new millennium, there has been an emphasis on the "less is more" training philosophy. In May of 2007, Rodale Press published the book, *Run Less, Run Faster: Become a Faster, Stronger Runner with the Revolutionary FIRST Training Program.*

The authors, Bill Pierce, Scott Murr, and Ray Moss, are marathon experts who developed their long distance training program at the Furman Institute of Running and Scientific Training (FIRST) in Greenville, South Carolina. The book received rave reviews and explained how to run successful road races with only three run workouts per week. In April 2012, Rodale Press published a revised second edition endorsed by Amby Burfoot, *Runner's World* executive editor and 1968 Boston Marathon winner. He praised the FIRST training program as, "the most-detailed, well-organized, scientific training program for runners that I have ever seen."

An increasing number of coaches advocate low mileage. The focus is on quality, not quantity. They use the phrase "junk mileage" to describe slower-paced recovery runs. I admit most of my runs in my heyday were "easy". A typical week for me meant three intense workouts and six runs at a more comfortable, relaxed pace. I never bought into the "less is more" philosophy for marathon training.

Running guru and Olympian Jeff Galloway introduced athletes to his "run/walk" concept in the 1970s. It took off and four decades later millions of people do the "run/walk." Galloway deserves credit for helping thousands of people complete the marathon. He made it a sport which is enjoyed by everyday novice athletes, not just the gifted and committed elites of long distance.

Jeff Galloway (born July 12, 1945) ran in the 1972 Olympics and represented the USA in the 10K event. He is the author of the book, *Galloway's Book on Running*, first published in 1984. The second edition of his book was printed in 2002. Beyond a doubt, Galloway revolutionized the marathon.

Previous to his best-seller, the marathon was an endurance run in which a minuscule percentage of the running populace participated. Marathon runners were a rare species, an odd breed. Only seasoned runners attempted the torture of the distance. It was not an event for amateurs. It was the Holy Grail and seemed beyond the reach of most mortals. The ultimate goal for an extremely talented marathon runner was to run the race in sub-three. Other serious runners set the challenge to crack four hours. These lofty time standards disappeared from the minds of most runners in the post-Galloway era.

Charity programs, with their huge influx of former non-athletes turned into marathoners, owe Galloway a big thanks. Thousands of charity runners wouldn't have had the courage to embark on their six-month training programs if Galloway hadn't paved the path. His results helped build the confidence of the weekend athlete who became inspired and believed, "Yes, I can do a marathon!"

I respect Jeff Galloway, a lifetime runner, Olympian, and author. Jeff posted a 29:35 in the first round of the 10K in Munich at the 1972 Olympics, but it wasn't quite fast enough to make it to the finals. Some theorists think he would have fared better in the Olympics if he had run the marathon instead. He was a natural at the 26.2-mile distance.

The Galloway run/walk method dates back to 1974 when Jeff was asked to train a group of 22 novices who wanted to complete either a 5K or 10K race. In the first training session, his advice to the class was to walk 15 to 20 minutes but insert a few one-minute intervals of running. Over a 10-week period, Galloway tweaked the run/walk formula. Gradually, the class transitioned so they spent more time running than walking. By the end of the program, the participants became runners, though they still took a one-minute-walk break each and every mile. Galloway and his 22 students met with success. Everyone finished their 5K or 10K race.

Jeff observed that not one person suffered an injury during the training. He became convinced that he was onto something with this "run/walk" idea, even though traditional runners and coaches pooh-poohed his program.

Galloway expanded his training programs in the '70s, '80s, '90s, and '00s. He established running camps and has coached thousands of runners. He firmly believes that even veteran experienced runners receive significant benefits from the run/walk program. His theory is to insert walk intervals *before* one feels fatigued, and he suggests a walk break every mile from the get-go. The ratio of run/walk depends on one's time goal. Runners who hope to finish in three hours and 30 minutes walk a lesser percentage than a marathoner with a seven-hour time goal.

The only times I tried the run/walk method were during my two Medoc Marathons. On September 8, 2007, I ran my 28th and final marathon in Medoc, France. I did the run/walk, and I drank wine. It took me more than six hours to complete the marathon, which I viewed as a party, not a race. (I was compelled to return to Medoc because I felt gypped when I ran it in 2001 because that vacation turned into a disaster.)

Gone are the days of the 1990s when the majority of marathoners ran and walked only as a last resort. I am lucky to be one of the fortunate few who never "hit a wall" in a marathon. Certainly, some miles were tougher than others, but I managed to struggle through the difficult patches and was always able to run, be it at a slow pace.

We old-timers were running purists; our goal was to run the marathon. We trained long and hard to run as fast as possible. We strived to improve our race times and endurance levels. We walked only under severe circumstances.

When our feet were rubbed raw by painful blisters, we walked.

When diarrhea was imminent if we ran another step, we walked.

When our leg muscles cramped, we walked.

When our glycogen stores fell so low we felt in danger of fainting, we walked.

Since the 21st century, the run/walk concept has been universally accepted and practiced by the masses. The popularity of marathons has soared as a result. According to the non-profit organization, Running USA, there were 143,000 marathon finishers in America in 1980. By 2000, the number skyrocketed to 353,000. In 2010, a total of 507,000 crossed the 26.2-mile finish line. The 2014 report listed more than 550,000 marathoners. By all indications, the marathon is not a fad; it's here to stay and will continue to grow.

Since the influx of participants is made up largely of folks who do the run/walk, it is no surprise that marathon finish times have become slower. In 1980, the median finish time for male marathon runners in the United States was three hours and 32 minutes, slightly more than an eight-minute-per-mile pace. In 2008, it took four hours and 16 minutes for the average man to complete the race, a pace of nine minutes and 46 seconds per mile.

Women also have posted slower times. In 1980, the median female time was four hours and three minutes, a pace of nine minutes 16 seconds. In 2008, that median time increased to four hours 43 minutes, a pace of 10 minutes 48 seconds per mile. The 21st-century marathon runner is far less focused on speed than was his/her predecessor.

———

Prior to 1990, the marathon was an once-in-a-lifetime event for most. Dr. Timothy Noakes, the author of *The Lore of Running*, first published in 1991, recommended runners do no more than three marathons per year. He believed it took a tremendous amount of time to properly train and recover from this strenuous race.

Noakes, a South African professor of exercise and sports science at the University of Cape Town, ran more than 70 marathons and ultra-marathons. *The Lore of Running* delves deeply into the physiology of running, as well as the psychological, nutritional, mental, and social aspects of the sport. His book is the Bible on running. The first edition contains 804 pages, packed with valuable information. The fourth edition, published in 2003, is a lengthy 931 pages.

I've never read either volume cover to cover, but I have thumbed through both of them hundreds of times over the years. The first edition sat on my bedside table for a decade. It was my "go to" source for answers to the myriad of training questions which surfaced on racing, injuries, nutrition, stretching, and you-name-it.

Dr. Noakes's advice (1991 edition) to run only a few marathons per year is largely ignored today. Conventional wisdom has changed, and some runners do marathons on a monthly basis. Most don't actually *run* the entire marathon. They do the run/walk.

Noakes starts the virgin runner on a walk program. He cautions those new to the sport not to run a step until they reach their fourth week of exercise. The first three weeks is walk only. Then the newbie is advised to insert run intervals. Gradually, the run time is increased, and the walking decreased. After three months, more time is spent running than walking.

Most athletes are weaned completely off the walking within six months.

Noakes and Galloway share a similar training philosophy for beginner long-distance runners, except Galloway encourages walk breaks up to and including race day. Noakes does not.

———

An elite marathon club, "The 50 States and DC Marathoners Group USA" was founded in 1989 by Dean Rademaker. Rademaker was born in the small rural town of Emden, Illinois in 1925. He became a runner in 1979 at the age of 54 upon his doctor's advice. His physician became concerned about Dean's rapid heart rate and urged him to begin some sort of aerobic exercise. Dean took to running and the marathon became his passion.

Rademaker knew of others who had run a marathon in every state, but none of them were interested in forming an organized group. Rademaker took it upon himself to do so. He vowed to keep the database of the 50 states finishers and also publish a newsletter. He made good on his promises, and the club has flourished. Walter Herman of Ontario, Canada is reported as the first person to run a marathon in every state. He accomplished the feat in 1983. Rademaker himself completed the 50 states and D.C. circuit in 1994.

Gerry and I know the third person on the 50 states roster. It is Al Becken of San Antonio, Texas. Al finished his 50th state in 1986. We met Al at the 39th annual RRCA Convention in Knoxville, Tennessee in May of 1996. Over the next 15 years, we saw Al frequently in cities coast to coast. He was an avid RaceReady customer and would visit our RaceReady booth and stock up on shorts and socks. I think he had more RaceReady shorts in his bureau drawers than I did in mine.

As of December 2016, the 50 States Club (50anddcmarathongroupusa.com) listed 487 finisher names. Some obsessive runners don't stop after one tour of the states. Thirteen runners (all men) have done "the tour" five times. Take Jim Simpson of Huntington Beach, California, who has done the tour 10 times and ran his *1,000th marathon* on January 1, 2013 at the Texas Marathon in Kingwood, Texas at the age of 71. Simpson's other claim to fame is that he has slept overnight in his camper in a Wal-Mart parking lot the night before a marathon in all 50 states. The youngest member of the club is Beverly Paquin, a nurse from Carlisle, Iowa. She completed her quest in October 2010, when she crossed the finish line of the Mount Desert Island Marathon in Bar Harbor, Maine, at the age of 22.

––––––

In the mid-1980s, a friend of mine joined a training group in the Washington, D.C. area to train for the fall Marine Corps Marathon. The coach, Phil Fenty, was an accomplished marathoner and ultra-marathon runner. Fenty was also the owner of the DC Fleet Feet Sports running store, which he opened in 1984 in Washington, D.C. His was the first East Coast franchise of the highly reputable Fleet Feet stores.

Fenty thought that only seasoned runners, those who had been running for at least a year, should attempt to train for a marathon. He did not agree with the premise that anyone can come off the couch one day, lace up a pair of running shoes, and begin to train, and then run a marathon six months later. He firmly believed that a runner needed a strong running base before he or she embarked upon a marathon-training program.

Fenty was of the old school of coaches who encouraged a runner to do at least three 18-mile runs in his/her marathon preparation. He did not advise runners to go much farther than 20 miles because of the increased risk of injury. A serious injury such as a torn muscle or pulled ligament takes time to heal and often forces the runner to miss valuable weeks of training. If you fall behind and miss more than a few weeks of training, most likely you'll have to forgo the marathon. Fenty thought it better to be safe than sorry. He wanted his athletes to make it to the start line injury-free on race day. His theory contrasts with the Galloway program which suggests a 26-mile run/walk before the race.

Fenty's Fleet Feet store carried *Galloway's Book on Running* when it was first published in 1984. He sold the Galloway book for several years. But after Fenty talked with runners who purchased the book from him, he learned that most did not read the book in its entirety. Instead, they jumped right into the chapters focused on the marathon. In his early chapters, Galloway talks about the importance of building up to the marathon distance slowly. However, this sound advice was not seen by the average reader who skipped these pages. Fenty grew exasperated and stopped selling the book in his store. He didn't want his local runners to buy the Galloway book and read a mere chunk of it and come up injured.

———

Fleet Feet Sports was a good retail customer of RaceReady in the 1990s, as was Marathon Sports in Minneapolis, Minnesota. The owner of Marathon Sports was Steve Hoag, a gifted, accomplished runner. Hoag ran a 2:11:54 in the 1975 Boston Marathon, fast enough to finish second place. (Bill Rodgers was two minutes ahead of him and finished first in a time of 2:09:55.) Hoag founded his Marathon Sports store in 1985 and operated it for 20 years until 2005 when he sold his business and retired.

In the late 1990s and early 2000s, Marathon Sports bought a slew of our products, mainly our popular LD (Long Distance) shorts. I often talked with Steve when he phoned in his orders. Steve reminisced about how the sport had changed. "These days, runners overly prepare. They carry fanny backs loaded with multiple bottles of fluid. They are laden down with snacks, gels, and a first aid kit. It looks like they are prepared to enter a combat zone instead of a mere run in the neighborhood park!"

Sales of fanny packs have soared. Most large-scale training programs require participants to carry water with them on their weekend long run. I've noticed these runners weighed down with their fuel belts and packs. It doesn't look comfortable; the packs bounce up and down with each step the runner takes.

In the 1980s and 1990s, I seldom carried water with me, except perhaps when I ran a 20-miler on a hot summer day. Yet, I stayed hydrated. I made sure my route passed by a water spigot or gas station with a water fountain. I gulped down bottles of water before and after my long run and drank several glasses of water every day.

I never suffered symptoms of dehydration which include increased thirst, nausea, dry mouth, headache, and lightheadedness. Severe dehydration leads to muscle cramps, chills, disorientation and heat stroke. I didn't know the word hyponatremia, a situation that occurs at the opposite end of the spectrum when a runner is *overly* hydrated.

According to an article published in the *New England Journal of Medicine*, 12 percent of the runners in the 2002 Boston Marathon experienced hyponatremia to some degree. The condition is caused by drinking too much water during exercise. The level of sodium in the blood decreases to a dangerously low level.

It is alarming to learn that such a high percentage of *Boston Marathoners* were afflicted. The Boston field is composed of the elite and experienced runners. One can only guess the occurrence of hyponatremia in the run-of-the-mill marathon which draws the average novice runner. Exercise physiologists say it can be more dangerous to drink too much water than to be mildly dehydrated. Listen up, Team TNT and other charity runners!

Dr. Noakes wrote an article on the issue of hyponatremia in his paper, "Water Intoxication: A Possible Complication During Endurance Exercise." The article appeared more than 30 years ago in the June 1985 issue of *Medicine & Science in Sports & Exercise*. MSSE is the flagship monthly journal of the American College of Sports and Medicine. ACSM is the largest sports medicine and exercise science organization in the world, with more than 45,000 members whose mission is to offer practical applications in the field of sports based on scientific research.

Noakes's article was greeted with skepticism when it first appeared. It wasn't until 10 years later that the issue of hyponatremia started to be taken seriously. Additional scientific studies were conducted on endurance athletes and hydration, which led to similar conclusions: hyponatremia is very dangerous and potentially fatal.

Sports drinks saturated the market in the 1990s. It was no longer a choice of water or Gatorade. The makers of these new-age concoctions came up with powerful, creative literature and commercials to get across their important message to "Stay Hydrated." Weekend warriors were encouraged to drink copious amounts before, during, and after exercise.

One beverage company advised runners to guzzle as much as a liter (four or five cups) of their product each hour of exercise, which translates to 20 cups of fluid for the four-hour marathon runner. This just begged for hyponatremia to occur.

Running magazines preached, "Don't wait until you are thirsty before you start to drink. By then it is too late. You are probably already dehydrated." Nutritionists and dietitians urged even sedentary folks to drink eight 12-ounce glasses of water per day.

Marathon training programs in the 1990s encouraged the runner (or walker) to drink each and every mile of a long training run or race. Nearly all major marathons started to offer aid stops every mile. Coaches instructed, "Slow down and stop if you have to, but don't dare miss an aid station in the marathon."

In 2001, Dr. Noakes revisited the hyponatremia topic with his report for the International Marathon Medical Directors Association (IMMDA) titled "Advisory Statement on Fluid Replacement During Marathon Running." In his report, Noakes recommended that marathoners drink between 400 to 800 milliliters per hour, which translates to 13 to 27 ounces. This amount is less than half the fluid intake that was recommended by the American College of Sports Medicine. Exercise physiologists couldn't seem to agree on how much to drink.

Five years later, in 2006, the International Marathon Medical Directors Association released their highly-anticipated report on hydration guidelines. The bottom line was that runners should simply drink when thirsty. If they followed this concept, runners were likely to be protected from the hazards of both dehydration and hyponatremia. It's a mantra often repeated, "Everything in moderation."

Moderation is the current training theme. Gone are the days of the 1990s when most marathon runners did regular "double workouts." Doing a double meant lacing your shoes up twice a day for a six-miler in the morning and another six in the evening. The pace wasn't important; the main goal was to put in the mega miles, which I certainly did. I've added up the mileage of my yearly training logs. The tally comes in at more than 50,000 lifetime miles. The earth's circumference is 24,901 miles, so I've run around the world twice.

The concept of cross-training became popular in the 1990s. It is in contrast to the principle of the specificity of training. Most elite runners concentrated solely on running, and they often ran 80 to 100 miles per week, which left little time and energy to cross-train. Two top female distance runners, Ingrid Kristiansen and Grete Waitz, were the exception and amongst the earliest elites to cross-train.

Norwegian runner Ingrid Kristiansen, born in 1956, placed fourth in the first Olympic women's marathon, in Los Angeles, 1984. She won the London Marathon several times, was first female in Boston in 1986, and won the New York City Marathon in 1989. Profiles written on Kristiansen mentioned that she included cross country skiing twice a week as part of her vigorous training regimen. She retired from competitive running in 1993 but continued to cross country ski near her home in Oslo, Norway.

Grete Waitz was another famous Norwegian runner (October 1, 1953 – April 19, 2011). Waitz put in long periods of solid training during the frigid winters and frequently substituted skiing for running. The average high temperature in Oslo is 30 degrees for five months of the year, more ideal to ski than to run. Waitz finished second in the 1984 Olympic Marathon. She won the New York City Marathon a record nine times.

Although Ingrid and Grete cross-trained in the great outdoors, most latter-generation runners cross-train in their local gyms, which feature air-conditioned comfort and state-of-the-art equipment.

NordicTrack became a national fitness craze in the 1980s. People became obsessed with the idea of working out indoors at home. In 1986, NordicTrack hit annual sales of $15 million. The boom lasted another 10 years; but by 1995, NordicTrack was on a downswing and gym memberships skyrocketed instead. People signed up at their neighborhood gym and engaged in a variety of cross-train options. Rowing machines, stationary bikes, elliptical trainers, stair-master machines, treadmills – you name it – all was available at the gym.

I became somewhat of a gym convert during my last decade of running when my knee couldn't take running every day. I balanced my gym workouts with hikes and bike rides. I prefer to get my exercise in the great outdoors, and I will always be a runner at heart.

CHAPTER EIGHTEEN
Ultra Running

MORE AND MORE people have been drawn to the extreme sport of ultra running. The standard definition of ultra running is any run that is over the 26.2 marathon distance. It was a fringe sport with few participants until the 1990s. According to *Ultrarunning Magazine*, there were 15,500 ultra finishers in 1998. That number jumped to 36,106 finishers in 2009. By 2013, the magazine reported a whopping 69,573 finishers of races longer than the 26.2-mile distance.

As more runners are attracted to the ultra races, the demand is often greater than the supply. Many of the popular ultra races now are on a lottery system. The famous Western States 100 starts in Squaw Valley, California at 6,229 feet elevation and finishes in Auburn, California at 1,292 feet. This trail race is limited to 369 runners. Ninety-nine spots are given to race administrators, sponsors, previous top finishers, and overseas runners. The remaining 270 spaces are filled via a lottery. In 2005, Western States received 791 applications for the 270 spots. In 2014, 2,700 applied for the coveted 270 positions, which meant a 10 percent chance of being accepted into the prestigious race.

Diane Eastman, an accomplished ultra runner, is a good friend who is 17 years older than I am. She is attractive (blonde hair, a lithe body, and a winning smile), and she always has a positive attitude. She was the one who suggested The Skyline 50K Endurance Run for me to do as my first ultra. She ran it several years earlier; in her words, it was an "easy 50K." I don't think "easy" and "50K" even belong in the same sentence. A 50K is 31 miles; it is guaranteed to be difficult. But I listened to Diane that spring, and registered for the 16th annual Skyline Race, which was scheduled for the first Sunday in August 1997. I was excited to train that summer and to become an ultra runner.

———

Diane did ultras for more than 30 years. She competed quite well at the marathon distance, but mostly she considered marathons as training for her passion, her ultras. In 1987, Diane ran the Angeles Crest 100-miler. As a local, she trained for many months on the course. She got familiar with the terrain and ran on the trails for more than 100 miles each week for several months prior to the race. She was assisted by her running friends and her husband Skip, who set up aid stations (stocked with fluids and salty foods) for her on her training routes. Skip also put together her crew and team of pacers on the day of the race, which included her mom and dad who had booked flights from their home in Massachusetts to support their daughter Diane in California.

It was sunny, but a very cool race day on Sept 26, 1987, and Diane became hypothermic. When she approached an aid station mid-race, she sat down and wrapped herself in a blanket and drank a cup of hot soup. Within 15 minutes, she warmed up and was ready to get back on the trail (with dry clothes on her body and a hat on her head). There were only four women in the race, and they were all ahead of her. It took her 45 more miles, but she passed them all. She was the first female to finish, with a time of 28 hours and 41 minutes. Of the 72 runners who started this prestigious race, only 43 finished. Nine runners completed the race in fewer than 24 hours, the cut-off time to receive the highly-coveted award, a race buckle.

Diane insists that she did not do the race by herself. She attributed her success to not only her spirit and determination but the help and support of her crew and the numerous volunteers. Her pacers kept her moving. Diane believes that it takes a community for a single ultra runner to succeed.

Diane also ran Western States four times. The Western States 100 runs through some of the most pristine forests in the High Sierra Mountains. Temperatures can be brutally cold in the morning but soar to more than 100 degrees in the canyons during the heat of the day. Runners face several stream and river crossings. It is a hilly course, with both a gain and loss of thousands of feet; it is definitely not a race for the meek. Diane's most difficult race was in 1998, the year of severe snow. At the age of 56, she finished in 29 hours 41 minutes, a remarkable accomplishment. In her words:

"We were not allowed to have cleats or poles for aid. I spent a lot of time falling, and so I ended up sliding downhill on my butt. I had no ski experience and my balance sucked. But, sliding on my butt was certainly easier than falling all the time. When I got to the first aid station, I was way behind my goal time. I wanted to break 30 hours. I met my crew at 55 miles, when it became dark. We chugged along to 70 miles, but then I fell hard. My body was a mess, but my crew bandaged me up and off we went. My pacers cajoled, prodded, told stories and jokes. They harassed, teased, told me I was doing great, made me eat and drink, and kept me warm and dry. They made it happen. I was black and blue all over from falling, and my knees were a mess, but I managed to walk to the platform to receive the 100 mile buckle for completing the race in less than 30 hours."

———

Seven of my friends from the Flyers also registered for the August 3, 1997, Skyline 50K, including Diane and Chuck. We trained hard in June and July and did long runs of 20 miles nearly every weekend. I felt strong, confident, and nearly invincible as race day approached.

The day before the race, I jogged an easy three miles in the wee hours of Saturday morning on the streets of my neighborhood. Then, I caught a 9:00 a.m. flight to Oakland. It was a short flight, just over an hour. I opened my book, *Snow Falling on Cedars*, by David Guterson. It's a love story that describes the discrimination against the Japanese-Americans during and after World War II. But I couldn't concentrate and focus on the characters. I was too nervous about the next day's 31-mile adventure.

The Skyline race starts at 7:00 a.m. on the side of Lake Chabot, a beautiful regional park in the Castro Valley. The nearby town is San Leandro, about 10 miles south of Oakland, where Gerry and I and the other Flyers booked hotel rooms. We made dinner reservations for our group of eight at Paradiso, an upscale Italian restaurant, which had opened the previous year to rave reviews. I carbed out with one of their signature dishes: linguini with prawns, a delicious choice of homemade pasta topped with shrimp, fresh herbs, feta, sautéed Roma tomatoes, and plenty of garlic. We all ate well, and the waiter repeatedly brought us more baskets of freshly baked bread. Chuck and I toasted with our customary glass of wine.

Our conversation was all about the next day's race. Everyone was nervous. Chuck had pre-registered for the optional 6:00 a.m. early start. The early starters were ineligible for awards, which wasn't an issue for him. He knew it was unlikely that he would place in the top three of his age group. He was happy for the extra hour of cool weather to be gained from his early start time.

Gerry posed the question to our table. "At what mile, do you think Mary will catch Chuck? Let's place a bet." Some people guessed I would pass Chuck as early as mile 10. A few others thought I wouldn't catch him until mile 20.

Skyline was an excellent choice for my first ultra. The race took care of first-timers like me. We were given a special color-coded race bib, which meant that volunteers and medical staff knew we were virgin ultra runners, and they paid extra attention to us. I appreciated their care and concern. At every aid station, they asked, "Are you OK? Do you need anything?" The course was quite hilly, with a 4,000-foot elevation gain. (I'll never know why Diane defined the race as "easy." My conclusion is she lied to us, but with good intentions to get us to register!)

Diane and other experienced ultra runners had advised, "Start out slow. Conserve your energy. Jog the first few miles." I followed their advice. I went out at a conservative nine-minute-per-mile pace, though I felt I could have easily handled eight-minute miles. I caught up to Chuck shortly after the mile 12 marker, and we ran a quarter-mile together before I went ahead. (Gerry won the previous night's bet with his guess I would meet up with Chuck at mile 13.) I picked up my pace during the last half of the race and clocked off several eight-minute miles.

We were allowed pacers the final five miles of the race. Gerry met me at the last aid station at mile 26 and ran with me to the finish line. He witnessed my struggle on the very steep downhill stretch, which was scary steep. Gerry held my hand at a few spots to prevent me from falling. I came close to doing a face-plant a couple of times. Running downhill over loose rock and gravel was never my forte.

I passed Chrissy Ferguson, an esteemed ultra runner a year younger than me, at mile 27. I was not even close to the first-place woman in front of me, Jennifer Pfeifer, a 25-year-old who won the female race and finished 15th overall with a fast time of 4 hours 25 minutes. I crossed the line 11 minutes after Jennifer, at 4 hours and 36 minutes. I was the second female finisher and 21st of the total 213 finishers. I felt happy, proud, and exhausted.

————

Ultra running has grown, but some aspects of the sport remain unchanged and are very similar to the way they were 30 years ago. Smart, conscientious race directors (often runners themselves) understand how to orchestrate a race so all the components come into play, with the safety of the runner as their top priority. This includes well-marked trails (so runners don't get lost), well-stocked aid stations with electrolyte drinks and real food (such as cut-up baked potatoes, soups, homemade brownies, pretzels, and fresh fruit). Dedicated volunteers (doctors, nurses, and experienced runners) are available and on call to assist runners who face medical problems.

Ultra runners are a laid-back community. They represent fewer than two percent of all runners. But this special group of people has broken away from the fringes and has entered the consciousness of the mainstream. They have gained the respect and admiration of fellow athletes and the general public.

The camaraderie among them is everlasting. They have their own unique culture; one that dictates assisting a fellow runner no matter what. Ultra runners embrace fellow runners on the trail with big hugs and high fives. They stick together and will never desert a runner who has fallen down or has suffered cramps or severe dehydration during a race. They ensure that their fellow compatriots have enough food and drink and encouragement to finish. *"You can make it!"* they chant.

Ultra running is here to stay. In 2014, there were more than 800 annual ultra marathons on the calendar, more than double the offering of 10 years previous. A classic illustration is the "Way Too Cool 50K", a popular race in Northern California. It exploded from 135 runners in the mid-1990s to more than 850 runners in 2013.

More women participate in ultras than ever before. Both younger and older women have embraced the sport and have met with success and satisfaction. Arguably, the best ultra runner of all time, male or female, is Ann Trason. Ann is the 14-time women's champion of the Western States 100. She held the women's course record for 18 years, which she set in 1994 when she ran Western States in 17 hours 37 minutes.

Trason won the 56-mile Comrades Ultra in South Africa in June of 1996 and then returned to California and won the Western States 100 mile race 12 days later. She repeated this duo victory the following year in 1997. I met Ann several times and also talked with her on the phone. RaceReady made the official shirts for the Dick Collins Fire Trails 50, an ultra held October in Northern California. Ann and her former husband, the talented ultra runner Carl Anderson, were the race directors for 10 years, from 2000 to 2010.

————

How does one train for an ultra? Coaches agree that the runner should build strength and endurance over an extended period of time. Most people have at least a few years of running and a marathon or two behind them before they attempt an ultra. Personal trainers and dietitians offer special nutritional guidance for long-distance runners. They cater to the increasing number of vegetarian athletes and others with dietary concerns.

Many ultra runners just want to have fun and don't care how fast they do their mega miles. They enter races and wear special creative costumes. Colorful, flamboyant sportswear is popular. Leg warmers and caps are flaunted in bright colors and patterns. Skirts and neon-colored shoes are all the rage. Groups of runners will dress alike as a "team" with specially designed t-shirts and caps.

Ultra running is a way to experience the mountains and nature on off-the-beaten-path trails. Some ultras encourage pay-back to the sport and to the environment. Western States 100 and the Angeles Crest 100 require a certain number of hours of service as an entry requirement for the race. The service can involve help with trail maintenance. (Work days are usually scheduled on weekends, so it is convenient. Or, it can require participation as a volunteer to assist at aid stations in ultra races.)

The shoe and clothing industries have developed and expanded their lines to suit the ultra runner. Nearly every type of foot problem imaginable, as well as every type of surface (hard, rocky, roots, mud, rivers, rain, and sand), has been addressed. Fanny packs, water bottles, and backpacks are available in various shapes and sizes.

Ultrarunning, one of the popular cult magazines on the market, is geared to the fanatics of the sport. The articles are written by runners, race directors, pacers, and volunteers. Each issue is filled with stories and pictures of ultra events, along with special articles on nutrition and training. Often, there are in-depth profiles of individual runners and commentaries that explain the latest scientific research on the endurance athlete.

I hope that the sport of the long, long distance will continue to grow. I can't help but think of ultra running when I hear the Neil Young song, "Long may you run."

CHAPTER NINETEEN

What to Eat?

WHAT IS THE optimal runner's diet? The answer depends upon whom you ask, and when you asked the question. Fad diets change every few years. No wonder we're confused!

As of 2018, the current craze is a gluten-free diet. We can find gluten-free pizzas, tortilla chips, pastas, beer, and much more. Kale is the "in" veggie which you can't escape. Restaurants promote their kale salads; cooking magazines feature recipes for delicious kale soup, and grocery stores stock kale chips in their snack aisle.

The athlete's diet has run the gamut from high carbs to low carbs, high protein to low protein. Low-fat diets were once popular, as were the 40-30-30 ratio diets of carbs, protein, and fat. It can be a challenge for a runner to decide what and how much to eat. Prescribed diets need to be tweaked because women require different nutrients than men, and younger runners gobble down more calories than do seniors.

In the late 1980s through the 1990s, training books advised runners, "Consume a high-carbohydrate diet to perform at your best." This was good advice since carbs are an important fuel for both the body and the mind. They are the first source of energy used. If your carb tank becomes empty, the body resorts to stored fat and protein. Though fat is a rich source of energy for the body, it does nothing for the brain. When runners "hit the wall" in long races, it is because they are out of carbs. They can't think straight, and they become dazed and confused.

High-mileage elite runners chow down twice as much as sedentary folks, yet they tend to be rail thin. Most people don't realize that these athletes run more than 100 miles each week. They burn thousands of calories, which justifies repeat trips through buffet lines.

Timing is everything. We learned that it was just as important when you ate as what you ate. By the late 1990s, much hype was given to protein and its importance for recovery. Exercise physiologists stressed that it was crucial to ingest some protein within 30 minutes after a tough workout to rebuild muscles. If you waited for longer than this amount of time to consume protein-rich food, your recovery would suffer, and you would recuperate at a slower rate.

I became a fan of the protein supplement, Jog Mate. I first sampled it at a race expo in San Diego in the late 1990s. I listened to the sales pitch from the young, handsome jock who worked their booth. He promoted the convenience and benefits of their product. Jog Mate was a pudding-like substance, packaged in a four-ounce pink tube, similar to toothpaste. You could easily stock your kitchen cabinet or the glove compartment of your car with several tubes of Jog Mate. It was convenient to open a tube of Jog Mate post-run, suck it down, and let the muscle recovery begin. Each tube contained a mere 100 calories, so it was hardly a meal, but it was a quick picker-upper that began the refueling process.

I tried it and it seemed to work for me. My muscles felt less "hung over" the next day after a strenuous workout. I became convinced and used Jog Mate to help with recovery after nearly all of my long runs. Serious cyclists also swore by it. One avid cyclist from Texas gave his testimony, "It used to be, if I hammered one day, I could hardly ride the next day. A friend turned me on to this stuff, and it made a HUGE difference. Now I am ready to ride nearly every day."

Jog Mate debuted in September of 1996, a trademark of Otsuka Pharmaceutical Company of Tokyo. Although the product was heavily promoted at running and cycling expos, it never really caught on with the masses in America. It disappeared entirely from the United States market within 10 years of its introduction. By 2005, protein bars had become the rage. Endurance athletes preferred to chomp down on solid food after an intense workout, rather than suck down "toothpaste."

———

Brian Maxwell was Canada's top-ranked marathon runner in 1980. Unfortunately, he didn't participate in the Olympics, which were held in Moscow that year. The United States (President Jimmy Carter at the time) and Canada boycotted the games in protest of the Soviet Union's invasion of Afghanistan. Maxwell was among the throngs of athletes who had trained for years but were denied their opportunity and participation in the Games because of the politics.

Maxwell got the idea for his product after he "hit the wall" and bonked during a marathon race in England in 1983. He sacrificed his lead in the late stages of the race, when severe stomach cramps forced him to slow his pace. He finished seventh, very disappointed. He returned to his home in Berkeley, California, determined to come up with a formula for something he could eat pre-race that was low-fat and palatable. Toast and jam were not sufficient, yet he couldn't handle a Snickers bar and Coke, like some of his training buddies could before they raced.

In 1985, Jennifer Biddulph, a 20-year-old sophomore at the University of California at Berkeley and cross country runner, began to date the 32-year-old divorced Maxwell, who was the coach of the UC Berkeley men's cross country team. Jennifer was a nutrition and food science major. She volunteered to help Brian test and develop recipes.

At first, they made "this horrible sort of glop," admitted Brian. But the couple did not give up easily. They kept at it and made batch after batch of recipes which combined simple and complex carbs. Their goal was to make a tasty, easily digestible, nutritious and convenient product (which did not cause stomach distress) for the endurance athlete. By 1986, they felt they had perfected their formula and were ready to take the product out of their home kitchen and into the marketplace. They launched their company and called it PowerBar.

Maxwell invested his life savings of $55,000. His start-up budget left no funds for advertising, and it was a tough go. They barely broke even with their initial production of 35,000 PowerBars, which he and Jennifer sold at local sporting events in Northern California.

"For us, marketing meant standing in the rain at 5 a.m. at races and handing out PowerBars with coupons that told people how they could order them," remembered Brian. Jennifer agreed, "We lived and breathed PowerBar!" The couple married in 1988. They grew their company into a multi-billion-dollar business. In 2000, Nestle bought PowerBar for about $350 million.

Sadly, Brian Maxwell passed away four years later on March 19, 2004, at the young age of 51, after suffering a heart attack while on a run near his home in San Anselmo, California. He is survived by his wife Jennifer and their six children: Alex, Justin, Christopher, Julia, James, and Andrew.

———

I tasted my first PowerBar in the spring of 1989. It was malt-nut, one of the two original flavors. The other one was chocolate. I had never heard of PowerBar until a friend handed me one after a local 10K race. "Try this for breakfast before your next race. It's the greatest!" I followed his suggestion two weeks later. On the morning of my 10K race, I ate the Power-Bar along with a piece of dry toast. I raced well and thought the PowerBar might have had something to do with it. I had thrown away the wrapper and was clueless as to where I could find more of these PowerBars.

During the next few weeks, I dialed local nutrition stores and inquired, "Do you sell PowerBar?" I got nowhere. No one with whom I spoke had even heard of it. PowerBar was scarce; impossible for me to find.

Frustrated, I called 411 (directory assistance), and asked the operator for the phone number of a company called Pow-erBar. Back then, it was common to dial 411 to get the phone number of a person or company. It cost perhaps 25 cents for a 411 call. There was no option of doing a Google search for phone numbers. This was years before the Internet went main-stream.

I called the number I was given, which had a Northern California area code. It was answered on the second ring. "Hello, this is Jennifer. May I help you?"

"I hope so. I live in Los Angeles and I would like to buy a dozen PowerBars."

"We only have two distributors in Los Angeles. One is a 7-Eleven Store in West Hollywood. The other is in San Fernan-do Valley."

At that time, I worked for Marvin Davis in nearby Centu-ry City. The 7-Eleven was a minor detour, so I swung by the convenience store a few days later on my way home from work and stocked up on PowerBars. During the next year, that 7-Eleven was my source for PowerBar.

By the summer of 1990, PowerBar was readily available in at least three dozen nutrition and running stores throughout the greater Los Angeles area. The company grew by as much as 40 percent a year in the early 1990s. Sales for 1994 reached $30 million, and PowerBar finally began to advertise.

The success story of PowerBar inspired others to enter the highly profitable energy bar market. In 1994, Gatorade, well known for its sports drink, introduced Gator Bar. Other smaller companies came up with their own innovations; creative knock-off versions of PowerBar.

PR Bar appeared on the scene around 1992. PR stands for Personal Record, an acronym understood by most runners. The company founder was Bill Logue of San Diego and his wife Sheri Sears. Sheri's brother, Barry Sears, was the creator of another popular energy bar that emerged on the market, Balance Bar. PR Bar and Balance Bar were similar. Both were designed upon the nutritional 40-30-30 ratio; 40 percent carbs, 30 percent protein, and 30 percent fat.

PR Bar was a vendor at all the major marathon expos in the early 1990s. You couldn't miss them. They had a massive booth (easily double the square footage of our 10 x 20-foot RaceReady booth) which they staffed with half a dozen attractive 20-year-olds who could pass as models. They handed out samples of PR Bar and signed up customers on the spot to place orders for monthly deliveries of the bars. It wasn't long before PR Bar reached the number three slot on the bar charts, behind only PowerBar and Clif Bar.

PR Bar mysteriously vanished from the expo scene and disappeared in 1998. (They had sold out to a nutrition company, TwinLabs, which filed chapter 11 bankruptcy in 2003.)

In order to keep their competitive edge in the market, PowerBar expanded their flavors. They rolled out a berry flavor, followed by peanut butter, then oatmeal-raisin. Still, many runners and cyclists complained about the chalky texture of the PowerBar. Sure, it was packed with nutrition, but it didn't taste very good. It lacked the chewy, candy bar taste which many crave.

Clif Bar became a player in the nutrition bar market in the early 1990s. Clif had its own humble beginnings. Gary Erickson (a passionate baker, cyclist, and mountain guide) was on a 175-mile bike ride in 1990. When he couldn't stomach the taste of the PowerBar that he tried to scarf down, he got the idea for his nutrition bar. He later coined this his "epiphany ride."

He went to work in his mother's kitchen. The eventual result was his not-yet-named energy bar. Erickson planned to debut his bar at the September 1991 Interbike Trade Show, held in Anaheim, California. It was the bicycle industry's largest trade show which featured 600 vendors.

Gary Erickson struggled, but he couldn't drum up a name for his bar. Finally, a few days before the show, he decided to name his bar after his father and mentor, Clifford. Clifford was the dutiful and wonderful father who had introduced Gary to the mountains and sparked Gary's passion for the great outdoors. Clifford, shortened to CLIF, also fit with the climbing imagery of a cliff. Gary thought it was a perfect name for his new product.

CLIF Bars met with immediate success. In its first year, sales exceeded $700,000, fueled primarily by strong sales in bike shops and the growth of the natural foods movement. CLIF boasted that it used only quality, organic, all-natural ingredients in its bars. Sales doubled each year, and revenue surpassed $20 million in 1997.

The CLIF company has set its priorities - minimal packaging, planet-friendly transportation, and very few landfills. It launched its volunteer program, Project 2080, in 2001. An employee works 2,080 hours per year, based on a 40-hour work week times 52 weeks. CLIF set the goal of committing that many hours to community service each year. The company easily met that challenge and has increased volunteer work in subsequent years.

As of 2013, 98 percent of CLIF employees participated in Project 2080. They collectively devoted more than 9,200 hours of labor to their favorite non-profit causes, which brought the grand total of CLIF "sweat donated" hours above the 60,000 mark.

Energy bars come and go. Since they first appeared on the scene, dozens of companies have entered the energy bar market, which has clearly gone mainstream. No longer are they found solely in nutritional specialty stores. Instead, they take up half an aisle in the grocery store. Offerings are numerous and diverse. Here's what I saw offered at my local supermarket in December 2016:

Balance Bar - Caramel Nut Blast
Garden of Life - Organic Summery Berry Bar
Kashi Bar - Go Lean Chocolate Almond
Healthy Warrior Chia - Coconut, Chocolate Peanut Butter
Kind Bar - Dark Chocolate Nuts, Blueberry Pecan and Fiber
Lara Bar - Apple Pie, Cherry Pie, Cashew Cookie
Luna Bar - S'Mores, Chocolate Peppermint Stick, Lemon Zest
PowerBar - Apple-Cinnamon, Banana, Chocolate
Promax Energy Bar - Cookies N' Cream
Snickers Marathon Energy Bar - Chewy Chocolate Peanut
Soy Joy whole soy and fruit - Dark Chocolate Cherry, Pineapple

A bar to suit everyone's taste!

———

Nutritionists have begun to raise a red flag. Dietitians are concerned that the average person consumes far too many energy bars than is healthy. Because they are convenient, some people gobble up energy bars in lieu of a healthy diet of "real food," such as fresh fruits and vegetables, wholesome grains, and lean meats. Energy bars should be a pre-workout snack or an afternoon pick-me-up, but not a meal substitute for breakfast, lunch, or dinner.

I read the excellent book by Michael Pollan, *The Omnivores Dilemma*. Pollan provided a simple answer to how we should eat. His advice: "Eat like people did a century ago, when preservatives, artificial flavorings, and colorings did not exist. Eat plenty of fruits and vegetables."

He advises grocery shoppers to check the list of ingredients for the product. The healthiest bets tend to be the foods with the fewest ingredients. A long list of ingredients generally indicates a poor choice. Wonder Bread turns out to be not so wonderful, with at least a dozen ingredients: unbleached wheat flour, water, sugar, oat hull fiber, yeast, soybean and/or canola oil, wheat gluten, salt, soy flour, cultured wheat starch solids, vinegar, and soy lecithin. What even is soy lecithin? If you don't recognize a word that is an ingredient, it's probably a good idea to avoid the product.

If the food didn't exit when grandma was around, you probably should ignore it. (Purple yogurt squeeze, for example.)

———

Runners are better informed and make healthier food choices than they did decades ago. In 1934, when he was one of the race favorites, Jock Semple followed the wisdom of the time and ate a fat two-inch steak an hour before the start of the Boston marathon to properly "fortify" him. On Commonwealth Avenue, the final stretch of the race, he suffered extreme nausea and puked his marathon victory dreams away. (Semple was the race official for the 1967 Boston Marathon who attained worldwide notoriety when he attempted to tear off the race bib number from Kathrine Switzer, the woman who had entered the race under the name of K Switzer.)

A popular race in Southern California is America's Finest City Half Marathon, which takes place in late August in beautiful San Diego. The point-to-point course starts at Cabrillo National Monument and follows a scenic route to the finish in downtown Balboa Park. The course features a screaming downhill between miles two and four, but you "pay the piper" toward the end of the race at mile 11, where an uphill that seems to last forever awaits you. It is a steep climb of more than a mile. It is a challenge at this point in the race (with weary legs that have already pounded the pavement for well over an hour).

I ran the AFC race a half-dozen times during the 1990s and early 2000s. Each and every time, I passed by "Margaritaville," a curbside aid station staffed right before the uphill at mile 11. The aid station was staffed by rogue volunteers. They set up speakers which blared the 1977 Jimmy Buffet tune "Margaritaville" non-stop. They handed out ice-cold plastic glasses containing the frothy alcoholic cocktail made with tequila, triple sec, and lime juice. The stop was a hit with the back-of-the-pack runners who could care less about their finish time and didn't mind getting wasted away. I was tempted a few times to stop, but I never did. Probably a wise decision, as far as my race results were concerned!

Alcohol on the race course goes back a hundred years. In the 1908 Olympic Marathon in London, Canadian Tom Longboat, the 1907 Boston Marathon winner, closed in on the leader at mile 15. He sipped some champagne to quench his thirst, but he then dropped out of the race two miles later.

———

My advice on nutrition is to listen to your body. It will let you know when it's hungry. I ran the Boston Marathon eight times. The week after the Boston race, I was always ravenous. I became light-headed mid-morning and could not wait until noon for lunch. I would eat a sandwich before 11:00 a.m. and then have a snack a few hours later. It enabled me to concentrate and be productive at work. It also helped my disposition. I am not a pleasant person to be around when I have hunger pangs. I become "hangry" (hunger + anger = hangry).

I ran 60 to 70 miles nearly every week back in the mid-1990s. I consumed mega calories. I had to in order to stay healthy and survive my mega-miles of running. It was protocol for me to have a dish of ice cream each night before bedtime. I rarely turned down "seconds" at dinnertime. I thought of my body as a high-performance car, which required high-octane fuel to perform at its optimum.

Diets come and go. We've seen the craze of the high-protein/low-carb diets as well as the reverse. There are bizarre, creative, and extreme diets, which tempt with their promise, "Lose 20 pounds in 20 days." They advise us to avoid certain foods, such as no bread for the first month of a diet. Many people buy into these diets and pay a lot of money to lose weight, when what they really need to do is simple: eat less and move more.

CHAPTER TWENTY

Expo Tales

A N ENJOYABLE PART of our business was traveling to expos throughout the country. I loved to talk with fellow runners and customers as they came by our booth. The days were often long and involved standing 12 hours straight, but it was worth it. Sales were lucrative and almost always surpassed our expectations. We often worked the two-day show and then ran the race on Sunday. Or, we would do a long run on our own instead, such as the scenic 17-mile Drive in Pacific Grove, California and the gorgeous trails of Rock Creek Park in Washington, D.C. I have fond memories of our RaceReady trips. The stories abound.

There's the time we got "squeezed" at the Marine Corps Marathon Expo in Washington, D.C., in October of 1993. It was during the infancy of our business. We were pretty much clueless about expo contracts, but it seemed simple enough.

We plunked down $500 six months in advance to reserve our 8' x 10' booth for the two-day expo, which took place in the ballroom of the Sheraton Hotel in Arlington, Virginia. The show hours were Friday and Saturday, 8:00 a.m. until 10:00 p.m. I thought, "Damn. I'm probably not going to run much that weekend!"

Our good friend Chuck offered to fly east to D.C. with us and help at the expo since we anticipated a busy show. Marine Corps is one of the most popular and well-respected fall marathons. The race boasted 12,030 official finishers in 1993, an all-time-high record at the time.

The three of us stayed with Gerry's Aunt Rita and Uncle Lyle. They lived in a beautiful home in the tranquil nearby town of Fairfax, Virginia. It was a heavily-forested area, with colorful deciduous trees, including red-leaved maple, sugar maple, yellow buckeye, black walnut, and birch. The timing was perfect to enjoy the fall foliage, a true feast for the eyes.

Our 9:00 a.m. Los Angeles flight touched down in D.C. at 5:00 p.m. that Thursday afternoon. We pulled into Rita and Lyle's driveway at 6:45 p.m. When they opened the door to greet us, I breathed in the heavenly aroma of roasted pork. We sat down to a scrumptious meal of pork tenderloin, mashed potatoes and gravy, green beans, and flaky dinner rolls. Conversation was focused upon RaceReady. Rita and Lyle were intrigued with our company and asked us dozens of questions. They sincerely wanted to understand what we did and learn about the running apparel industry.

After our dessert of homemade apple pie, Chuck, Gerry, and I strategized about when we could fit in a run. We concluded our best bet was to run *very early* the next morning, before the 14-hour expo.

We tiptoed out the door, pre-dawn at 5:15 a.m., and figured we had enough time to fit in a 45-minute run. It seemed surreal, since 5:15 a.m. in Virginia is 2:15 a.m. California time.

We carried flashlights and ran along a grassy median. Since we run at different paces, we didn't run together. However, we agreed we would each turn around at 22 ½ minutes to be back "home" and finish together at 45 minutes. I almost took a spill a few times because the terrain was both dark and unfamiliar.

After quick showers, Rita fed us a hearty breakfast of bacon, eggs, hash browns, toast, coffee, and juice. We drove to the Sheraton (on schedule for having to be there shortly after 7:00 a.m. to set up our booth). At the time, RaceReady had a very limited clothing line. We only offered singlets, one style of shorts, and socks. Surely an hour was ample time for us to put up our display posters, hang a few signs, and lay out the clothing on the two tables.

A Marine Corps volunteer ushered us toward our booth. No way was this an 8' x 10' booth! Minus a tape measure, we merely eye-balled it, but we agreed it was a 6' x 6' space, tops. Meanwhile, our "neighbor's" space appeared twice the size as ours. We figured out what had happened. Vendors who had checked in hours earlier had expanded their footprint and cut into the space of later arrivals like us. It wasn't fair, but there wasn't much we could do about it.

We barely had enough time to unload our boxes of clothing and get set up before show time. At least 200 runners waited in line for the doors to open.

Thus we learned the valuable expo lesson, "Arrive early before a show and stake out your space!"

Squished though we were, we nearly sold out of all our clothing. By early Saturday afternoon, we had nothing to sell except for a few lonely singlets and a couple of XL socks. The last eight hours were frustrating. The best we could do was engage runners in conversation and tell them about *(not sell them or show them)* our line of apparel.

RaceReady returned to Washington, D.C., each October for 18 years. Marine Corps Marathon consistently ranked in the top three of our annual show sales. By 1996, the show hours were shortened to a more reasonable 10-hour workday of 10 a.m. to 8 p.m., which allowed us time to enjoy long early morning runs on the beautiful rails-to-trails bicycle and walking paths in Northern Virginia. It became our tradition to do a longer 12-to-15-mile run on Sunday morning, followed by brunch and window-shopping in Georgetown, before we flew back to Los Angeles early Sunday evening.

Our second year at Marine Corps Marathon in 1994, we stayed with my sister Anne, who lived in a two-bedroom apartment in Arlington, Virginia. It was within a few miles of the Sheraton, very convenient. We packed far more product than we did the previous year, and we arrived plenty early at the Sheraton to set up our booth and "secure" our space.

1994 was seven years prior to the September 11 attacks, when flying was actually a somewhat pleasant experience. The seats were comfy, and flight attendants fed you decent meals served with real silverware. Airlines were lenient and generous with baggage allowance. They permitted three free bags per ticketed passenger. Our "bags" were enormous boxes stuffed with RaceReady apparel and our heavy toolbox. We tried to keep them under the 50-pound weight limit. We checked curbside; if a box weighed in at 52 pounds, a generous tip to the baggage handler ensured it would fly.

Gerry and I had the booth set up in good time (before the show opened at 8:00 a.m.). All was fine, except I had screwed up when I had packed the boxes in Los Angeles and forgot to include size medium socks. We offered four different sock patterns at the time.

The doors opened and our first customer appeared within minutes at the RaceReady booth. "I would like to buy three pairs of the medium white socks, but I don't see them."

I sheepishly replied, "Sorry, but we forgot to pack them." I handed him our catalog and offered to ship him the socks the following Monday from Los Angeles, free shipping. He didn't take me up on it.

Anne and her friend John planned to help us during the expo crunch time of 10:00 a.m. to 4:00 p.m. John was a tall, good-looking guy in his mid-twenties. He was a non-runner who could easily pass as a runner with his slim physique and clean-cut appearance. I quickly showed them our products and gave them a few selling pitches. I explained my faux pas and that we were void of medium socks. John corrected me, "Mary, you didn't forget to pack the medium socks. Just tell the customers, 'Sorry, we're sold out.'" So that's what I did with a poker-face for the next two days. I'm not sure how many people believed me. It looked fishy because we had hundreds of size small, large, and extra-large socks clearly visible on the display racks.

———

I had the opposite packing problem earlier that year at the Peachtree Road Race expo in Atlanta, Georgia, when I packed *way too much* of a certain product.

Peachtree was one of my favorite shows and also my favorite 10K race. The expo took place on July 2nd and July 3rd in the ballroom of the luxurious Hotel Nikko, which was located in the ritzy Buckhead neighborhood of Atlanta. The race was held the 4th of July. RaceReady was a vendor at the expo for a dozen years, 1993 through 2004. We lost money on the show our final few years, but we justified the trip because it was fun to run the famed race and celebrate Independence Day in Atlanta.

Georgia is referred to as the Peach State. It is well known for its juicy, tasty peaches. An image of the fuzzy, succulent fruit appears on the state license plates. Atlanta cafes serve homemade peach pies and cobblers. You can't seem to escape the splendid fruit.

Our first Peachtree, we focused on the patriotic colors of red, white, and blue. We barely sold any of the black, teal, and purple shorts and shirts we offered. In 1994, I came up with the brilliant idea to cash in on the peach theme. Early in the spring, I suggested to Gerry, "Why don't you try to procure some peach-colored nylon fabric? We can make special shorts and singlets for the Peachtree Expo. Women will go wild over them. I'm sure they will be a hit."

Gerry found the perfect bright peach-colored material at a reduced price. We made hundreds of peach shorts and shirts. When I packed the women's apparel, I took more peach-colored apparel than all of the other colors combined. That's how confident I was.

We made special signs for the show, which advertised our "Buy a Peach" special. The special knocked a few dollars off the price. Peach shorts and singlet cost $30, instead of the standard $32 combo price. We had peach decal stickers to hand out, free with every purchase.

Sad to say, my idea flopped. Atlantans may like their peaches, but the runners don't like to wear the color. We quickly sold out of everything we had in red, white, and blue. We barely made a dent in the steep stack of peach singlets and shorts piled high on our display tables. When the show closed, I packed up about 80 percent of the peach apparel to take back home to Los Angeles.

The boxes of peach shorts and shirts were stashed away in a remote corner of our RaceReady warehouse for the next decade. We finally got rid of them in 2005 when we included them in a package deal to our friend Rigo. Rigo was a dark, handsome, talented runner three years younger than I. He lived in Los Angeles, but his roots were from El Salvador. He visited his native country a few times each year, where he knew the owners of several running stores. He would sell them 'seconds' and close-out inventory that USA sports apparel companies wanted to dump. We gave him a huge discount and were happy to say goodbye to the peach.

———

Atlantans talk differently than Angelenos. We finished our dinner at an outdoor café in Buckhead and the waiter brought us our bill. He drawled, "Thank y'all fer dinin' with us. We sure do 'ppreciate it."

The next morning at the expo a woman stopped by our booth and asked me, "Do y'all carry that short in a size large navy?" I never heard the word "y'all" spoken as many times in my entire life than I did in two days in Atlanta.

Another peculiar phrase of Atlantans is "draw up." I thought "draw up" was an activity a painter might do, or perhaps an architect. During the 1994 expo, I slipped into my schpeel and touted the benefits of our fabulous shorts to a potential customer. She was polite and gave me her full attention. When I finished speaking, she leaned toward me and whispered, "I was wondering, do y'all shorts draw up?" I had no idea what she was asking me. She continued to talk, "I simply hate it when ah (I) do mah (my) laundry and afterwards ah try to squeeze mah-self into a pair of shorts to find they have drawn up on me!! And ah can no longer wear them because they are a size too small!"

I finally understood. "Draw Up" is two words for "shrink."

I answered her. "No, RaceReady shorts do not draw up, unless you put them in a hot dryer, which we do not advise. Wash the shorts on a gentle cycle, hang dry, and they will not draw up."

————

Our share of funny and memorable experiences also took place farther north. The distance between Los Angeles and Boston is roughly 3,000 miles. The coast-to-coast flight kills the day. You depart from LAX before 9:00 a.m. and touch down in Logan Airport after 5:00 p.m. For nine years straight, RaceReady did this trip each April for the Boston Marathon. I ran the WGM (World's Greatest Marathon) seven of those years.

We operated on a budget and did not splurge at fancy hotels. We never stayed in downtown Boston, which was quite pricey on marathon weekend. Instead, we booked a hotel in Westborough, near the race start town of Hopkinton. Prices were much cheaper in the small towns and villages 30 miles southwest of Boston. Our friend Terry joined us every year. The highlight of his race calendar was the Boston Marathon. He ran it all nine years he made the trip with us. RaceReady covered his hotel and meals in exchange for his help at our busy expo booth.

Our itinerary included the flight to Boston on Thursday, expo set up on Friday, long show hours on Saturday and Sunday, a marathon race on Monday, and flight home on Tuesday. It was an exhausting six-day schedule!

It's roughly an hour commute between Boston and Westborough and a miserable drive. Boston is known for its poor drivers, who are also incredibly rude. We learned early on that it is a bad idea to use your turn signal on the highway. If you signal, other cars become aware that you want to change lanes. They seem to conspire and plot against you, and make it almost impossible for you to do so. It's easier and safer to make a lane change if you *don't* signal.

We landed at Logan Airport on a chilly Thursday evening in 1995. We rented a van and stuffed our nine boxes of clothes and our three bodies into the vehicle and headed to our hotel in Westborough, Massachusetts, 30 miles down the turnpike. We picked up the "ticket" from the toll booth when we entered the turnpike near the airport. The drive was horrendous. We hit it right at rush hour, and we inched along with everyone else for more than an hour. We were elated when we finally reached our exit at Westborough.

The attendant at the toll booth asked Gerry for our ticket so he could calculate how much we owed. Gerry turned to us, "Which one of you two has the ticket? I don't have it."

Terry and I both dug deep into our pockets but came up empty handed. "Well, it's got to be here. Look under the seat," Gerry said. We did, but to no avail.

We were holding up the line. The driver behind us loudly honked his car horn. Others behind him followed suit. The toll booth guy also grew impatient. "Let's get on with this. People are waiting. Just tell me where you are coming from."

The three of us responded in perfect deadpan, "Los Angeles." He rolled his eyes. "Are you a bunch of wiseacres? I'm trying to do my job here and charge your toll for the turnpike. I don't give a damn that you are from Los Angeles. I want to know where you got on the bloody turnpike! The hell with it! I'll assume it was the Logan entry. Give me $10. You should be grateful I'm not charging you double."

———

By our 1999 trip to Boston, we had hit our prime. Expo sales were at an all-time high. Most customers back then paid with cash. Some people used their credit cards, and others wrote a check, but cash was clearly the preferred method of payment. (It was vice-versa 10 years later; with two-thirds of the buyers using their credit cards.)

On Saturday evening after the busy show at the Hynes Convention Center, I felt exhilarated by our lucrative sales, but I was worn out. We straightened up our booth, restocked the clothing for the next day, and exited the expo hall as quickly as possible. I was hungry and looked forward to our traditional Saturday evening dinner at Bertucci's restaurant in Newton. I could almost taste the piping-hot, fresh-from-the-oven buttery rolls the waiter brings to the table after he takes your order.

(My aunt and a few cousins often joined us. We always chose a variety of pizzas and engaged in some serious carbo-loading. We purposely ordered more than we could possibly eat in order to have several leftover slices of pizza. It made the perfect lunch to scarf down the next day at the expo.)

The light drizzle began to intensify as we scurried across the plaza from Hynes toward the parking garage. We carried no umbrellas. It was only a quarter-mile distance, but we were drenched when we reached the parking structure. We quickly descended the two flights of stairs to the level where we had parked our van 10 hours earlier.

Gerry turned toward me. "Mary, do you realize your backpack is opened? Why can't you remember to keep it zipped?"

I panicked. I'm the accountant and the one who always carried home the cash after a show – *in my backpack!* I yanked it off my shoulders in two seconds. Gerry was right; it was wide open. I fished around to see if the clear plastic bag of cash was still inside the pack. This was a hefty bag of neatly organized dollar bills: hundreds, twenties, tens, fives, and one-dollar bills. Rubber-bands held the various denominations together. The tally of the bag totaled several thousands of dollars. And this bag was *not* in my pack; I double-checked.

I sprinted faster than I ever had in my entire life, up those two flights of stairs to the plaza, Gerry and Terry by my side. On the pavement, a few feet from the staircase, I saw the bag of cash. It had not been touched, which was a miracle. There it sat, pummeled by the downpour. I breathed a deep sigh of relief. Someone up above was looking out for us. I learned my lesson. Since then, I always made damn sure the backpack was zipped tight when I exited an expo hall!

———

"Destination Marathons" became more and more popular. Runners planned their vacations around the race. Famed USA cities also drew an international crowd. Europeans visited San Francisco in July to see the Golden Gate Bridge and run the marathon. Runners from all over the world flocked to the betting capital of the world, Las Vegas, to play and run.

Thousands visited Disney World in January to combine a family vacation with their race. RaceReady was present at the annual Disney World Expo in Orlando for 11 years, 1999 through 2009. It was highly profitable for us, but an expensive race for the runner.

It cost a fortune to run at the "Happiest Place on Earth." The entry fee was steep, $150 in 2009. Lodging and food were not cheap either (not to mention the price of the plane ticket for the out-of-towners.) A three-day stay in Disney World could easily tally up to a $1,000.

But, it was good for our business. A $35 pair of RaceReady shorts was peanuts compared to the runner's other expenses. Nobody ever balked at the price of our apparel at the Disney expo and we sold shorts by the hundreds.

We did not sign up for the show in 2010 because it had become too expensive. In 1999, we paid $2,800 for our 10-by-

20-foot booth. In 2002, the price jumped to $3,200. Three years later in 2005, it rose to $3,900. In 2007, it was $4,550. In our final year of 2009, we paid $5,000.

We received the exhibitor package mid-2009 for the January 2010 show. The asking price for a booth at the three-day show was $8,000! We did the math. It cost us approximately $600 to ship our product UPS from California to Florida. We operated on a conservative budget; we stayed at 2-star hotels, and ate at inexpensive restaurants. Still, it cost about $2,000 for flights, hotels, and meals. Given the $8,000 expo fee, we could no longer justify making the trip. It was time to say, "So long, Mickey."

We were not the only ones to call it quits with Disney. Other small companies balked at the show price and no longer participated. Nike, Asics, and Brooks – companies with huge marketing and advertising budgets – were the only ones who could afford the steep fees. These larger corporations have dominated Disney and the other major marathon expos since 2010.

In 2014, runners paid between $160 and $190 to run the half or full marathon in Disney. If you pre-registered six months in advance, you paid $160; later registrants paid $190. The "Goofy Challenge" was also an option. Goofy runners did the half marathon on Saturday *and* the full marathon on Sunday. They received a special commemorative Goofy finisher's medal. $340 was the early-bird price tag of the Goofy race if you paid six months in advance. Then, it jumped to $400 after that. *Goofy indeed!*

There's even a Dopey Challenge, billed as the ultimate endurance challenge (a total of 48.6 miles of running fun). Participants do a 5K on Thursday morning, the 10K on Friday morning, the half on Saturday, and the full marathon on Sunday. In 2014, it cost $500 to be Dopey.

(Fine print: Admission to the theme park is not included with the race fees. The races start at 5:30 a.m., and runners exit the Magic Kingdom at mile 8, long before the Park opens to the public at 9:00 a.m. There are no runner discounts should you return to the Magic Kingdom later in the day.)

———

The weather forecast for race day was always the key factor which determined what would sell at the expos. I kept an eye on the extended forecasts before I packed for our trips to Boston, D.C., Orlando, Las Vegas, and other out-of-town shows.

Orlando is usually a warm, sunny destination; the perfect place to escape the frigid cold of the North and the Midwest. In 2001, a deep cold snap hit the Southeast and the thermometer dipped below freezing. I nearly froze when I stepped outside the hotel in Kissimmee at 6:30 a.m. on Friday morning to get in a brief half-hour run before we headed to the expo for a 12-hour workday. Kissimmee is the town immediately outside the Disney World gates, a convenient place for us to stay. I wore tights, two long sleeves, gloves, and a wool cap, but I never warmed up on my short run. I shivered until I took my hot shower 40 minutes later.

We had set up the infrastructure in our booth on Thursday afternoon. All we had to do on Friday morning was lay out the clothes on the tables before the doors opened to the public at 9:00 a.m., which didn't take us very long. We were ready with 20 minutes to spare, so I took a stroll and cased the floor of the expo. I checked out our competition and noted which apparel manufacturers were present and what products they had on display.

I became excited. I returned to the RaceReady booth and reported to Gerry, "Except for us, no one in the entire show has gloves for sale!" The extended forecast called for even chillier temperatures on Saturday and Sunday.

We were swamped with customers from the moment the doors opened. Nearly everyone who came by our booth bought a pair of gloves. We had packed only 200 for the show, which were gone in no time.

At noon, I called our office in Los Angeles and spoke with Stela. She worked for us part-time when we were in Los Angeles, but full-time (and often over-time) when we were away at shows. "Stela, I need your help! Please prepare as many gloves as you can before the UPS driver comes at 4:00 p.m. Ship them overnight for a Saturday delivery to the World of Sports Complex in Disney World."

It was expensive to ship UPS overnight for a weekend delivery, but I had a hunch we would sell every single pair of gloves she could "prepare." Preparation meant careful inspection of the gloves, trimming loose threads, and attaching RaceReady hang tags which indicated the size of Small, Large, or Jumbo. (And of course, she had to verify that the "pair" included one right and one left glove.)

Stela got busy and shipped more than 300 pairs of gloves to Disney, but we still sold out by noon. Latecomers to the expo were out of luck. Even the local running stores in Orlando didn't stock gloves since it only dips below freezing maybe three nights a year.

Against the odds, a similar scenario enfolded the following year. Once again, the coldest weekend of the year in Orlando was Disney race weekend. But this time, the extended forecast had predicted the cold front, and we came prepared (or so I thought.) We packed more than 600 pairs of gloves and, despite some competition from another vendor who was also selling gloves, we sold out by mid-day on Saturday.

———

Another memorable expo weather story took place in Huntington Beach. The Surf City Marathon is held on Super Bowl Sunday in Huntington Beach. The two-day Friday and Saturday expo venue was the Big Top "waterproof" tent, which was temporarily set up 100 yards from the sand and surf on the massive asphalt beach parking lot. I loved the views at sunset from our booth when I looked to the west and peered through the flaps of the tent to view the colorful red-orange sky as the sun disappeared from the horizon over the Pacific Ocean.

The race originated as the Pacific Shoreline Marathon in 2000. The Huntington Beach City Council voted in 2007 to change the race name to Surf City USA Marathon, which sounded much more hip. The race grew from its humble beginnings of 500 participants in the year 2000 to more than 15,000 by the year 2010.

I liked this show because it was close to home, and we didn't have to fly clear across the country to attend. We simply loaded our van with boxes of apparel and drove an hour southwest to Huntington Beach. When the expo closed at 6:00 p.m., we returned home to eat dinner and sleep in the comfort of our bed. It was a no-hassle show, and the booth price was reasonable - $2,000 for a 10 x 20-foot piece of real estate.

Nasty, soggy weather was predicted for the 2010 race weekend. Weathermen warned of spotty, heavy storm cells which could drop up to several inches of precipitation in an hour. We always kept backup inventory of our shorts and shirts in boxes stored underneath the display tables, which we restocked every few hours during a show. We came prepared for the vicious weather with the forethought of putting "diapers" on our boxes to make them weather-proof. We had wrapped multi-layers of heavy-duty plastic packing tape around their bottoms and sides. It did the trick.

Early Friday, just after the show opened, it started to rain. We learned that the "waterproof" tent was anything but! The tent sprung numerous leaks in the roof. Although our clothes under the display tables were protected, those atop the table got dripped upon.

Customers and vendors also got soaked. The expo staff worked feverishly to patch the tent, but to no avail. So they set up dozens of plastic buckets on the astro turf floor of the tent to catch the leaks from the ceilings. It barely helped. People were miserable as they walked through the expo; they were shivering cold with wet feet. It didn't bode well for sales since people didn't want to linger and shop for shorts. They wanted to pick up their race packet and get the heck out of the Big Top to someplace warm, dry, and comfortable.

I became fed-up as my shoes became waterlogged. It was not fun to stand for hours on end with cold, soppy feet. On Friday evening, we drove home quite chilled. I immediately took a long, hot shower and heated up some soup, but it took more than an hour before I could wiggle my toes and feel some warmth. I dreaded the next day's return to Huntington Beach for the Saturday show. It was predicted to be just as wet.

Suddenly, I thought of my Sorrel boots! Sorrels are often used in the mountains as après-ski foot wear. They are known to keep the feet warm and cozy in sub-freezing temperatures. I had my Sorrels stashed away somewhere in a closet. I hadn't worn them since the early 1990s on a Christmas trip to Breckenridge, Colorado.

I dug them out of the back corner of the closet and brushed off a layer of dust. I tried them on, and they still fit. I wore them Saturday at the expo and my feet stayed nice and toasty. At the end of the show, I thought, "This is a funky-ass world when the only time I wear Sorrel boots is at the beach in Southern California!"

CHAPTER TWENTY ONE

Lost and Found: A Busy Retirement

IT WAS NOT your typical waiting room. Rock and roll posters graced the walls. The sound system played the Rolling Stones 1969 hit, "Honky Tonk Woman," followed by Bruce Springsteen's 1975 "Born to Run."

I was at Stetson and Powell Orthopedic Sports Medicine in Burbank. Dr. Scott Powell was a founding member and vocalist of the famous 1960s rock band, Sha Na Na, who performed at Woodstock and toured Europe and Japan in their heyday. Powell quit the band in 1980 to pursue his career in medicine. He and his current team of doctors had a stellar reputation.

Finally, my name was called and I walked into the inner chambers for my appointment with Dr. Bojan Zoric. Dr. Zoric was a handsome, athletic man in his thirties, with sandy-blonde hair and sparkling blue eyes. He was the physician to the U.S. Women's National Olympic Soccer Team. I liked the fact that my doctor worked with competitive female athletes. It instilled confidence that he would do everything in his power to get me back in the sport.

He plastered the X-rays on the wall and then he proceeded to explain them to me.

"You have bone-on-bone arthritis." He pointed to the X-ray of my left knee. "Do you see that gray color that surrounds the kneecap?" I nodded my head. "That's cartilage," he informed me.

"Now look at the right knee. There is not even a strip of gray along the side of the joint. And you tell me you ran eight miles on Saturday?" Again I nodded.

"I don't see how that is even possible." So I gave him my long story short.

I knew I was in trouble the past year and a half. I simply couldn't run as often or as far as I had in previous years. 2008 was the first time in 18 years that my annual mileage dipped below 2,000 miles. It became a struggle for me to run three times a week. Even then, a 10-miler left me limping for days afterward. I had seen two other doctors a few months earlier whose advice was, "Don't Run!" Here I was for my third opinion, and I was desperate. Dr. Zoric at Stetson & Powell was my final hope.

He didn't mince words. "You will probably require knee replacement surgery sooner or later. If you stop running now, you might be able to hold off the surgery for several years. Knee replacements only last about 20 years. Since you are not yet 50 years old, if you have the surgery within the next year or two, it is likely you will need another knee replacement when you turn 70. The success rate isn't that great the second time around. If I were you, I would switch over to a sport with no impact on the knees, like swimming or perhaps cycling. Hiking in moderation might be OK, too."

The date was Wednesday, March 18, 2009, the day I lost running.

———

I cried and felt sorry for myself. I knew that I was acting childish and that I ought to be grateful instead. My personal odometer read 50,547 miles at my final finish line. That's higher than what was recorded on my Honda. I had run hundreds of races all over the country, and even in Ibigawa, Japan, and Cabo San Lucas, Mexico. I was fortunate to have participated in the 2000 Olympic Marathon Trials. I should be appreciative instead of angry.

One of my most cherished awards is the beautiful Waterford crystal bowl that I received from the Boston Athletic Association in 2001 when I finished 10th master. (The B.A.A. awarded this treasure to the top 15 open runners and top 10 masters.) Etched into the crystal in a simple but elegant style are the B.A.A. marathon logo, the year 2001, and the words, "Masters Division Tenth." It sits on the coffee table in my living room and I look at it nearly every day.

My finish time in 2001 at Boston was 3:00:27. It was bittersweet to me; although I was thrilled with the Waterford

Crystal, my personal era had come to a close. I was no longer a "sub-three" marathoner. My streak of 20 consecutive sub three-hour marathons was done. It had begun on November 3, 1991, in Orange County, California and ended on April 17, 2000, in Boston.

The sport *had* been very good to me. I truly did work, play, and live the running life for nearly two decades. Yet after my appointment with Dr. Zoric, thoughts spun in my mind...such as, "If I had fewer mileage over the last 10 years, could I be running now?" "If I hadn't pushed myself so hard, could I have pushed longer?" "If I hadn't had knee surgeries (1973, 1993), might I have run better?" I'll never know the answers.

I felt like a smoker diagnosed with lung cancer, told by his doctor to quit. I gained compassion for people who stop their habit cold turkey. It isn't easy to stop a lifestyle you have enjoyed for 18 years.

I called my friend MaryJane three days after my appointment with Dr. Zoric to clue her in. "I'll miss our Wednesday evenings, but I can no longer run, so I can't join you anymore," I explained.

MaryJane was one of a handful of us who met in Griffith Park at 6:00 p.m. every Wednesday for our five-to-six-mile run. This mid-week run had been our routine for more than a decade. Even in the cold, dark evenings of winter, we ran. We wore headlamps and just took it a bit slower due to our limited vision.

MaryJane is 10 years older than I am, but she looks much younger than her age. She has been a runner since the 1980s and is one of the few women who ran trail races back then. We have been good friends for a dozen years. She was aware of the history of my right knee.

"Nonsense!" was her response. "You can hike, right? We'll just meet at 6:00 p.m. as usual and hike instead of run. I can always run some other time and place. This isn't about the run. It's about our seeing each other and getting together each week. That is what I care about and that is what matters." I gave her a big hug of appreciation the next time we met.

Later that week, I glanced out my car window at a guy on his evening run on the streets of my neighborhood and I suddenly became furious. I thought, "It's not fair. That should be me!" Then I saw another runner and almost shouted at him, "You better enjoy that run because you have no idea how long you'll be able to do it!" I obviously had anger issues to resolve.

I grew jealous when I heard friends babble about their upcoming races. I became cognizant of how much my social life involved friends who shared the passion of running. At parties and dinners, conversations revolved around running stories and adventures. The fact that I could no longer run broke my heart. I tried to be supportive of my friends, but I grew weary when I heard "running" nonstop.

What made it even worse is that Gerry and I still owned and operated RaceReady. Our business meant I had to talk to runners and store owners each and every day. There was no escaping it. We still attended marathon race expos in Los Angeles, Big Sur, San Francisco, San Diego, Las Vegas, Tucson, and other faraway locales, such as Washington, D.C.

In October 2009, I stood at our RaceReady booth in Long Beach, California, with a smile as I handed my customer the bag with his purchase, a pair of shorts. "Thanks so much. We appreciate your business. Have a good race tomorrow."

He politely replied, "Thanks. You too. You're running the race, right?"

I lied, "Yep. Maybe I'll see you out there." It was easier for me to pretend for the moment than to tell the truth. I didn't want to spill my guts to people I hardly even knew. I didn't need their pity or their advice.

The next month at Tucson, an expo customer with good intentions preached to me about it being a case of "mind over matter." He had heard from a mutual friend that I no longer ran. "If you think positive, your knee will get better," he insisted. "I know of a lot of runners who have overcome serious injuries. If running means that much to you, you will find a way to do it." It felt like a slap in the face. He seemed to imply that I was a quitter. He hardly understood the passion I had (have) for running. I couldn't wait for him to leave our booth, sale or no sale.

I stopped reading *Runner's World* and *Ultra Running*, whereas previously I devoured each monthly issue as soon as it arrived in the mail. I no longer cared about race reports, the bios of talented athletes, or the most scenic places in the country to run.

This whole "woe is me" attitude lasted a couple of years. Gradually, it got better, but I still missed running. I saw a huge improvement after we sold our business at the end of December 2010 and I didn't have to think about running 24/7.

Meanwhile, I hiked often and also went to the gym to swim and use the elliptical trainer. But it wasn't the same. I never felt anything close to the runner's high when I swam or exercised upon the state-of-the-art machines indoors.

In August of 2012, Gerry and I took a brief vacation in Colorado. I traveled to Denver and I visited my sister Anne and her family. She had a basic 10-speed bicycle in her garage that she used for short rides around town. Although I pedaled a stationary bike at the gym, I hadn't been on a real bicycle in nearly 20 years. I hopped on Anne's bike and road a few blocks in her neighborhood.

It brought back fond memories of when I was a kid. I remembered what a thrill it was to get on my bike and pedal. Back then, I covered a lot of ground and knew every street in Merchantville, New Jersey, and the surrounding towns. Most memorable were the rides to Friendly's for an ice cream cone. Friendly's was two miles from home and a perfect destination on a hot, humid summer afternoon. I went nearly every week and would order a double-dip butter brickle cone.

I decided that I wanted to take up bike riding again. When I was back in Los Angeles in September, I bought myself a birthday present. I chose a hybrid bike, which is a cross between a road bike with the super-thin tires and a mountain bike. I began to ride on the flat bike path along the Los Angeles River, a few miles from home.

After a few months, I gained confidence and started to ride on the neighborhood streets. Fortunately, several paved interior roads in Griffith Park are closed to vehicular traffic. These are hilly roads, and full of potholes, but it is a beautiful and safe place to ride. I soon discovered a 20-mile-loop ride from my house, which became part of my weekly routine.

I loved it! My Saturday three-hour ride in the hills of Griffith Park was very similar to my long runs of yesteryear. I registered for a 50-mile bike ride in Solvang in March of 2013 and bumped up my training mileage. After completing a handful of 30-mile hill rides, I was confident and ready for Solvang.

Friends joined us for the weekend. Solvang is a popular getaway respite for Angelenos. It is in rural wine country, less than a three-hour drive from Los Angeles. I was nervous for my first official bike ride, but need not have been. The course was well-marked, and we could stop and rest as often as we wanted. An official aid station was set up mid-race with plenty of beverages and snacks. A party awaited us at the finish line area where we were treated to a BBQ, beer, and live music. It was a fun celebration, and I felt proud of my achievement.

I like to push myself, so I next set a goal of a 100-mile ride, and I registered for the Ventura Cool Breeze Century Ride, August 15, 2013. This bicycle journey followed the gorgeous central coast. We pedaled through the towns of Carpinteria, La Conchita, Goleta, Mission Canyon, and Santa Barbara. My favorite part of the course was the hilly stretch in Montecito, the ritzy neighborhood above Santa Barbara. We started the ride shortly after 7:00 a.m. and finished close to 4:00 p.m. It made for a long, but glorious, day. I felt the "runner's high" pretty much the entire time.

I miss running, and probably always will. I consider myself a runner at heart, even though I don't run. I've made the transition from a single-sport focus to multi-sport. I bike, hike, walk, and visit my gym to do a body-pump (strength training) class. I also practice yoga occasionally. I thrive on exercise, especially when it is outdoors in my beloved Griffith Park.

Since we sold RaceReady, I have spent much time and effort as an advocate for Griffith Park. I am one of the 12 founding Directors of a non-profit, Friends of Griffith Park. The mission of our organization is to protect and preserve Griffith Park (which contains more than 4,300 acres and is the largest urban park in the country). Friends of Griffith Park work is a big time commitment, but it is rewarding.

I want to give back to my neighborhood (to the local community and the tourists, and especially to the runners.) Griffith Park is a special place that I am proud to call "home." I've covered most of the 53 miles of trails countless times. Probably half of my more than 50,000 lifetime mileage took place in Griffith Park.

I am grateful that I led the running life for nearly 20 years. It was an amazing trip which rewarded me with hundreds of memories I will always cherish.

ABOUT MARY BUTTON:

Mary Button grew up in Merchantville, NJ, a small town close to Philadelphia. Her running career began in high school, fall of 1973, when she took advantage of the recently passed Title IX legislation and ran with the boy's cross-country team.

Mary became a serious long distance runner after she moved to Los Angeles in 1986, and became focused on the marathon distance. Between November 1991 and April 2000 she ran 20 consecutive sub three-hour marathons. It is a feat that few women have achieved.

In 1992, she and her husband Gerry Hans started their business, RaceReady, a running apparel manufacturer. The company's niche was clothing for the long distance runner. Mary and Gerry traveled throughout the country, promoting their line of apparel at various race event expos.

Mary was privileged to meet many of the "players" in the industry, from store owners to race directors to other elite athletes. She got to know the sport from every angle – as a member and president of the Los Feliz Flyers, a grass-roots running club; as a nationally ranked competitive runner; and as the owner of a successful business in the industry.

The highlight of her career was as a participant in the February 2000 US Olympic Marathon Trials as a master. (She was one of only 17 masters in the starting field of 170 athletes, and the 12th master to finish.) The following year, in 2001, she placed 10th master in the Boston Marathon.